D0297964

U-BOATS
UNDER THE
SWASTIKA

U-BOATS
UNDER THE
SWASTIKA

Jak. P. Mallmann Showell

IAN ALLAN Publishing

First published 1973
Second edition 1987
Reprinted 1989
This impression 1998

ISBN 0 7110 1682 8

Published by Ian Allan Publishing

an imprint of Ian Allan Publishing Ltd, Terminal House,
Station Approach, Shepperton, Surrey TW17 8AS.
Printed by Ian Allan Printing Ltd, Riverdene Business
Park, Molesey Road, Hersham, Surrey KT12 4RG.

Code: 9808/3

Contents

Germania International
Germania International, the German Navy Study Group, was founded in May 1985 as an
independent English Language Group to help in bringing together people interested in the
history of the German Navies.
    Further information and a sample newsletter can be obtained from: The German Navy
Study Group, 78 Barnfield Crescent, Telford, Shropshire TF1 2EX, England.

Glossary

AA   Anti-aircraft.

aD   *ausser Dienst*: withdrawn from service, retired or decommissioned.

Abt   *Abteilung*: Department/Division.

AGRU Front   *Ausbildungsgruppe Front*; a technical branch to test men and boats before going on to operational service. This was the last stage of the training process.

AO   Artillery Officer.

Aphrodite   A German device for foxing radar by reflecting impulses.

Asdic   Initials of Allied Submarine Detection Investigation Committee. (Now known as Sonar.) A device for detecting the presence of submerged submarines.

ASV   Air to Surface Vessel. Radar used by the Allies.

Athos   A capstan-shaped radio detection aerial. The upper ring picked up 3cm and the lower ring 9cm radio waves.

Bachstelze   Name for *Focke-Achgelis*, a gliding helicopter or autogyro towed by U-boats to give lookouts a better field of vision.

Bali   Aerial for detecting radar waves.

Bauwerft   Ship-building yard.

B-Dienst   *Funkbeobachtungsdienst*: Radio Monitoring Service. Also provided intelligence to U-boat Command.

BdU   *Befehlshaber der Unterseeboote*: Commander-in-Chief for Submarines.

Betasom   The Italian U-boat Command in Bordeaux. Founded by *DivAdm* Parona in September 1940.

Biber, Beaver   Midget submarine.

Biscay Cross   Nickname for the first radar detection aerial used on U-boats. It consisted of a rough wooden cross with wires strung around the outside and was chiefly used in the Bay of Biscay.

Blockadebrecher   Blockade breaker or blockade runner. A merchant ship used to bring essential goods into Europe during the war.

Bold   An Asdic foxer. It was ejected from submerged U-boats to reflect the noises made by Asdic.

Boot   Boat. A warship whose commanding officer is not a staff officer and which does not have a first officer. The second-in-command in a U-boat was known as First Watch Officer.

Borkum   A Friesian island, also name for a radar detector.

BRT   *Brutto Register Tonnen*: Gross Registered Tonnage.

Cypern   Codename for a radar detector.

'Deadlight', Operation   *See* Operation 'Deadlight'.

Delphin   Dolphin. A midget submarine. Not operational.

Destroyer   The Germans often used this name to refer to small vessels of the type used for convoy defences, although in English other terms such as frigate or corvette were used.

Dienst   Duty.

Dienstgrad   Rank. *See* Rank.

Dienststelle   Headquarters.

D-Maschine   Diesel engine.

Dräger   *Dräger Tauchretter*: the name of a firm which made submarine escape apparatus. The German equivalent of the British Davis Submarine Escape Apparatus.

DT or DeTe Apparatus   Technicians knew this as *Decimeter Telefoniegerät*, while others called it *Drehturm Gerät* (revolving turret apparatus). It was the name given to the first German naval radar.

Einbaum   Dugout. Nickname for Type II.

EK   *Eisernes Kreuz*. Iron Cross.

Elefant   Elephant. Name for an experimental midget U-boat.

E-Maschine   Electro motor.

EMA, EMB, EMC, etc   *Einheitsmine Type A*. Universal Mine type A. All types of mines.

Engelmannboot or **Engelmannversuchsboot**   Engelmann's boat. An experimental submersible boat with high speed propulsion unit. Also known as VS5.

Englisch   During the war virtually everything British or even Allied was called *Englisch* by the Germans.

Enigma   The name of the German code writer. There was a special naval version known as *Schlüsselmaschine M* (M=Marine).

FAT   *Federapparat Torpedo*: also known as *Flächenabsuch Torpedo* by some people. A special anti-convoy torpedo. It would travel in a straight line for a predetermined distance and then zig-zag.

FdU   *Führer der Unterseeboote*: Flag Officer for Submarines.

Feindfahrt   Operational cruise.

Flak   *Fliegerabwehrkanone or Flugabwehrkanone*: anti-aircraft gun.

Fliege   Fly. Name for radar detector.

Fliegerführer   Air Force Commander.

Flugzeugfalle   Aircraft trap.

Freikorps   Free Corps.

Freya   Radar detection apparatus.

Front Boot   Operational boat used to fight the enemy. Not training or experimental craft.

Führer   Leader, flag officer, commander, chief and in the case of Hitler, dictator.

FuMB   *Funkmessbeobachtung*: radar detection.

FuME   *Funkmesserkennung*: radar recognition.

FuMG   *Funkmessgerät*: radar equipment.

FuMO   *Funkmessortung*: radio direction or radar.

Funk   Radio.

Funkbeobachtungsdienst or B-Dienst   *See B-Dienst.*

Funkmess   Radio/radar detection.

Funkpeilgerät   Radio direction finder.

Goliath   Name for powerful radio transmitter near Magdeburg.

Goldbutt, Goldfisch   Names for experimental torpedoes with special high speed engines.

GRT   Gross Registered Tonnage. The total displacement of a ship.

Grundhai   Name for rescue submarine. Planned, but not built.

Hai   Shark. Name for a midget submarine which was never built. After the war the name of a Federal German submarine, ex-*U2365*.

Hauptquartier   Headquarters.

Hecht   Pike. Name for midget submarine.

Hedgehog   An anti-U-boat weapon. A type of mortar, which threw special bombs ahead of the vessel carrying it.

Hertha U-boat   This term is not often used, but refers to Type XXI.

HF/DF   'Huff Duff'. High Frequency Direction Finder. A device which could determine the approximate direction from which radio signals were coming.

HMAS   His/Her Majesty's Australian Ship.

HMCS   His/Her Majesty's Canadian Ship.

HMS   His/Her Majesty's Ship.

Hohentwiel   A German radar aerial fitted to U-boats that looked like a bedstead. One side was a radar aerial and the other a radar detector.

Hondo, Honduras   Type of radar detection aerials used with Metox.

Hundekurve   Dog's curve. The path taken by a U-boat when attacking a ship so that the smallest possible profile was exposed to the enemy at all times.

Hydroplane   A type of rudder for making submarines go up and down when submerged.

iD   *im Dienst or Indienststellung*: commissioned or commissioning.

IWO   Pronounced 'Eins W O'. First Watch Officer.

IIWO   Pronounced 'Zwei W O'. Second Watch Officer.

Kaiserliche Marine   Imperial Navy.

Kaleu, Kaleunt   Short for Kapitänleutnant.

Kalipatrone   Potash cartridge. Respirator which absorbed carbon dioxide.

K-Butt   A high speed torpedo with Walter propulsion unit. Probably used operationally by midget submarines shortly before the end of the war.

Kdo   *Kommando*: Command.

Kleinkampfmittel   Midget weapons.

Kleinkampfverband   Midget Weapons Unit.

KM   *Kriegsmarine*: Germany's equivalent to the Royal Navy. So called between 1935 and 1945.

Km   Kilometre.

Knot   The speed of ships is measured in knots. 1 knot = 1 nautical mile per hour.

Kommandant   Commanding Officer of a sea-going ship.

Kommandeur   Commanding Officer of a land-based unit.

Korfu   Name for a radar detector.

Krieg   War.

KTB   *Kriegstagebuch*: diary or log book.

Kurzsignal   Short signal. The system was introduced early in 1940 and the signals were thought to have been too short for Allied direction finders. However, HF/DF could get bearings on these.

K-Verband   Abbreviation for *Kleinkampfverband*. Midget Weapons Unit.

Leigh Light   A powerful searchlight fitted to Allied aircraft.

Lerche   Lark. A wire-controlled torpedo, which did not see operational service during the war.

LI   *Leitender Ingenieur*: Chief Engineering Officer.

Löwe   Lion. Nickname for Karl Dönitz (C-In-C for U-boats).

LT   *Lufttorpedo*: aerial torpedo.

Lt   *Leutnant*: Lieutenant.

Luftwaffe   Air Force.

LUT   *Lagenunabhängiger Torpedo*: a further development of FAT.

Marine   Navy.

Marder, Marten Midget submarine.
Meddo Similar to Rotterdam radar. Worked on 3cm wavelength. The first set to fall into German hands was in an aircraft shot down near Meddo in Holland.
Metox Name of a French electronics firm which gave its name to a German radar detector.
Molch Newt. Midget submarine.
Mondfisch Moonfish. A high speed torpedo which did not see operational service during the war.
Monsoon Group Long range U-boats which operated in the Indian Ocean and Far East.
MOV *Marine Offizier Vereinigung*: Naval Officers' Association. Founded in 1918.
MS M/S. Motor ship.
Mücke Knat. A radar aerial.
Naxos A radar detection device.
Niebelung Name for a German underwater detection device. Probably not operational during the war.
ObdM *Oberbefehlshaber der Marine*: Supreme C-in-C of the Navy.
OKM *Oberkommando der Marine*: Supreme Naval Command.
OKW *Oberkommando der Wehrmacht*: Supreme Command of the Armed Forces. No British equivalent.
Operation 'Deadlight' Codename for the British action when U-boats were sunk after the war.
Paukenschlag A roll on the kettle drums. German codename for the first thrust against the United States.
Peilgerät Radio direction finder.
RAAF Royal Australian Air Force.
RAF Royal Air Force.
Radar From Radio Detection and Ranging.
Radio Direction Finder Radar or a device for indicating the direction from which radio signals are coming. Used by U-boats to home-in on boats shadowing convoys.
Rank See the end of this section.
RCAF Royal Canadian Air Force.
Reichsmarine Germany's equivalent of the Royal Navy. So called between 1919 and 1935.
Ritterkreuz Knights Cross. Usually refers to the Knights Cross of the Iron Cross, but there was also a Knights Cross of the Distinguished Service Cross.
Rotterdam Apparatus The German name for British short-wave radar found in an aircraft shot down over Holland.
Schiff Ship. In the *Kriegsmarine* this term referred to a ship with first officer and whose commanding officer was a staff officer.

Schlüssel M Key M. the Naval code.
Schnorkel British equivalent of the German word Schnorchel. The term was coined by Karl Dönitz.
Schwertwal Narwhale, a midget submarine.
Sea Cow Nickname for large U-boats, such as Type IX. From the German *Seekuh*.
Sea mile Nautical mile (1.852km).
Sea wolves Term used for U-boats.
Seehund Seal, a midget submarine.
Seekriegsleitung Naval War Staff. The staff at the Supreme Naval Command responsible for conducting the war at sea. Abbreviated *SKL*.
Seeteufel Sea devil, a midget submarine.
SKL *See Seekriegsleitung*.
SMA (SMB) Shaft Mine Type A. A special mine developed for type XB U-boats.
SMS *Seiner Majestäts Schiff*, His Majesty's ship. This prefix was used during the Kaiser's reign. The *Reichs* and *Kriegsmarine* usually prefixed ship names with their type, eg *Panzerschiff Deutschland, Schlachtschiff Tirpitz*, etc.
Sonar American for Asdic, a term which has now replaced the word Asdic.
Sonderführer Special Commander, a title often given to merchant seamen who took special commissions in the navy.
Squid A device used by the Allied navies to throw mortars ahead of the ship which was carrying it.
Spatz Sparrow, nickname for a rescue buoy fitted to U-boats before the war. It consisted of a red and white striped buoy with flashing light on top, which could be jettisoned in an emergency.
Stapellauf Launch.
Sumatra, Samoa, Samos Aerials for detecting radar.
T5 The German acoustic torpedo (*Zaunkönig*).
Tauchboot Conventional submarine.
Tauchretter Submarine escape apparatus.
Tauchtiefe Diving depth.
Tauchzeit Diving time.
T-boot Torpedo boat.
TEK. *Torpedoerprobungskommando*: Command for testing torpedoes.
Thetis Either a name used for a number of German ships or a radar foxer.
TMA (TMB, TMC, etc) Torpedo Mine Type A. Torpedo mines were about half the size of a torpedo and could be ejected through torpedo tubes, if the tubes had been fitted with a special modification.
Trim dive A special dive to establish the proper balance of the submarine.

Tunis Radar search receiver, probably not used operationally.

Turm Conning tower.

TVA *Torpedoversuchsanstalt*: institution for experimenting with torpedoes.

Typ Type. In England the term 'class' tends to be used instead.

UA A submarine built for Turkey, but not handed over. She was commissioned in the German Navy as UA instead.

UAA *Unterseebootsausbildungabteilung*: the title suggests that this was a training department to teach men how to become submariners. This department also acted as clearing house for men waiting to take up positions in operational boats.

UAS *Unterseebootsabwehrschule*: a school for teaching anti-submarine warfare. It also served as cover name for the school where the first submariners were trained before the abolition of the Versailles Treaty.

UB The German identification of HM Submarine *Seal*, after she was captured.

Uboot U-boat, short for 'under water boat'. In German it is used to refer to a submarine of any nation, but in English it means a German submarine.

UD Identification for Dutch submarines which sailed under the German flag.

UIT Identification for Italian submarines which were under German control.

UJ *Unterseebootjäger*: submarine chaser.

ULD *Ubootslehrdivision*: U-boat Training Division.

USAF United States Air Force.

USCG United States Coast Guard.

USS United States Ship.

US-FL *Ubootsschulflotille*: Submarine School Flotilla.

Verb/Verband Unit.

verloren Lost, sunk.

vernichtet Destroyed.

versenkt Sunk.

VHF Very High Frequency radio, now the FM wavebands.

Wabos From *Wasserbomben*, depth charges.

Waffe Weapon or, when referring to a branch of the armed forces, an arm.

Walter unit A high speed underwater propulsion unit developed by Prof Helmuth Walter.

Wanze Nickname for *Wellenanzeiger*, a radar detection device which automatically searched various radar wavebands.

Werft Shipyard or dockyard.

Wintergarden Nickname for gun platform.

Wolfpack Translated from the German *Rudel*.

Zaunkönig The German acoustic torpedo, also known as *T5*.

German ranks, their abbreviations and British equivalents

Commissioned Officers:

	Grossadmiral	Admiral of the Fleet
	Generaladmiral	No British equivalent
	Admiral	Admiral
VA	*Vizeadmiral*	Vice Admiral
KA	*Konteradmiral*	Rear Admiral
	Kommodore	Commodore, Captain in a post usually held by an admiral
KS	*Kapitän zur See*	Captain
FK	*Fregattenkapitän*	Captain-junior
KK	*Korvettenkapitän*	Commander
KL	*Kapitänleutnant*	Lieutenant-Commander
OL	*Oberleutnant zur See*	Lieutenant-senior
LT	*Leutnant zur See*	Lieutenant-junior
	Oberfähnrich zur See	Sub-Lieutenant
	Fähnrich zur See	Cadet/Midshipman

Non-Commissioned Officers

Oberbootsmann (1, 2)	Chief Boatswain
Bootsmann (2)	Boatswain
Ober--maat (3)	Chief Petty Officer
--maat (3)	Petty Officer

Other Ranks

Matrosenhauptgefreiter (4)	Leading Seaman with more than 4½ years service
Matrosenobergefreiter (4)	Leading Seaman
Matrosengefreiter (4)	Able Seaman
Matrose	Seaman

1. More senior ranks were introduced during the war and prefixed with the term *Stabs*, eg *Stabsoberbootsmann*.
2. If the man had a special occupation, his trade would have been used instead of *Bootsmann*, eg: *Maschinist, Steuermann, Funkmeister*, etc.
3. The man's trade would have been used instead of the two dashes, eg: *Maschinenmaat, Funkmatt* or *Obermaschinenmaat, Oberfunkmaat*.
4. In naval circles, the word *Matrosen* was often left out.

Acknowledgements and Preface

Acknowledgements of the First Edition

I should like to express my sincere thanks to Kapitän zur See Otto Köhler for all the help and encouragement he has given me; I am especially grateful to Fritz Köhl who sailed in *U765* and *U1203* for supplying plans, technical information, an extensive selection of photographs and a series of comprehensive accounts of his nautical experiences. Without their help this book would never have been completed.

My grateful thanks also go to the following individuals and institutions who have kindly helped with this book: Buckinghamshire Public Library Service and in particular Mrs Iris Page and Miss Margaret Mackenzie of the Beaconsfield Branch; Michael Cooper for his help with factual information and proof-reading; I am grateful to Konteradmiral a.D. Eberhard Godt and Korvettenkapitän a.D. Adalbert Schnee for the assistance they gave to Michael in order to help clear up several problems; Grossadmiral a.D. Karl Dönitz for reading the proofs and making valuable comments; Roel Diepeveen for his help with schnorkels and Dutch U-boats; Ray A. Freeman of the Imperial War Museum; Hanni and Jack Fletcher; Heinz Kurt Gast; Ilse Hegewald, whose husband was killed whilst commanding *U671*; Bodo Herzog; the Imperial War Museum and in particular Mr M. Brennan and Mr R. E. Squires, the staff of the Photo Library, Reference Library and the Documents Section; Fregattenkapitän a.D. Max Kaluza of *Deutscher Marinebund* in Laboe for corresponding with Fritz Köhl and sending details of *U995*; Friedrich Kiemle; the National Maritime Museum and in particular Dr M. W. B. Sanderson, Mr Stonham and Mr G. A. Obson; Fregattenkapitän Karl-Heinz Nitschke; Mr A. Pitt; R. N. Karl; Adele and Heidi Prawitt; Kapitän zur See K. T. Raeder, Federal German Naval Attaché in London; Christiane Ritter whose husband helped to set up secret weather stations in the Arctic; Dr Jürgen Rohwer; Col G. Salusbury; the Science and Industry Museum, Chicago and in particular Mr J. E. Irwin; Staatliche Landesbildestelle in Hamburg and in particular Dr Diederich and his staff; Hans Staus who sailed in *U377*; Ulfert Tilemann; Anthony J. Watts; Oberleutnant zur See a.D. Herbert Werner.

I should like to thank the following for their kind assistance in the provision of information and addresses: R. Anderson of Arthur Baker Ltd; Henry Birkenhagen; Margaret Elsner; Dr Wolfgang Frank; Kapitänleutnant a.D. Wilhelm Spahr; Cdr G. A. M. Wermeskerken, Royal Netherlands Navy; George Allen & Unwin Ltd; Walter Kabisch of Verlag Ullstein; Schulte & Bruns of Emden; Herr G. Vannotti.

Preface to the Second Edition

I started *U-boats Under the Swastika* way back in 1970 after I had seen a book about German submarines and thought I could write something better. I have always had an interest in U-boats. My father disappeared with *U377* in January 1944 three months before I was born, and since an early age I have been collecting information in the hope of discovering the fate of the U-boat. Since those humble beginnings I have become increasingly immersed in the history of the German Navy; much of my research has been based on original documents, but these are useless without some background knowledge. Some of this can be gleaned from books, but verbal accounts from people who participated in the war bring an otherwise sterile collection of facts to life and it would have been impossible to produce this edition without such help from so many people. To list everybody who has contributed would be as difficult as providing a full catalogue of all the documents consulted, so I hope that a general word of thanks will be accepted by the people whose names are not mentioned.

A large proportion of my research has been conducted with the full support of the

German U-boat Archive and I am most grateful to Horst Bredow, its founder and director. I should also like to thank Axel 'Computer' Niestlé for his help and Klaus Schäle of *Uboot-Kameradschaft Kiel* for printing many of the photographs used in this book. My visits to the U-boat Archive would have been far less fruitful had it not been for Fregattenkapitän Peter Gladziejewski, CO *Marinefliegerhorst* (Naval Air School), Sylt; he must also be thanked for providing the support which has helped establish the Archive as one of the world's leading sources of information on U-boats.

In Britain I have enjoyed considerable help from Cdr Richard Compton-Hall and Gus Britton of the Royal Navy Submarine Museum at HMS *Dolphin*. The museum not only has an excellent collection but also a first class reference library. The use of these facilities together with personal advice and direction has proved invaluable.

The following people must be thanked for their contributions to this volume: Kapitän Otto Giese who served in the blockade breaker *Anneliese Essberger*, *U405* and *U181*; Wolfgang Hirschfeld who was radio operator aboard several U-boats and also at HQ U-boat Command, made a major contribution to U-boat history by keeping a secret diary during the war; and Franz Selinger.

Since the first edition of this book appeared I have traced the majority of men who served with my father in *U377*, but who did not participate in the last voyage from which the boat never returned. I should like to thank the *U377* family: Kpt.z.S. Otto Köhler, Fregkpt (Ing) Karl-Heinz Nitschke, 'Jumbo' Gerke, Heinrich Böhm, Hermann Patzke, Siebrand Voss, Sepp Fürlinger, Franz Albert, Werner Reinke, Werner Berns, and their wives for their help and encouragement.

I am also grateful to the following for their help: Korvkpt a.D. 'Ajax' Bleichrodt; Fregkpt Rudi Conrad; Kpt.z.S. Hans Dehnert who translated the first edition into German and provided a great deal of advice; Ralph Erskine; Frau Ursula von Friedeburg; Gerry Fowler, my local Labour MP for taking a lot of time to help me through the national red tape; Konteradmiral a.D. Eberhard Godt; Heinz Guske who served in supply ships and U-boats; Georg Högel of VDU Munich for his help with emblems; Geoff Jones; Kpt.z.S. Claus Korth; Karl Keller; Kpt.z.S. a.D. Hans Meckel; Dr Timothy Mulligan of the United States Archives and Records Service; Fregkpt Albert Nitzschke; Eberhard Rössler; Paul Preuss; Knut Sivertsen of the Army Museum in Trondheim; *Ubootkameradschaft Munich* of *Verband Deutscher Ubootfahrer* for putting up with me; Elaine Womack of Ohio; *Deutscher Marinebund* at Laboe near Kiel.

I am indebted to Maj Andy Postance for having made such a good job of reading through the manuscript before delivery to the publishers.

I should also like to thank the following for taking an interest in my project and helping to provide information: F. N. Beaney of HMS *Ark Royal*; Heinrich Blum of *U43*; Doug Campbell RCAF; Herbert Dittkrist; Bill Eddles RCAF; Victor Turon Garcia of Barcelona, Spain; Karl-Heinz Goetze of *U668* and *U751*; 'Gil' Gilmour RCAF; Walter Illig of *U473*; Adm Otto Kretschmer; Walter Lang of *U48*; David Lees of the German Navy Interest Group of the World Ship Soc; Christopher Lowe; Richard Linek of *U371* and *U410*; Ian A. Millar, founder of Sons and Daughters of US Merchant Marine Veterans of World War 2; Jack McKnight RCAF; L. L. von Münching; Hubert Plantenberg of *U71*; Heinz Pressler of *U71*; Donald Ream; R. S. Robertson, Town Clerk of Kirkwall in the Orkneys; Kpt.z.S. Hans Rösing; Richard Russon of the US Coast Guard; the Federal German Embassy in London, particularly Fregkpt P. Siedenburg; Karl Wahnig of *U802*; Gordon Williamson; George Young and Garry York.

The following have kindly supplied photographs: *Ubootsarchiv* (Horst Bredow); Kapt Otto Giese; Royal Navy Submarine Museum at HMS *Dolphin*; Karl Keller; Paul Preuss; Knut Sivertsen; Imperial War Museum; Otto Köhler; Franz Selinger; Hans Staus; Heinrich Böhm; Walter Illig; Ernst-August Gerke; Ajax Bleichrodt; Ursula von Friedeburg; Walter Lang.

The mystery surrounding the disappearance of *U377* was finally solved a few years ago when the release of Enigma documents showed *U377* to have sent a short distress call after it was hit by a torpedo. However, the signal was not picked up in Germany. The Royal Navy investigated the matter at the time and found that the torpedo had not been launched by an Allied vessel. Therefore *U377* was almost certainly sunk by a German torpedo. *U972* commanded by OL Klaus-Dietrich König suffered a similar fate during the same month.

1

The Birth of the U-boat Arm

At the end of World War 1 and with the abdication of the Kaiser in 1918, Germany became a republic governed according to the terms set out in the Treaty of Versailles, which imposed harsh penalties on the subjugated nation. This treaty was not negotiated, but dictated by the victorious Allied powers to exact revenge and to prevent a resurrection of Prussian militarism. The German military establishment was emasculated by the Versailles settlement: manpower was considerably reduced and the total strength of units was dictated; Germany was not permitted to station troops west of the Rhine; neither was she allowed to build or own heavy artillery, tanks, military aircraft, aircraft carriers or submarines.

The *Nationalsozialistische Deutsche Arbeiterpartei* (NSDAP — National Socialist German Labour Party; Socialists were nicknamed 'Sozis', thus the NSDAP became 'Nazis'), advocated the abolition of the Versailles Treaty. Adolf Hitler had been Chancellor of Germany for just two years when on 16 March 1935 he repudiated the Treaty with great publicity and ceremony. To many people's astonishment large parts of the previously prohibited forces were already in existence: the Luftwaffe (Air Force) had been functioning as a civil flying club; men had been trained in groups which posed as sports clubs; barracks had been built in the guise of factories. Although this repudiation also triggered off a new era of U-boat construction, it was by no means the beginning of the story because submarine development had been in progress since the gloomy days of 1922, some 10 years before Hitler came to power.

At that time the Imperial Navy, which had re-established itself after the war under the new name of *Reichsmarine*, encouraged the formation of a clandestine 'Submarine Development Bureau' to keep abreast of the latest underwater developments. Under the leadership of Hans Techel, (formerly director of Submarine Construction at Germaniawerft) and KK a.D Ulrich Blum (a former Military Adviser at the U-boat Inspectorate), the Bureau established itself in small, well-hidden offices at Germaniawerft in Kiel. Taking the name of *Ingenieurskantoor voor Scheepsbouw* in 1925 it moved to The Hague in Holland where it remained until the end of the war. Briefed originally to keep abreast of submarine development, the Bureau later worked with at least 19 nations to develop more than 50 projects. Many of these never progressed beyond the initial design stage and a number were not laid down until after the re-establishment of submarine construction in German yards, but sufficient programmes went ahead to give Germany a good start when she resumed building in 1935.

Progress was not without its difficulties and the first project to build three boats for Turkey could only be instigated after the German Navy had made a considerable financial contribution. The first boat of this contract, named *Birindci Inönü*, was launched in Rotterdam as early as 1 February 1927 and delivered to Turkey by a German crew.

Personal connections between King Alfonso of Spain and FK (later Admiral) Wilhelm Canaris were responsible for the Development Bureau building a boat in Cadiz for the Spanish Navy. These plans were interrupted by the Civil War however, and the submarine had to be sold to Turkey where it was commissioned under the name *Gür*. The boat underwent extensive tests under the leadership of KL a.D Robert Bräutigam, who had worked with the Submarine Acceptance Commission before the end of World War 1. The design was adopted for Soviet service, several dozen ships being built in the Series IX, IX-bis, and XVI variants. Several of these boats are considered by the Soviets to have amassed excellent war records, and one, *S56*, survives today as a memorial in Vladivostok. Other projects which led to the completion of boats before 1935 involved the construction of several boats in Finland and one in Sweden. The 'Vetehinen' class, built in Turku became the forerunner of the Type VII, and the now famous *Vesikko* was further developed to become the Type II. Other interesting projects were the construction of the smallest submarine of the day, the 99-ton *Sauko*, launched on 2 July 1930 in Turku, and the *Delfinen*, launched in Malmö, Sweden, towards the end of 1934.

By that time a considerable easing of the political situation had allowed the Development Bureau to assemble parts for about 10 small coastal submarines in Germany and its role of building for foreign countries diminished, although the Bureau continued to work on export boats for some time to come. The prohibited U-boat parts, lying in a secret store at Germaniawerft in Kiel, were only small problems, which hardly came within range of thought at the Supreme Naval Command in Berlin. Many people there thought the Allies would prevent their assembly, even if the German government gave the green light. Only a few optimists saw visions of a few coastal submarines being attached to torpedo boat flotillas for harbour defences. Other people were of the opinion that the parts would have to be sold at a considerable loss, just like the first contract with Turkey. So, in 1934 there was no need for concern about the utilisation of these few submarine parts, especially as permission to assemble them was strongly refused in November when Admiral Erich Raeder (C-in-C of the Navy) asked to go ahead with the project.

By the spring of 1935 it was in the British interest to permit an expansion of German naval forces beyond the severe restriction laid down by the Versailles Treaty and thus the British government was happy to enter into negotiations which would scrap the terms dictated only 15 years earlier. The result of these discussions was the Anglo-German Naval Agreement signed in June 1935, which was far more generous than anticipated by the German High Command and left the door open for legal U-boat development in sufficient numbers to form several autonomous flotillas; definitely too many submarines to be administered by torpedo boat officials alone. Hitler responded to the successful conclusion of the agreement

---

Below left:
Dr Erich Raeder, Supreme C-in-C of the German Navy from 1928 to 1943, is seen here on an inspection in Wilhelmshaven; the stripes on his sleeve indicate his rank as Generaladmiral. He was promoted to Grand Admiral in April 1939, at the same time as the battleship *Bismarck* was launched in Wilhelmshaven.

Below:
A close-up of *U24* shows the early type of conning tower with the national emblem on the front. The eagle also serves as emblem for boats of the 21st (Training) Flotilla in Pillau. A horseshoe-shaped life belt can be seen on both sides of the tower.

Above:
These two Type IIC boats are both slightly different: filler caps for fuel and oil were accommodated behind a flap marked with four squares, as can be seen at the bottom of the tower. The conning tower of *U61* is unusual, being similar to those more commonly found on Type IID boats.

Below:
Three typical prewar conning towers with numbers painted on the sides and the national eagle on the front. *U52* is a Type VIIB with 88mm quick firing gun whilst the other two are of Type IIC. The walls of early conning towers were smooth and without wind or spray deflectors.

by saying that the signatory day was the happiest of his life and Adm Raeder told his officers that they could not have hoped for better conditions in the next decade. But this unexpected expansion brought several unforeseen problems for the immediate future, especially as far as submarines were concerned. Plans for an administrative network had not been formulated and at this critical stage coincidence and fate stepped into the limelight. The light cruiser *Emden* with FK Karl Dönitz as captain sailed into world history. Fregkpt Dönitz! What a character and what an opportunity!

Dönitz has often been described as a successful U-boat commander of World War 1, which is most misleading because he had been in the navy for 25 years since 1910, and had only spent a little more than the last two years of the Great War with submarines. He was not a submariner at heart and had no longing to leave his prestigious post in *Emden*, especially as such a move could take him out of the running for the position of cruiser squadron commander. He had never even undergone a fully comprehensive training programme for submarines. Instead Dönitz had gone through a crash course before being pitched into action in *U39* as apprentice to the ace Walter Forstmann, the second most successful U-boat commander of World War 1. Yet, despite this limited experience, Dönitz had two terrific advantages over those with better U-boat qualifications: he had been a successful commander during the difficult times of the 1920s and had commissioned two brand new units: firstly, the 4th Torpedo Boat Half Flotilla and secondly *Emden*, which had been brought back into service with a new crew after a refit. The move from *Emden*, meaning promotion to Kapitän zur See, but returning to the type of post he had held seven years earlier as Korvettenkapitän, has been interpreted as a definite move to clip his wings, which is untrue, for Raeder did not have any hard feelings towards Dönitz. He appreciated the talents of this gifted officer and felt certain Dönitz would fit into this most difficult position, where a tactical commander with great organisational skills and a mature outlook was far more important than a submarine expert.

Dönitz was sent to Weddingen Flotilla because nobody else was available; he was left free to develop his own ideas because there was no naval policy for the employment of submarines and not because he was an expert in this field. In any case, Dönitz's appointment had only been a stopgap measure until a new commander could be found. This was due to have been Hans-Georg von Friedeburg, four years younger and with a similarly mature commanding character, but without submarine experience. Von Friedeburg underwent a period of training in a U-boat and then the war started before the switch in leadership could be made. The Naval Command thought it would be better to keep Dönitz in the position of Flag Officer for Submarines, while von Friedeburg was given the opportunity of running the far more complicated Organisation Department, which dealt with everything from commissioning new boats, to training the crews, checking their weapons and getting them to the front.

Above:
Generaladmiral Hans-Georg von Friedeburg, C-in-C of the U-boat Arm's Organisation Department and also known as the 2nd Admiral — U-boats. He is wearing the Knights Cross with Swords of the Distinguished Service Cross (*Kriegsverdienstkreuz*) around his neck. Long before the end of the war he told his wife that he would commit suicide rather than face humiliation as a prisoner-of-war. He took poison when the Dönitz Government was arrested.

2

The Essence of the Battle of the Atlantic

A considerable volume of literature on the Battle of the Atlantic has appeared since the first edition of this book was published in 1973. However, the widely accepted pattern of the war at sea has hardly been challenged. This is rather curious because that long-established image was created shortly after the war when access to information was still restricted and people had been given little time to digest the full implications of the available evidence. One would have expected at least a modification in emphasis as more information and a better analysis of statistics became available. Yet, this has not been the case. Instead, misconceptions have become further ingrained and to understand the Battle of the Atlantic, it is necessary to have a fresh look at some of the statistics.

First, let us consider the number of U-boats employed by Germany during World War 2 because the often quoted figure of 'over a thousand' is most misleading. After the war, the Royal Navy tried to account for every U-boat and found 4,712 to have existed in German records. 3,552 of these had not been completed, indeed the vast proportion had not even been laid down. That left 1,160 U-boats commissioned during the war. (This figure does not include midget submarines.) On a recent recount, Horst Bredow of the U-boat Archive on Sylt came to the conclusion

that 1,171 U-boats had been commissioned. When considering the Battle of the Atlantic, the exact figure is somewhat erroneous because it bears no relation to the number of boats which attacked and at least damaged ships. These details, calculated from the latest edition of *Axis Submarine Successes* by Prof Dr Jürgen Rohwer, are as follows:

25 U-boats attacked and at least damaged 20 or more ships;
36 U-boats attacked between 11 and 19 ships;
70 U-boats attacked between 6 and 10 ships;
190 U-boats attacked between 1 and 5 ships.

This adds up to a total of 321 U-boats. A few more can be allowed for calculation errors, but there is still an incredibly high figure of 850 U-boats which appear not to have sunk or damaged anything throughout the entire war. School boats, supply tankers, experimental craft, boats commissioned towards the end of the war and similar categories were never in the position to sink ships. So a few hundred boats could be accounted for, but it still leaves a vast gap between the total number of boats and those which actually sunk ships.

When examining this from a slightly different angle, by considering ships to have

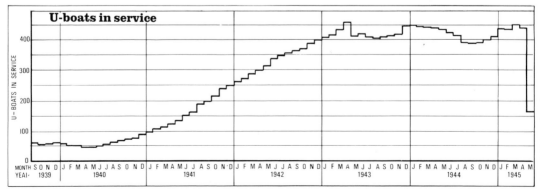

Above left:
U377 in Norway beneath a stormy summer sky in 1942. The cradle in the foreground and the scaffold at the top of the conning tower are part of the torpedo loading gear and were usually dismantled when the boat put to sea. Note the water-tight tampion on the 88mm quick-firing gun.

Above:
This shot of *U24*, a Type IIB, shows how low the conning towers were and it is not difficult to imagine how rough it must have been for lookouts in bad weather.

Left:
KK Heinrich 'Regge' Lehmann-Willenbrock talking to men of *U377*. My father, Jak Mallmann, has dressed up for the occasion by wearing a bow tie. 1WO Ernst-August 'Jumbo' Gerke, who later commanded *U673* and *U3035*, is on the left.

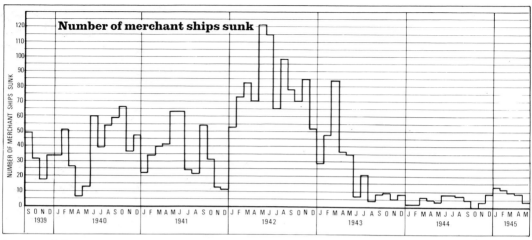

Number of merchant ships sunk

Y-axis: NUMBER OF MERCHANT SHIPS SUNK (0–120)

X-axis: S O N D 1939 | J F M A M J J A S O N D 1940 | J F M A M J J A S O N D 1941 | J F M A M J J A S O N D 1942 | J F M A M J J A S O N D 1943 | J F M A M J J A S O N D 1944 | J F M A M 1945

been sunk by men rather than machines, one comes to an even greater contrast in the statistics: about 2,450 merchant ships were sunk or seriously damaged by U-boats in the Atlantic, and the total rises to about 2,775 when other theatres of war are added. It might be interesting to add that German wartime records claim about 3,500 ships to have been sunk. Just under 800 of these ships were sunk by 30 commanders. In other words 2% of the U-boat commanders were responsible for sinking almost 30% of the shipping. Eight of these commanders joined

---

the navy before 1927, 19 of the men joined in the period 1930-34 and three belonged to the 1935 class. Therefore, almost 33% of all Allied shipping was sunk by 30 older men who joined the navy before Hitler reintroduced national conscription in 1935.

Theoretically the number of merchant ships lost was directly related to the quantity of U-boats at sea and the commissioning statistics, shown on page 133 have been quoted to illustrate the size of German patrol lines. These statistics, although reflecting the number of boats in service, fail to give an accurate picture of what was happening at sea because it does not account for the sizeable proportion which was never in a position to make a significant contact with the enemy. It is necessary therefore to use the U-boat Command's calculations of the daily average number of U-boats at sea, which are shown on page 22. This includes boats on their way out and on their way home and only about 33% of that figure was actually in the operation areas. During the first successful period in the autumn of 1940, the so-called 'Happy Time', there were not enough boats at sea to form wolf-packs. Occasionally when sufficient numbers were brought into the same area, a devastating group attack resulted such as the massacre of Convoy SC7, but on the whole numbers were insufficient to form packs.

The terrific bulge towards the latter half of 1942 and the first quarter of 1943 can be explained by the harsh preceding winter, when thick ice prevented training but production lines kept running. Consequently an unusually large number of boats went through the training establishments during spring 1942 producing the bulge in the graph on page 22. This also shows the

Above:
U106 (KL Jürgen Oesten), a Type IXB, running
parallel to *Anneliese Essberger* in an attempt to
exchange cigarettes for fresh bread on 9 September
1941. The U-boat had been ordered to escort the
blockade breaker for the final part of her voyage from
Japan to Bordeaux.

Below:
The commissioning of *U354* (KL Karl-Heinz
Herbschleb) on 22 April 1942 in Flensburg fitted with
a typical early Type VIIC conning tower with 20mm
AA gun. The white circle with line to the right (on the
forward part of the tower) is an identification mark for
training and was carried by seven boats: *U352*, *U354*,
U360, *U364*, *U369*, *U1303* and *U1307*.

Right:
The object seen here on the foredeck *U68* (KK Karl-Friedrich Merten), a Type IXC, is the head of the sound detection apparatus, which could detect propeller noises of ships when they were still invisible to lookouts on the conning tower.

Below:
A brief moment of light relief aboard *U405* in Norway during 1942. The fishing nets make good improvised camouflage, helping to break up the stark distinctive outline of the boat.

slow start of the war, mainly because Hitler was still hoping for a negotiated peace with Britain and so he seriously curtailed U-boat activities. Surface ships were even worse off and the two pocket battleships at sea, *Deutschland* (KS Paul Wenneker) and *Admiral Graf Spee* (KS Hans Langsdorff), were given orders to cease hostile action. Permission to attack shipping was only issued to them during the night of 25/26 September, some three weeks after the start of the war. Early in September 1939, Hitler agreed to an escalation in naval construction, but he did not authorise the delivery of the necessary steel until the end of the year, and it was not until the fall of France that he ordered a drastic increase in the production of submarines.

From the figures given so far, it is possible to calculate the number of ships sunk per U-boat at sea and these results are shown below. It has often been claimed that Britain came within a measurable distance of defeat during the war. This may be correct, but somehow the statement does not reflect the picture from the German side. For example, during the first 'Happy Time' in the autumn of 1940 U-boats were sinking up to 5½ merchant ships each month per U-boat at sea, but there were only 10 U-boats at sea. At least half of these were not in a position to make contact with the enemy, so Britain was indeed facing defeat by an incredibly small number of men. When the second 'Happy Time' reached its peak in May 1942 U-boats

were sinking two merchant ships each month per boat at sea, although the number of boats at sea for that month had climbed to 61. On reaching the so-called climax of the Battle of the Atlantic in February-March 1943, U-boat numbers had risen to a staggering 116 at sea, but their achievements had dropped dramatically to often less than half a merchant ship sunk each month per U-boat at sea. In other words, sinkings had dropped from over five ships per U-boat to two U-boats being required to sink one ship. So, the vast majority of boats at sea never came within shooting distance and the carnage in the convoys was created by a very small number of boats.

While collecting these details from *Axis Submarine Successes*, it became evident that during the first 'Happy Time' it was possible for U-boats to make a number of successful attacks over a period of several days. This changed from the end of 1940, when most boats which managed to sink or damage more than one target could only do so in one single attack. In other words, multiple sinkings could only be achieved if the boat managed to get through the escort screen and then shoot several torpedoes within a few minutes. From 1941 onwards it was usually not possible to get into such a shooting position more than once.

Sinkings in American waters during the first half of 1942 can be disregarded in this statistical analysis because the United States not only failed to chase their attackers, but

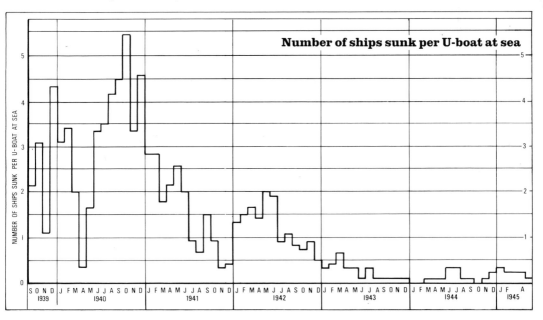

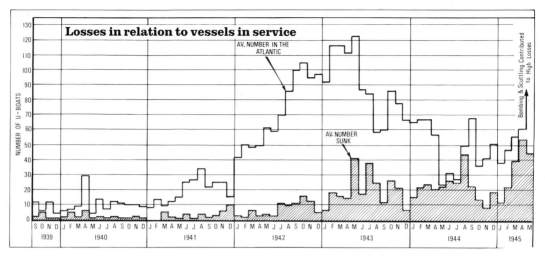

Losses in relation to vessels in service

AV. NUMBER IN THE ATLANTIC

AV. NUMBER SUNK

NUMBER OF U-BOATS

Bombing & Scuttling Contributed to High Losses

S O N D | J F M A M J J A S O N D | J F M A M J J A S O N D | J F M A M J J A S O N D | J F M A M J J A S O N D | J F M A M J J A S O N D | J F M A M
1939 | 1940 | 1941 | 1942 | 1943 | 1944 | 1945

also offered easy targets and good navigation aids to U-boats. The high figures of the second 'Happy Time' were not achieved by any noteworthy contribution by Germany, but as a result of negligence by the Americans. Germany would never have had such high successes if the counter measures already taken by the Royal Navy had been extended to American waters.

The effect of the U-boat offensive declined rapidly from the end of 1940 onwards, as is shown on page 21. The term 'offensive' is rather ambiguous in this context because it suggests a complex plan involving considerable numbers and there were usually less than a dozen boats at sea. Even the term 'U-boat Arm' over-emphasises the small number of boats with which Karl Dönitz (C-in-C U-boats) was fighting the battles from the German side. However, the effect of this small number of boats diminished dramatically and rapidly from the end of 1940. This was shortly before U99 (KL Otto Kretschmer), U100 (KL Joachim Schepke) and U47 (KL Günther Prien) were sunk, and one must look to this period of time to find an explanation for the collapse of the U-boat offensive. The view that the U-boat offensive started to collapse in 1941 instead of in 1943 is supported by the U-boat Command's war diary, where the critical year of 1941 contains an ever-increasing number of exasperated statements about U-boats failing to achieve their objectives.

U-boat losses remained low in 1941 because the Royal Navy did not have sufficient ships to hunt and sink them. British Special Intelligence gained to a large extent from being able to understand the German secret radio code, which made it possible for Allied convoys to avoid the vast majority of the small number of U-boats at sea. When contact was made, escorts could only put the attacker down because they had instructions to return to the convoy as quickly as possible. The small number of escorts made it impossible for ships to remain behind, hunting suspected U-boats. But despite this, in 1941 Britain was already in possession of the winning hand which would ultimately defeat the U-boats. The German move into American waters gave Britain valuable time to perfect technology, increase numbers and improve training for the bitter onslaught of early 1943. By that time U-boats had increased to such numbers that it was often possible to have at least two wolf packs in the operations areas at the same time, covering too vast an area to be avoided by convoys. Confrontation became inevitable and resulted in large convoy battles, but the effect of each individual U-boat had already declined to small proportions.

May 1943 has often been considered as the critical month when the U-boat offensive collapsed. The U-boat losses were certainly a bitter blow to Germany, but one needs to take the drama out of the situation and consider the facts objectively. The fateful month of May 1943 becomes less important when one considers that it is relatively easy to sink a submarine! Once submerged, it is comparatively immobile and without defences against well-placed depth charges. The major problem in the procedure is to get the depth charge launcher to the right place at the right time. So the turning point for the Allies came when they could locate U-boats closing in during the hours of darkness and turn them away before they reached their targets.

3

Steps to Unrestricted Sea Warfare

In 1939 international laws regarding the conduct of war against merchant shipping were based on foundations laid at the Paris Congress of 1856, with modifications established at the Second Hague Convention in 1907 and the London Declaration of 1909. These points were brought up to date by the London Protocol of 1930, when the main maritime nations agreed on a variety of limitations regarding the use of submarines and Germany signed this document on 6 November 1936, a year after she had reintroduced U-boats to her Navy. The Protocol did not dictate how each participating nation should implement the agreements and a general instruction to the armed forces to obey the rules would have been sufficient. However, in Germany the regulations were drawn together and passed through the legal system under the title of 'German Prize Ordinance', to be made law on 3 September, the day on which Britain and France declared war.

At 14.00hrs on that fateful day, the German Supreme Naval Command sent a signal to all ships at sea ordering them to start hostilities, and one hour later U-boat commanders were especially warned to follow Operational Orders when attacking merchant shipping. This was nothing new to them as it formed the basis of their thinking since the vast majority of them had been in command. The rules made it necessary for merchant ships to be stopped and searched; they could only be sunk if they were carrying war goods for the enemy. Submarines had been considered in the same light as surface warships and were therefore expected to ensure the safety of the crews before sinking any ships. Lifeboats were considered unsuitable accommodation on the high seas, making the regulations virtually impossible to honour because submariners either had to take the merchant sailors into their already overcrowded boats or operate close to land.

U-boat Command had provided little in the way of training to enable submariners to board merchant ships at sea, and at the start of the war, U-boats tried to concentrate on targets which could be attacked without warning. Six categories of merchant shipping were listed in an exclusion clause in the agreement and, like warships, these could be attacked without previously being stopped for an inspection of cargoes. These were: troopships, armed merchant ships, merchant ships sailing with a warship escort, ships sailing in convoy, ships participating in military action (which included the passing on of military intelligence), and ships identified as carrying war goods.

Germany's desire to observe Prize Ordinance Regulations and not to strike the first blow at sea was given a severe blow on the first day of the war when KL Fritz-Julius Lemp (*U30*) sank the 13,581grt passenger liner *Athenia*, thinking he had an auxiliary cruiser or troopship in his sights. This single action has often been blamed as having given the Royal Navy the impression that Germany was disregarding previous agreements and had ordered a state of unrestricted sea warfare. Britain allowed her forces more freedom in the attacking of Germany, while this incident led to Hitler enforcing even tighter restrictions upon naval operations. His immediate reaction to the *Athenia* sinking was to forbid attacks against all passenger ships. At the same time, on 6 September, the German government issued an order to exclude merchant ships carrying food to the United Kingdom from military action, and the two pocket battleships *Admiral Graf Spee* and *Deutschland*, were ordered to cease all hostilities, except in self defence, until 25/26 September.

The varying interpretations of the London Protocol by different nations made it necessary to amend the German Prize Ordinance Rules less than two weeks after they had been made law, and on 12 September the government revised its definition of the term

Right:
This photograph of *U405* is worth showing to naval buffs to see whether they notice anything odd: there is a minesweeper escort sailing ahead which is producing the double bow wave configuration.

Below:
U50 (KL Max-Hermann Bauer), a Type VIIB seen here during the winter of 1939/40, cruising past the locks of the Kiel Canal. The cold weather helps to make the diesel exhaust clearly visible. The 20mm AA gun on this type of boat was first placed on the upper deck, just aft of the conning tower as can clearly be seen. Also of note is the net cutter on the bows of the boat which was still a standard feature at this time.

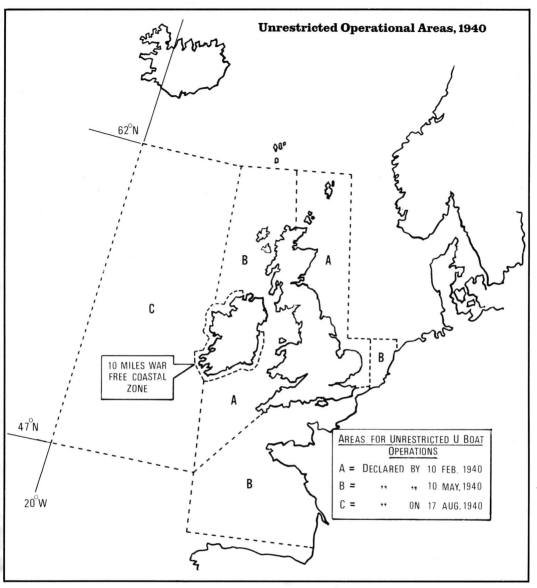

Unrestricted Operational Areas, 1940

62°N

47°N

20°W

B

A

C

10 MILES WAR
FREE COASTAL
ZONE

A

B

B

AREAS FOR UNRESTRICTED U BOAT
OPERATIONS

A = DECLARED BY 10 FEB. 1940
B =   ,,   ,,   10 MAY, 1940
C =   ,,   ON 17 AUG. 1940

'contraband'. Initially it had been taken to mean goods used directly by armed forces for the conduct of war, but Britain announced she would also include food and a number of other non-military items. Therefore Germany felt it necessary to follow by including such items as well and as a result of the Anglo-French Contraband Declaration of 4 September, they issued a detailed list of prohibited goods. Items were graded for their use as 'war goods' and a type of circular slide rule was produced for officers at sea to dial in the type of cargo and read off what action to take.

Despite this hive of activity in government circles, the efforts hardly helped the men at sea who were perplexed by the constantly changing rules and by the impossibility of some of the instructions. For example, how were they to determine whether a potential target was carrying passengers or troops? The U-boat Command complained to the naval hierarchy, saying Prize Ordinance was hardly working because merchant ships were sending special 'SSS' distress calls as well as taking evasive, and on some occasions agressive, action against U-boats which were trying to stop them. Frequently such distress calls brought aircraft to the scene, causing unpleasant incidents, some of which could

Above:
KL Dietrich von der Esch (left) on the bridge of *U586*. There was little for him to do at this stage because a canal pilot had control of the boat.

Right:
The U-boat conning tower hatch: at sea this was usually the only way in or out of the boat. The torpedo hatches cut through circular supports which meant sections had to be unscrewed every time they were used. The other opening, the galley hatch just aft of the conning tower, was generally not used at sea because it was too easy for water to wash in and closing it could delay diving during an emergency.

have led to the loss of U-boats. The German government responded on 24 September by allowing U-boats to attack if the target used its radio, taking the view that the sending of the special SSS signal with position constituted a passing on of military intelligence, but it was emphasised that the crews of sunken ships were to be saved. (Ordinary SOS calls were replaced by SSS meaning attack by submarine. RRR was also introduced for when the attacker was a surface raider. Later on in the war the letters were repeated four instead of the initial three times to become RRRR.) A week later such incidents led to the abandonment of Prize Ordinance Regulations in the North Sea and the approaches to the Baltic because it was felt that retaliatory action could lead to the sinking of U-boats in these waters.

Two weeks later on 2 October 1939, the Naval War Staff also gave permission for U-boats to attack merchant ships which were not displaying normal lighting at night because it was assumed such vessels would probably be carrying war goods. However, this action was restricted to a relatively small area around the British Isles, extending to 7°W and from 44°N to 62°N. Meanwhile, Britain was also taking steps to intensify the war against U-boats by fitting more armaments to merchant ships and early in October the Admiralty in London suggested that merchant ships might try ramming U-boats which attempted to stop them. Hitler responded on 4 October by allowing U-boats to attack without warning not only ships seen to be armed, but also those listed as armed. This hardly satisfied the U-boat Command, who feared the enemy could be using disguised ships as submarine traps, as had been done in World War 1, and two weeks later Hitler bowed to demands and gave permission for all suspicious ships to be

Above:
With her engines at rest, *U24* (OL Helmut Hennig), a Type IIB, gently rises and falls with the swell of the glassy sea. The entire crew, except for a few men manning the rowing boat from which this picture was taken, is standing on the upper deck.

attacked. This was followed by an enlargement to 20°W, of the area where darkened ships could be attacked without warning. On 19 October the U-boat Command ordered ships not to be boarded any more because there had been a number of attacks from aircraft while part of the crews had been aboard the merchant ship, meaning the U-boat had to dive without them and in some cases men were injured while trying to retrieve the boarding party. U-boats were still allowed to stop ships with their guns and wait for papers to be brought over, but they were ordered not to get involved in artillery exchanges and to sink all targets with torpedoes. Cartridges for the gun had to be brought up through the conning tower hatch by hand, and diving in an emergency took too long when the gun crew was on deck, with cartridges being passed along their only way of entry.

Passenger ships, although there was no special clause for them in Prize Ordinance Regulations, still enjoyed considerable immunity from attack. It was mid-November before Germany realised that they were being converted to auxiliary cruisers and gave permission for passenger ships with visible armaments, or those listed as having been armed, to be attacked, but the last restrictions of attacks against passenger ships were not lifted until August 1940.

The German government's desire to leave the responsibility for starting fighting at sea to the countries who declared the war, and the vague hope of still coming to a negotiated peace, resulted in French shipping also enjoying special exemptions from attack during the early months of the war. Despite France having declared war against Germany only six hours after Britain, U-Boats were initially instructed only to take defensive action against French ships and were not even allowed to stop them, meaning they received better treatment than neutrals. These rules were almost impossible to obey since U-boat commanders could not always establish the nationality, especially of darkened ships at night. Furthermore, the abandonment of a late stage of an attack, when the target was identified as French, put several U-boats into most dangerous predicaments where they had to extract themselves from a ring of enemy ships without being able to shoot. On 10 September the Naval Command lifted these regulations for a small area north of Brest, but only two weeks passed before the necessity to avoid conflict with French ships was again emphasised. Karl Dönitz protested most strongly, outlining the problems being faced by the men at sea, who were frequently being confronted with a combination of French and English groups. Consequently the restrictions were lifted on 24 October 1939, when it was ordered that French ships were to be treated the same way as the British.

Neutral shipping was still a problem at this time. There was an incident on 30 September when *U3* (KL Joachim Schepke) sank a Danish coaster at 10.00am and a Swedish ship at 10.00pm. (*Vendia* and *Gun*, both just over 1,000grt.) One of them turned on the U-boat in an attempt to ram her and as a result the German government warned neutral nations to instruct their ships not to indulge in suspicious actions such as zig-zagging, sudden changes of course, sending unidentifiable radio messages or failing to display the correct lighting at night. There followed no noteworthy incidents of interference from neutrals, although the minesweeper M1 (KL Hans Bartels) was confronted by three Danish fishing boats with more than the usual radio equipment and some British naval manuals. With insufficient evidence to molest them, but feeling certain they were in communication with the enemy, Bartels took the unorthodox step of sending his men below with instructions for all port holes to be closed. Then, alone on the bridge because he did not want to burden his men with any responsibility, he ordered full speed and used the cycloidal propeller to sink the boats. There

were no survivors, only a large hole in the bows of M1. Several neutral merchant ships were sunk as a result of the Royal Navy procedure of taking them into British harbours for inspection of cargoes. Consequently a number of innocent neutrals were subject to interference by U-boats and a few were sunk close to British waters.

The restrictive measures so far outlined, sounding more like the ingredients for a comic opera, placed the U-boat Command in a difficult position between the Supreme Naval Command and irate submariners. The latter frequently found themselves at the receiving end as a direct result of the limitations placed upon them. Karl Dönitz campaigned for more freedom, but it was almost three months after the start of the war, on 24 November 1939, before a positive initiative was taken by the German government. The first step was to send a warning to neutral powers, informing them that the safety of their ships could no longer be guaranteed in the waters around the British Isles and suggesting a number of safe routes for their traffic. At the same time secret instructions were sent to the U-boat Command, giving permission to attack tankers and certain other types of shipping, except those belonging to Russia, Japan, Italy, Spain, Greece and the USA. However, it was stressed that U-boats had to remain unseen and use only electric torpedoes which did not leave a wake, to give the impression of an internal explosion or a mine. Greek shipping, a large proportion of which was sailing under British charter, was included in the instructions on 30 December, when the Supreme Naval Command again emphasised the importance of U-boats remaining unobserved during attacks on such targets, to avoid political repercussions.

The operations area was enlarged as indicated on the map on page 25, but a situation of unrestricted sea warfare did not come into being until 17 August 1940, when Germany announced a blockade area around the UK in which merchant ships would be sunk without warning. Only clearly marked ships going to or coming from the Republic of Ireland were allowed to pass. However, this situation lasted for only a few months before U-boat action was curtailed further with regard to US ships in this total war zone. Even unlit American warships indulging in hostile action were not allowed to be attacked. Incidents involving 'neutral' US ships are now well documented and lasted until America joined in the war in December 1941.

4

The Wolf Pack Attack — from Vision to Reality

U-boats were drawn into the prelude to war at around noon on 15 August 1939 when KL Werner Fresdorf telephoned from the Supreme Naval Command in Berlin to confirm that submarines were to be included in the recently ordered state of naval emergency and the U-boat Command was to put the so-called 'Three Front War Programme' into immediate effect. This was designed in previous years to meet a possible conflict in the Baltic, North Sea and in the Atlantic. Karl Dönitz returned from leave in Austria the following day and the first boats were ready to sail one day later. However, they did not sail on that day because tradition has it that ships do not leave a home port on a Friday. So they weighed anchor in the early hours of 19 August and members of the U-boat fleet proceeded to take up waiting positions at sea.

Dönitz thought there could well be a lull in the flow of traffic because Britain and France had probably stockpiled vital necessities before declaring war, and since all U-boats were at sea with no reserves in port he considered it best to withdraw those furthest out to get them ready to meet an anticipated increase in merchant shipping later on. At the same time, he wanted to introduce the now famous 'Wolf Pack Attack'. Contrary to some modern views, this had not been conceived during World War 1 and perfected before the start of World War 2. The U-boat Command had been experimenting with the concept since 1936, but had come to no definite conclusions and only got as far as demonstrating that the idea might work. There was considerable opposition to the plan and even Dönitz was not certain he could solve the remaining problems. It was the

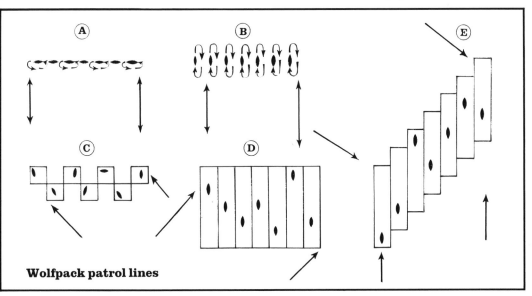

Wolfpack patrol lines

absence of any better suggestions which spurred him on and in theory the wolf pack attack, where a group of U-boats attacked a convoy together, offered good prospects.

The first attempt to put a wolf pack to sea was made during early October 1939, while U-boats were returning from the operations areas they had occupied from before the declaration of hostilities. U42 (KL Rolf Dau) became the first boat to leave Germany with the sole objective of forming a pack off Southern Ireland and five more boats, including U37 (KK Werner Hartmann) whose commander was to act as pack leader, followed during the next few days. The group never got into position to form a pack because three boats were sunk on their way out and another three were held up in port with mechanical trouble.

The second attempt of getting a pack to sea was made in early November, when U43 (KL Wilhelm Ambrosius), U41 (KL Gustav Adolf Mugler) and U49 (KL Curt von Gossler) were positioned to the northwest of Cape Finisterre. The next four boats to join this group were withdrawn at the last minute on instructions from the Supreme Naval Command, who wanted them to go into northern waters for an operation against warships and the other three boats were ordered into the Mediterranean, leaving the potential pack off Cape Finisterre rather short.

Sceptics who argued that the pack idea may have worked in the confines of the narrow Baltic during naval exercises, but that it would be too difficult for a group to converge on a point over the vastness of the Atlantic, were given something to think about during January 1940 when U34 (KL Wilhelm Rollmann) and U44 (KL Ludwig Mathes) were brought together from positions some 800sm apart, (910m or 1,490km), to work in the same area. Critics, who were saying wolf packs would be defeated because the enemy could pin point the positions from which radio messages were transmitted, were also defeated during this first winter of the war. Thanks to the Royal Navy using a fairly dated cypher system, it was possible for the German B-Dienst (Radio Monitoring Service) under Heinz Bonatz to understand a fair proportion of its radio messages. This intelligence showed Britain's smallest detection error to have been some 30sm, but usually there was a difference of 300 to 600sm, too great to be of any concern to U-boats. It was also argued that Britain would re-route convoys once the shadowing submarines had been detected,

but the U-boat Command maintained that since Britain did not know the positions of the pack, the Admiralty could just as well direct merchant ships towards the U-boats as away from them. Dönitz argued that it was important to keep a happy balance in the use of radio in order to keep the pack together, because total abstention could be self defeating and put Germany back to the single boat mode of operations of World War 1.

The intensive use of boats throughout the autumn of 1939 resulted in the vast majority needing to go into dock by the end of the year and consequently there was a lull in activity during the winter months. Operations were just getting under way again when all units were recalled to prepare for the invasion of Denmark and Norway, where machinery was put under such strain as to ensure another enforced period in dock before recommencing the offensive against merchant shipping. The first boats to operate in North Atlantic shipping lanes after the Norwegian campaign left Germany towards the end of May 1940 and appeared in large enough numbers for two wolf packs to be formed. Following the pattern established earlier, each group was under the control of a tactical leader, who was also a U-boat commander at the same time and the packs were identified by the names of these men.

At this stage U-boat operations against merchant shipping developed far better than anticipated and there followed a terrific carnage known as the 'Happy' or 'Golden Time'. U-boats were confronted with so many unprotected targets that they often expended their torpedoes by hitting solitary ships long before enough boats assembled for a pack attack against a convoy. Furthermore, once a U-boat had found a convoy, it often failed to get support because other submarines encountered different groups of merchant ships while converging on the given position and at times the situation became so confusing that a number of U-boats, thought to be tracking the same convoy, were in fact stalking different ones sailing close together. This successful period was the only time throughout the whole war when the U-boats could have won the upper hand in the bitter Atlantic battles, but there were not enough of them to inflict a decisive blow. The graph showing the daily average number of U-boats at sea includes those on their way home and travelling out. Thus the daily average in contact with the enemy was only about one third of the figures given in the graph. The terrific successes were mainly due to close

Above:
U377 (KK Otto Köhler), launched at Howaldts Werke in Kiel on 12 August 1941, showing the final development of deflectors on the conning tower. The lip at the top acted as a 'wind deflector' and half way up is the spray deflector. The bulge at the bottom houses filler caps for fuel and oil, and a magnetic compass. The compass housing was fitted with a light and periscope so that it could be viewed by the helmsman in the central control room.

Left:
U992 (OL Hans Falke) loading torpedoes. The storage container between the pressure hull and the upper deck can be seen hinged upwards, forward of the hatch.

Above:
U377 (KK Otto Köhler), a Type VIIC, during the
summer of 1942. The arrow points to the underwater
sound detection apparatus and the cradle in the
foreground is part of the torpedo loading gear.

Right:
Royal Navy Intelligence calculated that a lookout
would spend up to half an hour during each four-hour
duty spell cleaning his binocular lenses with a soft
leather. The periscopes also needed attention and here
KK Rolf-Heinrich Hopman, commander of *U405*, is
doing the job himself during the battle for Convoy
PQ18. The wires around the periscope were supposed
to have added additional stability by spiralling the
flow of water around it. A rope has been fastened
across the opening at the back of the conning tower to
help lookouts when they are washed off their feet in
bad weather.

range attack at night on the surface, something for which the Royal Navy was completely unprepared and had no counter-meaures to prevent the slaughter in the shipping lanes.

The U-boat Command was certain that this unexpected and advantageous state of affairs would not continue for long and Dönitz wanted to establish techniques for the wolf pack attack while the going was good and he still had the upper hand. The initial concept of this method had already undergone radical modification since the idea was first tried out three to four years earlier in Baltic exercises. One of the primary changes since the beginning of the war was the replacement of the tactical commander in a U-boat at sea with a land-based centralised control. Because radio communications were better than expected, the task could be accom-plished with greater ease from a land-based operations room. No one in the U-boat Command held the magic formula for success and generally people felt it would be better for each boat commander to make his own decisions once he had come within sight of his targets. Finding convoys in the first place, however, was still the major problem. Originally it had been thought that this task could be carried out by aircraft, but the lack of air support is well known today and it never played a significant role in the U-boat war. However, the German Radio Monitoring Service (B-Dienst) under Heinz Bonatz managed to provide the U-boat Command with details of Allied convoy positions, and submarines were then established in long patrol lines to make contact with the ships. The U-boat Command usually remained in direct control of the proceedings until the boats were within striking distance at which point permission was given for attack and commanders were free to carry on the best they could. A check was kept on convoy and pack movements at U-boat headquarters on land because at times the battle became too hectic and got out of control. One of the frequent occurrences was for all boats to withdraw after the battle to reload, leaving no one in contact with the convoy and in such an event Dönitz would interfere and order specific boats to shadow. Today it is usually assumed that only one submarine was used to keep tabs on the target, but Dönitz preferred to have a small group in contact because interference from escorts usually resulted in someone being pushed under. It must also be emphasised that as far as possible, U-boats shadowed convoys by sail-ing in front of the merchant ships, rather than following behind them.

The prospects of making contact with the enemy after the shock of the 'Happy Time' in the autumn of 1940 were slim unless the B-Dienst could keep up with a steady supply of convoy positions well ahead of the time when ships were due to arrive in the known location. Meanwhile in London, the Admiralty had perceived these difficulties and took the necessary action. The small number of U-boats available meant that only one or perhaps two small patrol lines could be established at any one time and the area to be covered was determined by the gaps between individual boats. They had to be close enough together to make it difficult for the convoy to slip through without being seen, and even if the weather allowed for large distances, spreading the eyes over too vast an area was self defeating because those boats furthest out might not reach the battle in time. The patrol lines had to be far enough from the UK to leave a few days steaming in which to attack an eastbound convoy and not too far west to run short of fuel when pursuing an outward bound group. It might be interesting to add that it was this factor which determined U-boat operations areas for the winter of 1940/41 and the Germans were not driven west because aircraft from RAF Coastal Command made waters closer to land too hot for them, as has been claimed.

The actual composition of patrol lines was given considerable thought with one of the first ideas being for boats to sail in line ahead, at right angles to the anticipated convoy. This proved quite successful in the narrow Baltic before the war but left each individual boat with very little freedom of movement. Prolonged bad weather as frequently occurs in the Atlantic made navigation difficult, and meant that radio beacons were constantly required to keep the chain intact. Further-more, speed and timing were vital; in poor weather some boats would close up to leave large gaps in other areas. The more favoured method was to establish the boats in line abreast to sail towards the anticipated convoy during daylight, and then turning to sail with it during the hours of darkness. Both these patterns declined in effect as the angle between convoy and patrol line changed from 90°, and in the Atlantic U-boats had to expect zig-zagging convoys coming from a variety of directions. Therefore the idea failed to find much support after the end of 1940.

To overcome this problem, patrol lines were established as two-dimensional patterns of slightly varying designs as illustrated by a typical formation in the diagram on page 29. Each U-boat had a small square shaped operations area and the increase in the depth of the line was thought to make it more likely for convoys to be spotted, no matter at what angle it approached. Such a net would also make it more difficult for enemy aircraft to determine the exact location of other boats, even if they managed to stalk upon the pack and perhaps spot several U-boats at once. This pattern was modified by enlarging each boat's operation zone from a square to a long, narrow rectangle, giving each commander more freedom of movement and making it more difficult for the enemy to recognise the exact make up of the pack. Furthermore, the direction of the patrol line could be changed by merely sliding the defined operational box for each boat, as is shown in the diagram, making it easy to challenge convoys approaching from any direction. The sighting boat had the difficult and unpleasant task of shadowing the merchant ships until sufficient numbers could be brought together for a mass attack. This task required not only a great deal of nerve, but also considerable skill to remain in touch with the objective even if attacked itself. The fact that this could actually be achieved was not demonstrated until the autumn of 1940 when U93 (KL Claus Korth) followed an outward bound convoy for four days and only failed to call in other boats because they were busy attacking convoys SC7 and HX72.

Bringing U-boats to the scene was done in three ways. First, details were radioed to U-boat Command, who would direct possible boats to the appropriate area. The shadow boat would also broadcast position, course and speed of the convoy at hourly intervals, and at the same time if requested, transmit radio beacon signals whose direction could be detected by other U-boats by using their radio direction finders. (The aerial of this device consisted of a circular loop fixed to the top of the conning tower and the signal usually consisted of the morse letter 'V' sent continuously for three minutes.)

At the start of the war equal importance was put on submerged and surface attacks, but as time progressed emphasis started to swing towards remaining on the surface because that offered far better performances for U-boats. By the late autumn of 1940, all night attacks were generally carried out on the surface, with submarines being used as torpedo boats. Diving tanks were not pre-

flooded and there were no standing orders for boats to dive, consequently some commanders hardly dived at all. It was also usual for the U-boat Command to prohibit daylight submerged attacks if there were chances of boats getting in for an attack during the coming night. This depended on the amount of fuel and on the location of the convoy: attacking close to land was considered too risky and it was impractical to follow merchant ships too far west.

Once darkness set in and U-boats started their run in to shoot, they would often report details to the U-boat Command and then approach as close as the commander dared, the actual distance being determined by the strength of the escorts. Originally it was thought best to go into the side of the convoy and shoot from a range of 1 to 3km. However, this distance was quickly reduced and some commanders like Otto Kretschmer pioneered the idea of actually sailing within the ranks of the merchant ships to shoot at point blank range from an unsuspected position, while escorts dashed around the outside in pursuit of the attacker. Shortly before daybreak, the U-boats had to vacate the convoy and vanish into the vastness of the ocean before they could be seen by escorts or by air cover, which usually arrived at first light. A skirmish late in the night could result in boats being put down and then losing the convoy for the next attack during the following night.

Today, it is well known that Britain gained the upper hand in the Battle of the Atlantic by being able to understand the German radio code, and as a result started to re-route convoys around known wolf packs. The German High Command failed to recognise how this was done and despite a constant analysis, U-boat headquarters never found out how patrol lines were discovered. It became blatantly obvious that the positions of wolf packs were known to the enemy and that they were avoiding the German formations. The U-boat Command had only one card left in its hand to play: that was to keep the pack constantly on the move, forming fast moving patrol lines to sweep across the Atlantic in the hope of catching merchant shipping in the way a trawler would catch fish. The first of these fast moving patrol lines formed to the southwest of Iceland on 6 September 1941, moving in an arc for 12 days to disperse off Cape Farewell on 18 September. Boats short on fuel returned to France, while four other boats (U109 KL 'Ajax' Bleichrodt, U208 OL Alfred Schliepner, U374 OL Unno von Fischer and *U573* KL Heinrich Heinsohn) were ordered west for a reconnaissance of the Canadian coast.

Wolf packs continued to feature in ever-increasing numbers until the end of the war, but Britain did not invest all her efforts in brute force and the production of more high explosives. Instead Britain turned to high technology to beat the U-boats, and antiquated submarines like Types VIIC and IXC, which had basically been conceived during World War 1 could not keep pace in the technological race. Even considerable modifications and pushing them out in ever increasing numbers did not help in winning what had become an Atlantic battle of high technology.

Below:
U203 (KL Rolf Mützelburg) in France after her 6th operational cruise. The attack periscope is slightly raised to hold the pennants showing the number of ships sunk. Each pennant, recording the victim's tonnage, represents one ship sunk.

5

Away from the Convoy Routes

The Black Sea

There were no prewar plans for naval engagements in the Black Sea and the only unit with direct access to this theatre, the Danube Flotilla, was equipped with special shallow bottomed river craft unsuitable for operations on the open sea. When the Army started the offensive on the Eastern Front, the Supreme Command of the Armed Forces (Oberkommando der Wehrmacht — OKW) over-estimated the performance of the Rumanian Navy, which was expected to fight alongside German troops and a number of minor set-backs occurred in Black Sea coastal regions as a result of enemy seaborne activity. Consequently, plans were made to bring German naval expertise to help in gaining supremacy on the water. The only feasible solution was to take boats as far as Dresden on the river Elbe, transport them by motorway to Regensburg and then float them down the Danube to a location with deep enough water to allow their reassembly. Bridges as well as shallow water presented considerable stumbling blocks and the process of moving naval units proved quite a challenge. Yet despite the difficulties, six U-boats, 16 motor torpedo boats, over 20 motor mine sweepers, almost 30 submarine chasers and a number of other craft were taken on the complicated journey to the Black Sea Coast.

The U-boats were among the most difficult to transport since they had to be split into several pieces before they could proceed upstream from Hamburg. However, it appears as if all the boats were dismantled in Kiel. The first stage was to cut each boat into three sections, remove engines and other heavy gear and lay the hulls on their side, to be carried by specially built pontoons. While this was in progress, 50-ton road transporters were manufactured for the overland stage. To make matters even more complicated, the pontoons had to be lifted out of the river Elbe and transported by rail to the Danube to carry the sections as far as Linz in Austria. There, the water was deep enough to allow reassembly and the U-boats continued their journey between two barges. One report states that these were intended as camouflage, while another account claimed there was a cradle between the barges to help support the U-boat.

To give some idea of the time taken for the journey, U9 (KL Hans-Joachim Schmidt-Weichert), the first U-boat, arrived in Kiel during April 1942 to be dismantled at Deutsche Werke and was recommissioned in the Black Sea on 28 October of the same year. At this time, U23 (KL Rolf-Birger Wahlen), the third boat of the first wave, arrived for stripping and she was recommissioned on 3 June 1943, winter weather having helped to slow the progress. The second boat of the first wave was U19 (OL Hans Ludwig Gaude), which arrived in Kiel at the same time as U9 and was recommissioned on 9 November 1942.

The second wave, U18, U20 and U23 (also Type IIB boats) left during the same summer but were not recommissioned until the middle of 1943. The first boat to end its life in the Black Sea was U9 (OL Heinrich Klapdor), which was destroyed during an air raid on Constanca on 20 August 1944. U18 (OL Karl Fleige) and U24 (OL Dieter Lenzmann) were also damaged by bombs and scuttled five days later. The remaining three boats continued until they ran out of fuel, when they made their way eastwards. There were plans to sell them to Turkey, but political problems prevented such a deal and they were finally scuttled off the Turkish coast. Quite a number of the Black Sea contingent managed to make their way back to Germany to see further service in other theatres.

The Mediterranean

The first thrust into the Mediterranean was ordered by the Supreme Naval Command

Above:
U24 after her 5th mission in the Black Sea. The large gun mount looks somewhat out of place under the small 20mm gun.

Above right:
Hans Staus of U377 wearing a life jacket with a whistle attached. His hat is the so-called 'Schiffchen' (Little Ship), which was popular becuse it folded flat when not in use.

Below:
The bow sections of two U-boats lying on pontoons for transport to the Black Sea. The vent configurations suggest that U19 is on the left and U23 on the right.

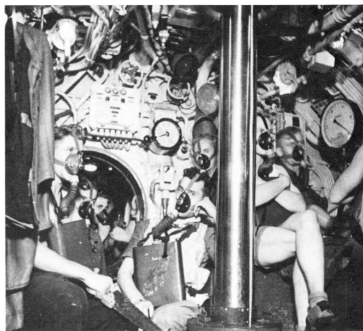

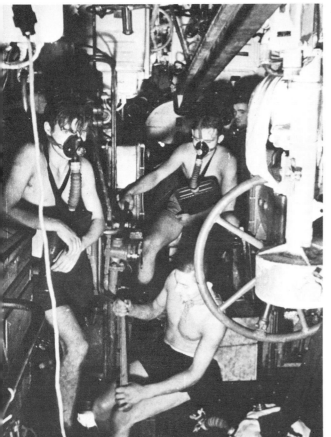

Above left:
U73's commander, KL Helmut Rosenbaum with a microphone at his mouth, gives the order 'Prepare to surface', after the aircraft carrier HMS *Eagle* had been sunk in the Mediterranean. His binoculars are at the ready, the navigation periscope is just behind him and the large dial shows a depth of 25m. It was only used near the surface and another gauge was used to indicate greater depths.

Above:
'Why did the old man attack an aircraft carrier?' The men of *U73* are paying for their success by having to remain submerged and undetected for a long time. They are breathing through *Kalipatronen*, an air purification apparatus which absorbed carbon dioxide. The large, shallow depth gauge, just to the left of the ladder on the right, shows the boat to be deeper than 25m. The engine telegraph (to the right of the circular pressure resistant door) indicates 'very slow ahead'. The black object above it and over the small wheel, is the viewing screen of the magnetic compass which was housed in the projection at the bottom of the conning tower. The periscope occupies the middle of the picture.

Left:
Crewmen of *U73* during a depth charge attack after the sinking of HMS *Eagle*, test the bilges with an indicator to check that none of the batteries have cracked. Acid turned the indicator red. The door to the rear torpedo tube can be seen in the background and on the top is a girder for carrying the winch when reloading. The wheel on the right is an emergency steering wheel.

shortly after the outbreak of hostilities and preparations to send three boats started while they were on their way home from the first action of the war. *U26* (KK Klaus Ewerth), *U25* (KK Victor Schütze) and *U53* (KL Ernst-Günther Heinicke) were ordered to break though the Straits of Gibraltar for a mining operation. Karl Dönitz, at that time Flag Officer for U-boats, was not keen on the idea because the long journey kept the boats from sinking ships nearer home and the break through the Straits of Gibraltar was considered most dangerous. The men in the U-boats also appear to have shared his view and *U53* broke off the attempt after she sighted a convoy and chased that instead of continuing with her original plan. Plans to refuel the boats in Spanish ports fell through and gave *U25* a good excuse not to carry on into the 'Gibraltar Mousetrap', leaving only *U26* to penetrate the narrow straits in early November. *U26* recorded the sinking of a ship with torpedoes, but this has never been verified and Jürgen Rohwer in his book *Axis Submarine Successes* considers it as dubious. Dönitz considered the whole undertaking as a waste of time because the boats could have sunk more shipping in the waters around the British Isles. By complying with the orders of the Supreme Naval Command he only proved the venture to have been the utter failure predicted before the boats left.

On 10 June 1940 Italy joined Germany in the war, throwing operations in the Mediterranean theatre into a new perspective. The U-boat Command was still against operating in those calm, clear waters, but was forced to detach boats from the Atlantic and send them through the 'Mousetrap', so called because the Germans considered it relatively simple to get in, but virtually impossible to get back out again. Currents flowing from the Atlantic helped boats on their eastward passage, but struggling against this on the return voyage was considerably more difficult. The hazards of such an undertaking are well illustrated in the television film *Das Boot* (The Boat), and men who actually made the attempt consider the episode in the film where *U96* tries to break into the Mediterranean past a destroyer and aircraft screen, to be most realistic. Once inside the Mediterranean, U-boats only remained under the jurisdiction of the U-boat Command for a short distance east of Gibraltar before control was transferred to the Mediterranean Command of the Navy. Administration and port facilities were still organised by U-boat men in the same way as it was done in France and in Germany.

U-boat life in the Mediterranean was more than difficult: clear, smooth waters made it easy for ships to spot them; observers in aircraft could see shadows of submerged submarines down to depths of about 20m; interiors got too hot for comfort and the boats had to remain submerged for such long periods that men often lived with breathing gear permanently on. U-boats were still without air purification systems and they only carried a supply of emergency air purifiers at the start of the war. These consisted of a mask worn over mouth and nose and attached with a flexible pipe to a tin containing potash, which absorbed carbon dioxide. Later on in the war, when remaining submerged for long periods became the rule of the day, boats had such equipment fitted to the walls and it was not necessary for men to wear a mask attached to their face.

Despite the difficulties of the Mediterranean, U-boats reaped some considerable successes: *U81* (KL Friedrich Guggenberger) sank the aircraft carrier HMS *Ark Royal* on 13 November 1941 and *U331* (KL Hans-Diedrich, Freiherr von Tiesenhausen) torpedoed the battleship HMS *Barham* on 25 November. As the stricken ship turned over, water flowed down her funnels to reach the boilers and the subsequent steam explosion tore the 30,000 tons of steel apart in a most dramatic manner. Despite this great blast, pictures of which have appeared in many books, the men in *U331* did not realise they had sunk the battleship until sometime after returning to port. The other major warship sinking was the aircraft carrier HMS *Eagle*, which was sent to the bottom by torpedoes from *U73* (KL Helmut Rosenbaum) on 11 August 1942.

American and Canadian Waters

Towards the latter part of November 1941, only a few weeks before the Japanese attack on Pearl Harbor, the Supreme Command of the *Kriegsmarine* ordered all U-boats to be withdrawn from the convoy routes of the North Atlantic. Boats with fuel and torpedoes were instructed to make for the approaches of the Mediterranean, while others were recalled to be prepared for supporting the North African Campaign. So on 11 December 1941, when Germany declared war on the United States, U-boats were either near to Gibraltar or in port. There were no U-Boats anywhere near mid-Atlantic which could be diverted to take advantage of new possibilities in the western Atlantic. Canada had so

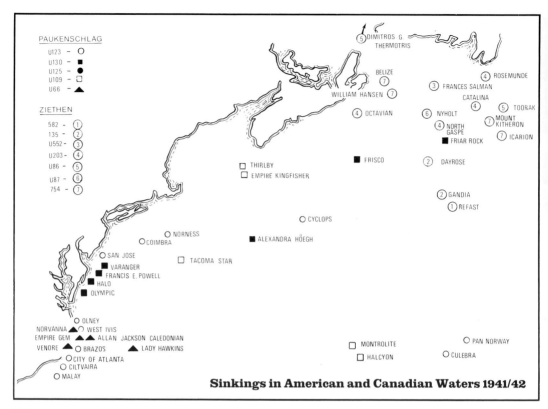

⑤ DIMITROS G.
THERMOTRIS

BELIZE
⑦

④ ROSEMUNDE

③ FRANCES SALMAN

WILLIAM HANSEN ⑦

CATALINA
④

⑤ TOORAK

④ OCTAVIAN

⑥ NYHOLT

④ NORTH
GASPE

⑦ MOUNT
KITHERON

■ FRIAR ROCK

⑦ ICARION

□ THIRLBY
□ EMPIRE KINGFISHER

■ FRISCO

② DAYROSE

② GANDIA
① REFAST

○ CYCLOPS

○ NORNESS
○ COIMBRA

■ ALEXANDRA HÖEGH

○ SAN JOSE
■ VARANGER
■ FRANCIS E. POWELL
■ HALO
■ OLYMPIC

□ TACOMA STAR

○ OLNEY
NORVANNA ▲ ○ WEST IVIS
EMPIRE GEM ▲ ▲ ALLAN JACKSON CALEDONIAN
VENORE ▲ ○ BRAZOS   ▲ LADY HAWKINS
○ CITY OF ATLANTA
○ CILTVAIRA
○ MALAY

□ MONTROLITE

□ HALCYON

○ PAN NORWAY

○ CULEBRA

Sinkings in American and Canadian Waters 1941/42

Below:
Stabsobermaschinist (Diesel) Jak Mallmann (my father) on duty in his engine room. He went down with the boat three months before I was born. The dial of the engine telegraphs can be seen and in the middle is the hand wheel which operated one of the many valves.

far enjoyed relative freedom from the U-boat campaign because a large proportion of the shipping in her waters belonged to the United States and Hitler had personally ordered all confrontation with that country to be avoided. Therefore, the vast majority of U-boats had been kept well clear.

America's entry into the war sparked off a concerted effort in planning a thrust into the eastern seaboard of the United States, but there were several problems which prevented an all-out onslaught. Firstly, Karl Dönitz was unhappy about the evacuation of the North Atlantic and wanted to resume operations there as soon as possible, despite the change in situation offering alternative action areas; secondly, the Supreme Naval Command insisted that the concentration of boats around Gibraltar and in the Mediterranean, which supported the North African Campaign, should not be diluted; and thirdly, the shortage of boats was a major stumbling block. There were less boats at sea than at the start of the war and Admiral Hans-Georg von Friedeburg (C-in-C of the U-boats Organisation Dept) made matters worse by reporting that skilled workers were being called up for service with the armed forces in such numbers that it was no longer possible to

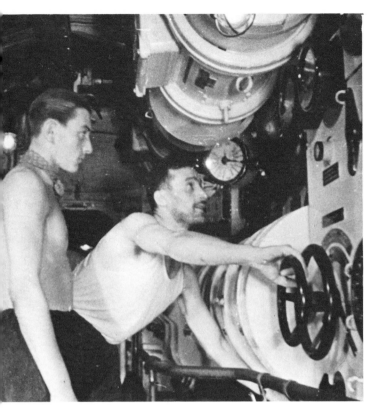

Left:
Electro-Obermaschinist Karl Keller with his assistant, *Maschinengefreiter* Schwerth, at the controls of the electric motors in *U73*. The telegraph dial suggests that the boat is on the surface with the diesel engines running.

Below:
A close-up view of a Type VIIC conning tower. The horseshoe on its side is a life belt. *U99* (KL Otto Kretschmer) — *The Golden Horseshoe* — had real horseshoes fitted.

Raincoat and sou'wester: oilskins were not issued to individuals and each boat carried a number which had to be shared.

forecast completion dates. The U-boat figures for December 1941 were as follows:

Number of operational boats	91
Number of boats at sea	37
Boats in a position to strike at the enemy	18
Boats on their way out or on their way home	19
Boats in port awaiting repairs and unfit for service	54

It should be remembered that U-boat successes declined throughout 1941. The year started with three 'aces', Günther Prien (*U47*), Joachim Schepke (*U100*) and Otto Kretschmer (*U99*) being lost and the fighting grew noticeably harder as the months progressed. This led Dönitz to fear that a move into American waters would be countermanded immediately and could lead to serious U-boat losses. However, he knew that the element of surprise was on his side and he thought U-boats might achieve slightly better results in the coastal waters than in mid-Atlantic. Therefore, he badgered the Supreme Naval Command for permission to send 12 long range Type IX boats west, arguing that these large submarines were unsuitable for operations in the narrow confines of the Mediterranean. The Naval Command eventually agreed to a strike by six Type IX boats, but mechanical trouble kept one in port, so Germany's attack against the world's most powerful nation was launched with only five U-boats. These were: *U125* (KL Ulrich Folkers) IXC sailed on 18 December 1941; *U123* (KL Reinhard Hardegen) IXB

sailed on 23 December; *U66* (FK Richard Zapp) IXC sailed on 25 December; *U125* (KL Ulrich Folkers) IXC sailed on 27 December; and *U130* (FK Ernst Kals) IXC also sailed on 27 December 1941.

Dönitz's fondness for dramatic code words contributed towards him choosing Operation 'Paukenschlag' (which has no English equivalent, but means a roll on the kettle drums) for the first thrust against the United States. Dönitz was certainly under no illusions of grandeur when deciding on this name, and his strict instructions for all boats to start their attacks at the same time was not an attempt to produce a great effect, as has often been claimed. Instead he was frightened of losing a high proportion of the boats and he did not want the first U-boat to trigger off a trap for the rest. Therefore, he felt it would be fairest to his men if they were all given the opportunity of striking together while the opposition was still off guard.

The campaign in American waters turned out quite unexpectedly in the U-boats' favour, with a terrific carnage being wrought which became known as the second 'Golden Time' or second 'Happy Time'. The majority of Americans living along the eastern seaboard of the United States did not want to impose a state of war because, among other things, that could bring a rapid decline in the tourist trade for the coming season and life continued as in peacetime. Illumination remained on, navigation lights continued to burn, radio was used as before, very little action was taken against the Germans and consequently U-boats enjoyed an easy time, running up high sinking figures. Prof Samuel Eliot Morison, the official US Naval Historian, described the U-boat attacks as 'a merry massacre'.

The experiences of February 1942 led Dönitz to remark in his war diary that the area off New York was proving to be an ideal training ground for inexperienced U-boat crews. Defences were weak and provided a good opportunity to send boats there to practise for hard times ahead. One month later he summarised his impressions of action in American waters by saying the defences were still poor, the opposition appeared to be untrained, their actions were badly organised and he got the impression submarine hunters only came out to sea because they got extra pay for going into U-boat infested waters. Their attacks were weak, un-coordinated and they gave up very quickly, making it easy for the already hardened U-boat men to escape.

Above:
First efforts of coming to terms with escaping from submerged boats: the diving tank at the Submarine School in Neustadt (Schleswig-Holstein).

Below:
Escaping from a submerged submarine: this photograph was taken in the training tower at the Submarine School and shows a man wearing a *Dräger Lung.*

Below:
The *Dräger Tauchretter* (U-boat Escape Apparatus) being used in the diving tank at Neustadt. The valve on the mouthpiece could be shut and the air bag inflated with oxygen to serve as life jacket once surfaced. A tin containing a chemical for absorbing carbon dioxide is situated inside the bag at the bottom of the breathing pipe, and oxygen in the bag could be topped up from a cylinder at the bottom. The tap can be seen at the left and there is an outlet valve just below the shoulder, above the cylinder tap.

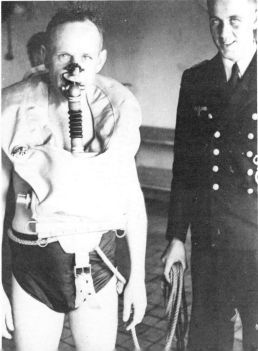

As extraordinary as it may appear, the U-boat Command did not know the maximum ranges of all their boats, especially of those types developed after the start of the war, because they had never been subjected to endurance trials. Performance details were based on figures obtained during tests in the Baltic or shorter runs on the European side of the Atlantic. The following were estimated before the start of the American campaign:

To Cabot Straight (between Newfoundland and Nova Scotia)

$\qquad$ 2,200sm = 9.2 sailing days

To Halifax, Nova Scotia

$\qquad$ 2,400sm = 10 sailing days

To Bermuda

$\qquad$ 3,000sm = 12.5 sailing days

To New York

$\qquad$ 3,000sm = 12.5 sailing days

To Trinidad

$\qquad$ 3,800sm = 15.8 sailing days

To Aruba (Caribbean)

$\qquad$ 4,000sm = 16.6 sailing days

To Galveston (Gulf of Mexico)

$\qquad$ 4,600sm = 19.2 sailing days

sm = Seemeile (sea mile or nautical mile)

At about the same time as the boats of the first thrust against the United States left France, a group of 12 smaller Type VII boats were being made ready for the first group attack on Newfoundland Bank. The vast majority of this Ziethen Group experienced freezing fog, snow and ice off the Canadian coast and it became clear to the U-boat Command that it was no longer possible for officers in the Operations Room in France to keep a tight control of the battles at sea. Distances had become too vast. Patterns changed between sailing from Europe and arriving in the operations area and in addition to this, boats in Canadian waters were experiencing considerably more co-ordinated opposition, making it difficult to drive home attacks, and once caught by escorts it was noticeably harder to get away. As a result, commanders of the boats following the Ziethen Group were given more freedom to decide exactly what they should do and where they might operate.

Two Type VIIC boats, U575 (KL Günther Heydemann) and U96 (KK Heinrich 'Regge' Lehmann-Willenbrock) left for Canadian waters during January 1942. Finding cold, foggy and empty seas, and having heard about the bonanza further south, they decided to head in that direction. This gave the U-boat command a most unexpected surprise because both U575 and U96 got considerably further than had been anticipated. Dönitz immediately grabbed the opportunity and sent a supply submarine to be stationed to the east of New York. At the same time another group of the smaller Type VII boats were made ready, each with strict instructions to keep to specified engine revolutions, to find the most economical speed over long distances. The results were most interesting: it was discovered that careful engine manipulation could increase the endurance by two to three weeks over the previously expected maximum. However, this could only be achieved if the men made a further sacrifice in their already spartan living conditions. Additional food stacked inside the boat meant there was not even enough room to stand upright! The surren-

Below:
2. Steuermann (2nd Helmsman) Karl Schuck (who took over as 1st Helmsman after this voyage), at the small chart table of *U73*. Helmsman is not a good translation because the Steuermann was an NCO responsible for navigation. Steering was done by a person of lower rank, who was known as *Rudergänger*. Schuck is wearing a sports vest with the national eagle on the front.

der of the men's meagre comfort was not without danger because every available tank had to be filled with something useful and the usual salt water ballast became a luxury. The taking on board of such large quantities of fuel oil had previously been prohibited because an early action could have resulted in it being spilled through the vents in the bottoms of the tanks, to float to the surface and give away the position of the submerged boat. However, action on the European side of the Atlantic was thought unlikely, therefore boats sailed with this extra fuel.

At first the main action concentrated off Cape Hatteras and in April 1942, when anti-U-boat forces started to make their presence felt, activity was moved southwards to avoid the hunters. U-boats continued to move southwards and eventually operated in the Caribbean and in the Gulf of Mexico, leaving little of those waters untouched. The Supreme Naval Command also instructed U-boats to attack land targets such as harbour installations and fuel stores. Dönitz did not like the idea and was proved correct by U130 (KK Ernst Kals), who was driven off Curaçao at dawn, after having fired only the twelfth shell from the 105mm gun against the oil installations. Once having vacated an area. Dönitz returned to vulnerable traffic junctions by sending in a small number of minelaying U-boats, which initially had quite reasonable successes.

Southern Waters

According to prewar plans, auxiliary cruisers and submarines were due to have operated together in far-off regions, but this never materialised because U-boats were employed more profitably nearer home. Karl Dönitz held the view that U-boats should be engaged in areas where they could sink the maximum number of ships in the shortest time at sea. However, sinking ships was not always the primary objective and the Supreme Naval Command considered it important to send submarines to places like Cape Town because that would encourage the Royal Navy to stretch hunting forces over a larger area. At the same time, it was thought such moves would force the enemy to adopt the convoy system over a wider area and thus slow the passage of vital war goods. When the long-range Type IX U-boats started to head south, they found exceptionally good hunting conditions. In his book 60 Jahre Deutsche Uboote, Bodo Herzog lists 16 high scoring U-boats for November 1942 (the month is important because a large number of boats were at sea and consequently many ships were sunk) and nine of them achieved their successes in the South Atlantic, one off North Africa, four in the Caribbean region and the rest were scattered over the North Atlantic.

The first major drive of sending a large number of U-boats into the waters of the far south was frustrated by a catastrophic loss of supply ships. The campaign coincided with the cruise of the battleship Bismarck (KS Ernst Lindemann) and the heavy cruiser Prinz Eugen (KS Helmuth Brinkmann) in May 1941 because U-boats could take advantage of the same supply ships. Unfortunately for Germany, the capture of U110 (KL Fritz-Julius Lemp) on 9 May 1941 made it possible for Britain to understand the radio code for this critical period and pin point the secret refuelling locations in lonely parts of the oceans. As a result nine supply ships were sunk during the first three weeks of June 1941. (These were Belchen 3 June 1941; Gedania, Gonzenheim, Esso Hamburg 4 June; Egerland 5 June; Friedrich Breme 12 June; Lothringem 15 June; Babitonga 21 June and Alstertor 23 June 1941.)

Only Spichern, captured by raider Widder as Krossfonn, was at sea as supply ship during this critical period and managed to return to port. U-boats already under way had to be recalled. At the same time plans went ahead to convert the fruit carrier Python into a special submarine supply ship. Another group of long range boats left French ports during the autumn of 1941 and auxiliary cruiser Atlantis (KS Bernhard Rogge) acted as a submarine supply ship to fill the gap until Python arrived in the South Atlantic. Britain had been unable to determine the exact movements of the surface raiders because radios were used too infrequently for cryptanalysts to crack the code. Once they came close to U-boats, positions were also broadcast in submarine cypher which could be broken.

The end of ghost cruiser Atlantis after 622 days at sea without putting into a port, is quite well known today. She was sunk on 22 November 1941 by the British cruiser HMS Devonshire while refuelling U126 (KL Ernst Bauer). The German Radio Monitoring Service (B-Dienst under KS Heinz Bonatz) intercepted her bogus British distress signal and guessed it spelled the end of Atlantis. Already under way, Python was diverted to pick up survivors but she only outlived the raider by little more than a week before suffering a similar fate. She was sunk by the cruiser HMS *Dorsetshire* shortly after supplying *U68* (KK Karl-Friedrich Merten). A rescue operation using a number of Italian U-boats succeeded in bringing a large number of survivors back to France.

Asia and the Far East

Hitler issued a secret directive to military leaders about co-operation with Japan as early as March 1941, in which he outlined the importance of engaging Britain in areas outside the Atlantic. He ordered that German military and technical experience should be made available to the Japanese, so that in the event of war Japan's contribution would have maximum effect. Germany already had a fairly strong presence in the Far East because a number of freighters had been cut off by the war and were prepared there for their blockade-breaking runs to Europe. However, this was not easy at first because Japan wanted to be seen as observing strict neutrality and there was little open co-operation until the end of 1941, when she launched her attack against Pearl Harbour. The idea of sending U-boats into Asian waters did not win a great deal of support in Germany until 1942, when it became clear that surface ships could no longer bring scarce commodities to Europe, and the backdoor route along the Siberian railway had also been closed since the previous summer. It was a case of doing without or sending submarine cargo carriers, as had been done during World War 1. Germany's economy was not so dependent on overseas influence as the British, but there were some products which could not be obtained in Europe, thus making contact with Japan more important. The idea was to send very long range boats of Type IXD2 to Japanese ports; where they were to fight their way out and then return as cargo carriers. Their capacity was very much limited to just over 220 tons of cargo, but that had to suffice since there were virtually no alternative ways of obtaining some of the essential raw materials.

The first 11 U-boats to be used for Far Eastern operations, christened *Monsoon Group*, left Europe during the summer of 1943. Only five reached their destination, the rest were sunk. Finding crews for this most difficult task of making contact with the Japanese and finding the best pathway through Oriental mazes was not easy, but scattered among U-boat crews were a number of men who had served with merchant ships in the region before the war. There were also people who had been in Asian waters with auxiliary cruisers earlier in the war, so it was not too difficult to find the unlikely combination of U-boat man, adventurer, diplomat and Oriental traveller. For example, KL Johannes Fehler, ex-demolition officer of auxiliary cruiser *Atlantis* became commander of *U234* and Otto Giese, Second Officer of the blockade breaker *Anneliese Essberger*, joined *U181* under KS Kurt Freiwald for voyages to Japanese-held territory. Freiwald also illustrates the importance that the German Command put on high qualifications for these delicate undertakings. He was one of the first U-boat commanders in 1935 and by 1943 had risen well above such a position, having been a most successful Adjutant to both Grand Admirals (Erich Raeder and Karl Dönitz). *U234* did not get very far because the war ended while she was sailing southwards through the Atlantic. Her cargo was most interesting because it included radioactive substances as well as parts required to assemble a jet fighter.

Boats which did manage to reach their destination encountered considerable difficulties. The humid, hot climate was unpleasant and the food was strange; spare parts were not always available and the crew had to carry out repair work which was usually done by dockyard workers, with tools which were often of poor quality. In addition to this, basic dockyard facilities were often most primitive and the vast distances between the major bases made communication difficult. Germany had an embassy with a naval attaché (KS Paul Wenneker) in Japan, and later a U-boat co-ordinator who covered the entire Far-Eastern theatre. This was FK Wilhelm Dommes, who made the voyage as commander of *U178* and then remained as Chief of the U-boat base in Penang. Later, when U-boats also ran into other ports, he was re-named as Chief of the Southern Area (Südraum). *U178* was taken back to Europe by her First Watch Officer, KL Wilhelm Spahr, who had been on a commander's training course before leaving Germany.

A number of the Far-Eastern boats were equipped with a novelty in the form of a gliding helicopter or autogyro, which was attached to the submarine by cable and kept airborne in a similar way to a kite. This Focke-Achgelis FA-300 was nicknamed 'Bachstelze' (Wagtail), and although quite

Right:
The *Focke Achgelis*, a type of gliding helicopter or autogyro, being tested in the Baltic during the summer of 1942 by *U523* (KL Werner Pietzsch).

Below:
U181 (KK Kurt Freiwald) undergoing repairs in dry dock in the Far East. The boat never made the return journey, because insufficient spare parts could be found to repair the wear and tear caused during the arduous outward journey. However, it was clear that such an undertaking would only be possible if the boat had a breathing pipe to negotiate the dangerous waters of the North Atlantic. A home-made schnorkel is seen here being fitted to the conning tower.

ingenious, it was really only a cheap substitute for Germany's non-existent fleet air arm. However, it did increase the field of vision from 10km to the horizon at boat level to 45km at the cruising altitude of 120m (400ft). The individual parts were stored inside the boat and assembled on the gun platform, where the flying machine was launched from a small pad attached to the rails. In case of an emergency, the rotors could be jettisoned for a quick descent and the observer usually carried a parachute to soften his landing. Museums took an interest in this unusual piece of equipment and quite a number have survived the war to be accommodated today in permanent displays.

The Arctic

The Arctic contributed very little to the overall war statistics, yet this harsh region saw an abundance of interesting activities and it was probably the only theatre of war where the enemy became the deuteragonist, with the natural elements taking the main role. Continuous daylight during the summer months, darkness for 24hr a day during the winter, icebergs, freezing fog, incredibly rough seas and extremely low temperatures all dominated activities. It was only possible to tackle the enemy when conditions were favourable as it was often impossible to find a target.

At first, standard boats fitted with a few additional heaters were sent north. This meant that the men had to sleep in two or three sets of clothing and still feel uncomfortably cold. Even when the duty watch returned with their seawater-drenched clothes frozen hard, they could not find a really warm place to thaw out. Hacking the ice off the exterior did not help because the ice also found its way into vents, pipes and interior. The only way to dive under such conditions was to descend slowly while speeding through the slightly warmer sea and hope that the water could be pumped out of the tanks faster than it flowed in until valves were cleared for closing. This hazard was later overcome by fitting special heaters in critical places to prevent the essential points from freezing.

Eternal darkness in winter probably acted in the U-boats' favour, but it was a major morale breaker. Submariners normally did not miss the sun because they operated mainly at night, but living in northern regions where they did not see daylight for several months of the year was most depressing for many men. After the apparently endless winter, the sun would appear on the horizon for a few minutes each day until eternal daylight set in. It had been known for sleeping commanders to have been shaken awake as though in an emergency, just for them to climb the conning tower and stare at the sun. Instead of queuing up for a smoke, men actually queued to take it in turns to look at the sun. The long hours of daylight presented another great hazard to U-boats because there was not enough cover of darkness to charge batteries or to escape from submarine hunters. However, U-boats were assisted by the fact that there were layers of different water temperature and salinity, which helped to refract Asdic impulses and provided a blanket to cover an escape. Icebergs presented a peculiar problem: on the one hand they had to be avoided because a collision could be fatal, but on the other hand large ice floes provided good protection where surface vessels could not follow.

There were several reasons for sending U-boats into the desolate cold wastes, the most obvious being to operate against Arctic convoys which ran to north Russian ports. The first group to hunt these convoys, named 'Ulan' (Lancer), was sent out during mid-January 1942 and consisted of three boats: *U134* (KL Rudolf Schendel), *U454* (KL Burghard Hackländer) and *U584* (KL Joachim Deecke). Much of the Arctic was within Luftwaffe range from Norwegian bases, therefore the subsequent battles saw a high proportion of aircraft which produced some magnificent results for the Germans. Other U-boats were sent out on explorative sorties to collect information about ice conditions, possible enemy convoy routes close to the permanent ice cap or about enemy ship movements in desolate areas. In mid-August 1942, *U255* (KL Reinhart Reche) carried out a reconnaissance of the area to the north of Spitzbergen and worked together with a Blohm und Voss BV-138 flying boat, which was refuelled and supplied by the U-boat. *U601* (OL Peter Grau) and *U251* (KK Heinrich Timm) went further east during this time to find a possible route for the pocket battleship *Admiral Scheer* (KS Wilhelm Meendsen-Bohlken), the idea being for her to head east to intercept a convoy known to be under way through the Siberian Sea Passage from the Bering Straits. Although a number of ships were sighted, the target was not found and the operation of *Scheer* and the two U-boats proved that neither were suitable

Above:
Obergefreiter Otto Kloninger (Action Helmsman) of *U376* (KL Karl Friedrich Marks). Steering is electric and he can move the rudder by pressing one of two buttons under his hands. To the left of his hand is a repeater from the gyrocompass, above it the engine telegraph. The magnetic compass is a little higher up out of view.

these in the hope of capturing a code writer, the Enigma machine which was used for translating messages into secret code. This caused the Germans to set up more stations, using U-boats to create land-based stations. Ironically Britain now made a noteworthy effort to prevent over-zealous commanders from planning attacks against these vulnerable positions because they were helping Britain in understanding the German code. The weather details were broadcast in a code, which cryptanalysts could understand and then re-broadcast by a more secret system, which had not been broken. By comparing the two, it was possible to gain a valuable insight into the composition of the German code writing methods.

The first weather stations established by U-boats were unmanned and fully automatic. *U377* (KL Otto Köhler) set one up on land in northern Spitzbergen during the early summer of 1942 and *U537* (KL Peter Schrewe) built another in Martin Bay in northern Canada during October of the following year. It is likely that several others were established as well. However, *U377*'s project did not work for long because ice froze the moving parts, causing them to seize up. *U537*'s station remained virtually unknown except to the men who were involved with the venture, and it was only discovered by Franz Selinger in 1980. Shortly afterwards when he led a salvage team to the spot, it was discovered that Schrewe's men had performed quite a feat in getting so close to the Labrador coast, but they had chosen a bad spot. Thinking their station was safe and well out of the way at the end of a long peninsula, it was in fact just the sort of area used by Eskimos to herd caribou. The radio station had been vandalised, but it was still recognisable and the various parts have been removed to form a museum display. Franz Selinger has also been instrumental in the recovery of many of the relics from Spitzbergen for museum displays in Norway.

The automatic land weather stations gave way to automatic floating stations and to manned meteorological bases. Small teams of scientists were taken to isolated locations by U-boats and the crew helped to build the base and frequently made several journeys to bring stores for the men to remain there throughout the Arctic winter. Once the base was well and truly frozen in and could not be reached by enemy forces until the thaw set in during the following year, the men started to make regular weather broadcasts.

for the harsh conditions experienced. *U589* (KL Hans-Joachim Horrer) and *U591* (KL Hansjürgen Zetsche) tried to lay mines, but only the first mentioned reached the target area of the Matochkin Strait between North and South Island of Novaya Zemlya.

The other major undertaking in the Arctic was concerned with the collection of meteorological data, something which was pursued with considerable energy by both the navy and air force. This was vital because much of the European weather is 'made up' in the Arctic and forecasting was most difficult without information from this region. At the beginning of the war, when Allied meteorological stations started to broadcast in code, Germany attempted to establish a variety of manned weather bases in converted fishing boats situated in lonely Arctic locations. Britain made a considerable strike against

6

Captured U-boats

Right from the start of the war, the Royal Navy was thinking of capturing enemy vessels and some escort commanders trained and maintained small boarding parties to be dispatched at an instant's notice. The Admiralty encouraged such action by stressing the importance of capturing U-boats. It was suggested that commanders might try to force a U-boat to the surface with shallow-set depth charges and then encourage the crew to depart quickly, without scuttling, by signalling that survivors would not be picked up if the U-boat sank. However, it was stressed that all survivors should be picked up whether the boat went down or not. This was not an open invitation to concentrate on captures and it was stated quite firmly that the escort commander's primary duty lay in ensuring the safe arrival of the convoy. U-boats were to be 'put down' as quickly as possible and captures only attempted in exceptional circumstances.

On the German side on the other hand, it had been a strong tradition that the enemy only set foot on their vessels as guests or prisoners and this was made exceptionally clear when the High Seas Fleet was scuttled in Scapa Flow after World War 1. Several Royal Navy vessels were in positions of getting close enough to board, but in almost all cases the last man out 'pulled the plug'. In fact, several men went down with their boats because they returned to the control room or engine compartment to flood tanks or break vents and then found the boat going down too fast to get out again.

The importance of the capture depended on the circumstances under which the crew was forced to surrender. During difficult missions, capture was foreseen and special secret material limited to only the one mission so the safety of other boats could not be compromised if this fell into enemy hands. The interior of boats was prepared for quick destruction: portable equipment such as the code writer was usually dismantled and each man given a vital part to throw away before falling into enemy hands. However, this procedure helped the Royal Navy when *U33* (KL Hans-Wilhelm von Dresky) was sunk during a mining operation in the Clyde Estuary. The attacker, HMS *Gleaner*, was damaged by her own depth charges and suffered a loss of power, making it impossible to scour the area for survivors. It is difficult to ascertain how some of the men from *U33* died during that February night of 1940, but a combination of injuries received during the attack and cold Scottish water was probably responsible. Whatever the cause, some corpses were later found with parts of the secret code writer still in their pockets. The Royal Navy sent divers to the wreck and a number of attempts were made to get inside. This was no mean feat because freezing waters with exceptionally strong currents made it a difficult dive. Secrecy was especially strong where the German naval Enigma was concerned and this prevented publication of details at the time. Much of the information has now vanished with the passage of time, making it difficult to find out what was actually extracted from the wreck and the corpses.

The first major effort to capture a U-boat was made as early as 20 September 1939, when a fishing boat sighted *U27* (KL Johannes Franz) in Scottish waters and 10 destroyers under command of Adm Forbes, were sent out to hunt her. HMS *Fortune* and HMS *Forester* eventually forced the intruder to the surface and men from *Fortune* managed to get on board, but the U-boat went down before a salvage operation could be mounted. The first submarine to actually be captured during World War 2 was a British boat, HMS *Seal* commanded by Lt Cdr R. P. Lonsdale. She was sent out to lay mines in the Kattegat where she was bombed by an enemy aircraft. The damage was slight and the operation continued, but submarine chasers were called to the area and dropped several well-placed depth charges, sending *Seal* to the sea-bed. Engineers aboard the crippled submarine worked for six hours, carrying out vital repairs in the hope of bringing her back to the surface. Eventually, after some fuel had been pumped out the boat began to rise, but the strategic predicament had not greatly improved because both electric motors were out of action and only one diesel engine would work in reverse. There was no hope of returning to Britain and Lonsdale could only see to the safety of his crew by cruising backwards into Swedish waters, where he hoped to scuttle the boat. There was virtually no electricity, enough only to power a few dimly-lit light bulbs, and the crew tried hard to destroy anything of value to the enemy. The lack of power made it impossible to jettison the six remaining torpedoes although smaller gear was thrown overboard. At daybreak a plane landed close by the boat and Lonsdale as well as PO Nolte were taken prisoners. After this, the trawler *Franken* (which had been commissioned as submarine chaser *UJ128* [Ubootsjäger]) landed a boarding party. *Seal* was towed to Denmark for emergency repairs and then went on to Kiel for a refit. During 1941 she joined the 3rd U-Flotilla under her new identification of *UB*. Her most important contribution was probably only her propaganda value, but the torpedoes did provide the Germans with valuable information on the detonation system, with which they were experiencing considerable problems.

The most important U-boat capture of the war was probably when *U110* (KL Fritz-Julius Lemp, who had fired the first torpedo of the war when he sunk the passenger liner *Athenia*) fell into British hands on 9 May 1940. The whole operation was carried out so quickly that none of the survivors knew their boat had been captured and they evacuated *U110* too quickly to destroy anything. The secret was so well kept that only a handful of people in the Royal Navy knew about the incident and the details only came to light after Capt Stephen W. Roskill had stated in his official history of the war at sea, that *U110* was sunk. On reading this, Capt A. D. Baker-Cresswell (Escort Commander) wrote to the author. Consequently Roskill wrote the book *The Secret Capture*, which is still one of the few sources of information on this remarkable incident.

It all started early in May 1941 after lookouts aboard *U110* had spotted a convoy on a clear night. The details of the convoy were radioed to base and this message was intercepted by *U201* (OL Adalbert Schnee). The two sighted each other at dawn on 9 May and after exchanging recognition signals came so close together that both commanders could shout to each other. Lemp's officers had suggested that they should wait a day or so before attacking because Royal Navy escorts were at their westerly limit and would soon

have to turn back. Lemp was not so keen on this because it meant wasting precious fuel and the two commanders decided to start the action with a submerged attack during daylight. *U110* was to go in first, followed about 30min later by *U201*. The morning was used for the manoeuvring into a favourable position and it was just two minutes before midday when the first torpedo left *U110*. The first one sank the British steamer *Esmond* (4,976grt) and the second the *Bengore Head* (2,609grt), but *U110*'s periscope was also spotted by lookouts in the escort HMS *Aubretia*, which raced over to drop depth charges. HMS *Broadway* and HMS *Bulldog* joined in the attack and attempted to locate the U-boat on their Asdics. They passed the position on to *Aubretia*, who cruised over the spot to drop more depth charges. After half an hour, *U110* appeared like a floundering whale on the surface and *Bulldog* went on a ramming course. Only a short distance from collision, it occurred to Capt Baker-Cresswell that a capture might come off and he changed course, while every available gun opened fire. *U110*'s crew came pouring out of the hatch and many jumped straight from the tower into the water. Lemp was last seen in the water by his men, asking about the fate of several of his crew. It appears as if he and some others tried to re-board to scuttle the boat, but the Royal Navy made sure no one got back into the control room.

HMS *Bulldog* lowered her whaler and the small boarding party led by Sub-Lt David Balme rowed over. Once inside *U110*, they found her to be empty and quickly set about picking up as many vital pieces as they could carry in their boat. The men's fear of being trapped inside a sinking submarine subsided as time went on and everything which could be moved was taken out. The whaler made several journeys backwards and forwards, each time carrying a heavy load of valuable booty. Nobody on the British side knew anything about submarines and nothing was done to improve *U110*'s buoyancy because Baker-Cresswell did not want to risk sinking her by accident. After everything which could be moved had been brought aboard HMS *Bulldog*, a line was fixed to the U-boat and an attempt made to tow the prize to Iceland, but *U110* sank the following day. Today it is known that the information collected was used to devastating effect in sinking all but one of the battleship *Bismark*'s supply ships as well as a number of raiders and U-boats. The secret code used by

Germany's surface raiders differed from the U-boat and other naval codes and was probably never broken during the war, but the positions of these ships were radioed to U-boats to prevent them attacking by mistake. Certainly the capture of the material in *U110* was one of the major events of the war. However, British access to the naval Enigma machine should not be considered in isolation with captured U-boats because the Royal Navy had already made special efforts to board a number of small surface ships and there is a full account in Jürgen Rohwer's book, *The Critical Convoy Battles of 1943*.

The second U-boat to be captured by British forces only three months after the secret *U110* incident was *U570* (KL Hans Rahmlow). This was a somewhat different affair because only the shell of a Type VIIC fell into British hands, and in the first instance, the boat surrendered to an aeroplane. Hans Rahmlow had commanded the small Type II *U58* and then became the first commander of the new *U570*. She was commissioned in March 1941 at a time when Germany was already building boats faster than training the specialised crews needed to operate them, and *U570* was one of the many boats which would have benefited from a longer running-in period. Instead the boat went to Norway and sailed for her first war cruise from Trondheim on 23 August 1941 with the intention of operating in the Atlantic whilst running southwards to La Pallice in France. It appears as if tempers flared on numerous occasions and some men suffered from sea sickness, making the boat hardly fit to face an enemy. On that fateful morning of 27 August 1941, *U570* was lying at a depth of 60m, out of reach of the turbulent Atlantic waves. Rahmlow surfaced cautiously. The boat was hardly moving as the blowing of the tanks produced a large area of foaming water right under Sqn Ldr J. H. Thompson's Lockheed Hudson 'S', who just happened to be right above the boat in the periscope's blind spot. The target was something every Coastal Command crew dreamed of — a helpless, stationary U-boat with AA guns not yet manned, and Thompson lost no time in straddling *U570* with several well-placed depth charges. When the spray from these subsided, he could hardly believe his eyes. Men on the conning tower were waving a white flag. Having no clue as to what to do next because nobody in the aircraft could claim their prize, Hudson 'S' called for help.

The Admiralty moved fast and ordered everything in the area to converge on the spot. There were no ships in the immediate vicinity, so Hudson 'S' continued to circle until the afternoon when Consolidated Catalina 'J', piloted by Flg Off E. A. Jewiss arrived. He had been ordered to remain with the U-boat until nightfall and if the Royal Navy had not turned up by then, he was to warn the Germans and sink the U-boat. This drastic action was not necessary because the trawler *Northern Chief* (Lt N. L. Knight) arrived at about 23.00hrs, some 12 hours after *U570* had surrendered. The sea was still rough with a near gale blowing, making it impossible to launch boats for boarding, so Knight sent over the message that he would depart if the U-boat sank and hoped she would remain on the surface until the following day. Reinforcements arrived during the hours of darkness, the first being another trawler, *Kingston Agate*, followed by the destroyer HMS *Burwell* and two more trawlers, *Wastwater* and *Windermere*, then finally the corvette HMS *Niagara*.

There was an anxious moment just after dawn as an aeroplane flew over to drop two depth charges. Luckily for the British they both missed their target. The sea was still too rough to launch boats and in the end, the first officer of the *Kingston Agate* (Lt H. B. Campbell) crossed in a life raft. Finally *U570* was towed to Iceland, where she was beached to be made seaworthy again for a trip to Britain under her own power. Commissioned under the new name of HMS *Graph*, she was used for extensive trials and later even shot torpedoes at *U333* (KL Peter 'Ali' Cremer), but missed. Despite only gaining a boat with much of the interior wrecked, the Royal Navy did learn quite a bit about the performance of U-boats. It made them realise that German submarines could dive considerably deeper than expected and depth charges were fitted with new deeper ranging detonators.

The next capture of a U-boat was also highly valuable and it looks as if the Royal Navy made definite efforts to board another U-boat throughout 1942. The reason being that Germany had changed her secret code in January of that year and British cryptanalysts needed one of the new four-wheel naval Enigma machines to break back into the U-boats' radio traffic. Even today it is difficult to gain access to information relating to Enigma, perhaps because much of it was not chronicled at the time, and thus it is difficult to come to definite conclusions. However, it appears as if an opportunity presented itself on 30 October 1942, when *U559* (KL Hans Heidtmann) was carefully chased by destroyers *Pakenham*, *Petard*, *Hero*, and escorts *Dulverton* and *Hurworth*, as well as an aircraft from No 47 Squadron RAF. Even Patrick Beesly, who worked in Operational Intelligence during the war, stated in his book, *Very Special Intelligence* that it is possible, but by no means certain, that the new code was broken as a result of material recovered from *U559*. So it seems highly likely that the truth will never be known, but Bletchley Park where the German secret code was deciphered, broke into the new naval code shortly after this capture. The recent release of Enigma documents suggests that a lot of valuable material was found in the wreck. Two men from HMS *Petard* went down with the boat while recovering it and afterwards an extremely difficult dive was attempted, which suggests something of value still eluded the Royal Navy. The precarious dive is described by Peter Keeble in *Ordeal by Water*. At the time of writing his book (1957), the author thought the U-boat he dived on was *U307* (OL Friedrich-Georg Herrle) rather than *U559*, but this appears to have been a mistake, made in the immediate postwar turmoil when U-boat identification was still difficult.

The year 1944 saw two interesting captures. The first happened on 3 May, when *U852* (KL Heinz-Wilhelm Eck), one of the long distance Type IXD2 (the so-called Monsoon Boats for operations in the Far East), was damaged in the Arabian Gulf by a Wellington bomber from No 621 Squadron RAF. There are still two versions of the story: one says that *U852* was driven ashore by the aircraft, and the other suggests *U852* was beached on purpose off Socorto by Cape Guardafui and then blown up. However, the crew did not make a good job of destroying their boat, since photographs show just a little damage forward and aft, but the central section appears to have remained intact. Forty four men survived the incident and it was not long before British forces made a thorough examination of the wreck, including the taking of metal samples for analysis. After the war, the commander, medical

officer and second watch officer were accused of shooting survivors from the steamer *Peleus*, (4,695grt), which was sunk by *U852* on 13 March 1944. They were found guilty and sentenced to death. This was the only proven case of U-boat men shooting at survivors in lifeboats.

The famous capture of *U505* (OL Harald Lange) by US forces followed on 4 June 1944, one month after the beaching of *U852*. An unlucky boat in many ways, *U505* was caught several times in the Bay of Biscay while on her way out and had to return to port for repairs. Her second commander, KL Peter Zschech, became so despondent that he committed suicide while out on patrol, and the first watch officer, DL Paul Mayer, brought the boat back to port. The commander was the only person in a U-boat trained in attacking and it was usually impossible for the watch officers to continue with a mission. For her last voyage under a German flag, *U505* left Brest on 16 March 1944 and made her way as far as the Ivory Coast in Africa. All seemed to go well until 11.00hrs on Sunday 4 June when the boat surfaced to charge batteries. At this critical stage she ran into an American hunter-killer group.

OL Lange was left with little choice: either attack with the little power he had left or be attacked by an aircraft carrier and at least two destroyers. The action appears to have been quick and concentrated, and ended with the U-boat being bombarded by shallow set depth charges causing it to go out of control, leaving Lange no choice other than to go on plummetting to the bottom or to blow the ballast tanks to surface.

The US Task Force was made up of the aircraft carrier USS *Guadalcanal* and the five destroyers *Pillsbury*, *Pope*, *Flaherty*, *Jenks* and *Chatelain*, which had sailed from Norfolk in Virginia under command of Capt Daniel V. Gallery, to seek and destroy U-boats in the Atlantic. Gallery, like his Royal Navy counterparts, had thought of capturing a U-boat and kept a number of special boarding parties for any opportunities of getting aboard a U-boat. Unlike earlier Royal Navy captures, some of these men were specially trained in submarines and knew what to do to prevent their prize from losing buoyancy, which paid dividends on this occasion.

USS *Chatelain* was first to make Asdic contact with *U505* and two fighters were launched at the same time as she went in to attack. Seeing the shadow of the U-boat in the depths, the aircraft marked the spot by shooting at it with their machine guns. A number of well placed depth charges produced large patches of oil, followed by the submarine herself. As the Germans came out of the hatch, the Americans opened fire with anti-personnel shells not only to discourage the manning of the AA guns, but also to prevent too much damage to the boat. Several U-boat men were injured, but only one man, *Bootsmaat* Fischer, was killed. While the crew jumped into the water, a whaler with the boarding party under Lt Albert David tried to get on board. This was no easy matter because *U505* was still moving at about 7kt. Once inside, it was discovered that the only scuttling action had been to remove one small cap from a water pipe, which was quickly replaced and a hosepipe lowered from a destroyer to pump the U-boat dry.

Gallery did not risk taking the U-boat to the nearby African coast because he felt certain that there would be German sympathisers who would either attack the boat or inform Germany of his secret capture (*U505* had not used her radio). So the U-boat was towed across the Atlantic to Bermuda. First she was used for tests and then her propaganda value was fully exploited. Now *U505* stands as a memorial to the Battle of the Atlantic at the Science and Industry Museum in Chicago. A few more U-boats can be added to the 'captured' list, although they did not remain afloat long enough to be of much use to their captors. The majority of these incidents took place towards the end of the war and any secret material recovered was probably only of limited use to the Allies by that time.

U501 (KK Hugo Förster) was forced to the surface on 10 September 1941 by HMCS *Chambly* and HMCS *Moose Jaw*. The U-boat became entangled with *Moose Jaw* and her commander jumped from his conning tower on to the destroyer, which the Germans considered to have been a serious case of abandoning command. Later on during the war Förster was exchanged for British prisoners, whereupon he committed suicide.

Another hunt by British and Canadian forces lasting one and a half days resulted in men from HMCS *Chilliwack* getting aboard *U744* (OL Heinz Blischke) to hoist the White Ensign and to collect a few documents. This took place on 6 March 1944 by which time most of the secret information was probably known to the Allies. *U1024* (KL Hans-Joachim Gutteck) was captured by HMS *Loch Glendhu* on 12 April 1945 in the Irish Sea

just south of the Isle of Man and taken in tow, but sank during the following day. *U175* (KL Heinrich Bruns) was boarded by Lt Ross Bullard from the US Coast Guard Cutter *Spencer*, with the aim of throwing a hand grenade down the hatch to kill any occupants before capturing the boat. Bullard saw the blood-splattered control room below his feet, the result of an earlier artillery action and found *U175* to be sinking but there was nothing he could do to save her. *U1195* (KL Ernst Cordes) was sunk by the destroyer HMS *Watchman* south of the Isle of Wight on 6 April 1945 and it seems highly likely that Royal Navy divers managed to get into the wreck. However, the war had come to an end before they could act on anything found in her. *U16* (KL Horst Wellner) was also boarded after she had been mined off the Goodwin Sands on 24 October 1939, but the crew saw to the destruction of the interior before scuttling her to the sands and it is highly unlikely that anything of great value fell into British hands.

There is one mystery U-boat, *U40* (KK Wolfgang Barten), that might be included in this chapter. She is reputed to have sunk after striking a mine in the eastern reaches of the English Channel on 13 October 1939. A few men in the rear compartment managed to get out and were the only survivors to be picked up. Forty years later I was asked to identify a Type IXA U-boat in the eastern Channel and at first questioned the type, thinking it was more probable that a U-boat from World War 1 had been discovered. However, there was no question of the type: the wreck had been located during a survey of the shipping routes with a view to widening the shipping channel, and the professional team was sure it was a Type IXA. Therefore it could only be *U40*. The interesting point is that she is lying on an even keel, with no external damage and the main conning tower hatch is open. One would expect a submarine which had struck a mine to exhibit some external damage however slight, and it seems highly likely that *U40* might have met some other end. That leaves the question as to whether the Royal Navy knew where she was and dived on her during the war.

The most obvious answer is that the identification of Type IXA is wrong and that could not be determined until the summer of 1987 at the earliest, when Martin Woodward of the Maritime Museum at Bembridge, Isle of Wight, intended to carry out a brief survey of the wreck.

Defeating the U-boats

Forecasting the Number of Boats at the Front

Towards the end of 1940, while losses of Allied merchant shipping in the Atlantic had reached catastrophic proportions, David Branchi (an interpreter of aerial reconnaissance photos) made a revolutionary contribution towards the Allied victory by inventing a method of forecasting the number of boats likely to appear at the front. This came about quite unexpectedly as a result of an increase in aerial reconnaissance providing pictures of what appeared at first glance as uninteresting shots of ship yards with uncompleted hulls on their slipways. Looking at the same yards over a period of time, it was possible to study the production process despite much of the work being hidden by camouflage. The erection of this cover was as methodical as the actual construction underneath, making it possible to guess the progress by the arrangements of the camouflage. For example, the removal of a few sections in the middle indicated work was about to start on the conning tower. David Branchi started by numbering individual keels as they were laid down before the camouflage was in place. Then over the months he followed the progress of each number until it became a boat in the water and when this disappeared he guessed the boat had been commissioned and was on her shakedown cruise.

By the end of 1940 there was sufficient data to calculate the time needed to complete boats by looking at photos of slipways, and by measuring the size of each hull it was possible to make a guess about the type of submarine being built. This information was first made available to planners at the Admiralty early in 1941 and met with disbelief until David Branchi appeared in person to explain his methods. Consequently his forecasts became a regular feature and certainly made a significant contribution

towards neutralising the effects of U-boats, especially later on in the war when huge wolf packs of previously unimagined proportions started to appear in the Atlantic.

Tracking U-boats at Sea

In the past, radar and similar inventions were thought to have been mainly responsible for the Allied ability to find U-boats at sea, but today it is known that anti-submarine forces were directed from German radio signals. The story of Enigma and how Britain managed to decipher the German secret code, including penetrating Hitler's supreme headquarters, is well known today and hardly needs detailed explanation here.

In 1971 while I was writing the first edition of this book, it became apparent that the frequently featured Submarine Tracking Room of the Western Approaches in Liverpool, with its huge chart of the Atlantic on which U-boat sightings and convoy positions were constantly updated, could not in itself have been the main instrument in locating so many U-boats. Records seemed to suggest that Britain did not have enough forces to cover all areas as had been assumed by the German leadership, and somehow the meagre resources had to have been closely monitored to either avoid U-boats, or later to sink them. In 1971 it appeared as if Britain's ability to understand the German secret code was the only feasible explanation as to how she succeeded in deploying her limited forces with such amazing effect. But suggesting this as a possibility always resulted in mild ridicule and firm assurances that Britain did not succeed in penetrating the code for any prolonged period. This made it easy for me to imagine how isolated the U-boat Command must have felt 30 years earlier when Dönitz suggested this as a possibility. Experts at the Supreme Naval Command assured him that to break the code was impossible and even

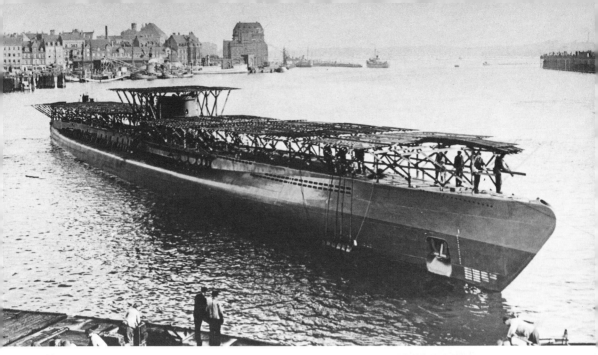

Top:
A minelayer of Type XB, probably *U219*, at the time of her launching. The scaffold on the deck was supposed to have served as camouflage, but this was erected according to strict rules and British Intelligence could work out the stage of progress by looking at the pattern of the screen on aerial photographs. It was made up of a simple wooden lattice, although early in the war sheets of iron were sometimes used as well.

Above:
The bridge of *U473* (KL Heinz Sternberg). From left to right: IIWO Lt Strohm; LI OL Gramms; *Rudergänger* (Helmsman) Obgefr Buddendieck; Commander KL Heinz Sternberg; IWO LT Schulte and *Obersteurmann* (Chief Helmsman and Navigator) Salzmann. In the foreground is a grid, covering the top of one of the ventilation shafts and on the extreme right is a circular dipole aerial for detecting radar transmissions. The object with the hood is the infra-red detection device, *Flamingo*, which could detect the presence of heat from engine exhausts at ranges of up to 10km. This was only fitted to a few boats for experimental purposes during operational missions.

considering such an eventuality was sheer madness and a waste of time.

Security was taken most seriously at U-boat headquarters, where procedures were under constant review. A possible leak in the radio code was considered shortly after the outbreak of the war, but each time experts from the Supreme Naval Command found alternative solutions. Several spy hunts in the U-boat Command resulted in the already small staff being cut even further and procedures revised so that U-boat positions were only made available to a fraction of these men. On top of this, essential details displayed in the operations room were written in such a manner that casual observers could not understand them. It is interesting to note that despite the Navy having been the most security-conscious of the three services, the Supreme Naval Command still had some strange procedures. For example, although there was a security clampdown at U-boat headquarters, the details of North Atlantic positions continued to be telexed to the Naval Commander of the Aegean Sea, who really had no need to know the exact locations of U-boats so far from his sphere of influence.

Security took on a new significance in 1941 when it became blatantly obvious that British forces were systematically avoiding U-boat formations. On several occasions Dönitz remarked in his diary that coincidence always seemed to be working to the advantage of the enemy. It appeared as if the Royal Navy was aware of U-boat locations and the ability to understand the radio code seemed the only solution. Each time Dönitz made such assertions, experts from the Supreme Naval Command considered individual incidents in detail and reached the same conclusions as they had come to a year earlier. They suggested feasible alternative solutions and insisting that a break of the German code would be impossible.

Dönitz, not being satisfied with these suggestions, demanded a change in radio procedures and when the Supreme Naval Command finally acquiesced, the German leadership made one of their biggest mistakes of the war. This disastrous story started towards the end of November 1941, when activities in North Africa caused the Supreme Naval Command to withdraw U-boats from the Atlantic to reinforce the Mediterranean and the area west of Gibraltar. As a result there were no boats in the shipping lanes of the North Atlantic and the convoy war came to a halt. The Japanese attack on Pearl Harbor took place during this temporary lull in hostilities and was followed by Operation 'Paukenschlag', the German move against the United States and the start of the U-boats' second 'Happy Time'.

When the German radio code was changed in January 1942 during this most turbulent period, it created a total blackout at the Operational Intelligence Centre in London but that was not noticed in Germany because virtually all the other parameters of battle were also drastically altered. Had the new code been introduced three or even two months earlier, the blackout would have coincided with regular convoy attacks and Germany would have been aware of the sudden change in situation. British cryptanalysts struggled with the new code until the autumn of 1942, and managed to regain some insight into the procedures shortly after U-boats shifted their main operations area from US waters back to the middle of the Atlantic, and again the change in theatres of war probably helped to cloud Britain's most important secret.

The secret Submarine Tracking Room at Naval Intelligence in London did not have to break all the radio signals to take appropriate action. There the process of determining U-boat locations started coincidentally after the scars of polio prevented Rodger Winn from passing the medical required for joining the Royal Navy. The person who shuffled him as a civilian into Operational Intelligence made one of the most significant appointments of the whole war because Winn came up with the revolutionary and hardly acceptable opinion that it was possible to forecast U-boat movements. On being taunted by his superiors, he replied by saying it would be better to have a go at attempting to predict the future and be correct for some of the time than never think about the enemy at all. So started the work of a genius, who had no counterpart in the German Navy and subsequently achieved fantastic results by studying the enemy's methods as well as the people who conducted the battles from the other side.

Winn established a top secret submarine tracking room with Naval Intelligence at the Admiralty on the south side of Trafalgar Square in London, and his research became so good that it was not always necessary to decipher a message in order to make use of the information. For example, despite the destruction of the Luftwaffe's 1,281-ton catapult ship *Ostmark* on 24 September 1940 by HM Submarine *Tuna* (Lt-Cdr Cavanagh-

Left:
OL Otto Giese with his Number One, keeping lookout on the bridge of *U181*. When asked for the name of the other man, Otto Giese replied, 'I can't remember. I always called him Number One.'.

Mainwaring) going unreported in many naval accounts, it was one of the critical sinkings of the war because it led to Winn being able to deduce when U-boats were on their way out into the open sea. The loss of *Ostmark* came after several serious attacks against submarines and the incident convinced Dönitz he could soon lose U-boats while they were on passage into the Atlantic. Consequently he ordered all outward bound boats to send a short signal when they reached 10°W. (Later when the enemy became more active in the Bay of Biscay, this was changed to 15°W). Being able to determine the approximate latitude of such transmissions, Rodger Winn could guess whether the boat was heading south, going to America or making for the North Atlantic and it thus became a small flag on his map. It did not take too long to establish the approximate cruising speed of U-boats and so keep an eye on each individual's progress, while an abundant supply of similar signals helped to update the information.

By the end of the war the Operational Intelligence Centre in London knew more about the locations of German submarines than the U-boat Command and at times even caught broadcasts which were missed in Germany, a classic example being the loss of *U377* (OL Gerhard Kluth) and *U972* (OL Klaus-Dietrich König). Germany's last records show the boats sending signals saying they were in contact with convoys, but Britain picked up later messages reporting both boats to have been hit by torpedoes. (Incidentally, following a Royal Navy inquiry it was discovered that these must have been German T5 torpedoes.)

Seeing in the Dark

Throughout 1941 Britain succeeded in detec-ting wolf pack formations and routeing convoys around the vast majority of the danger spots, but after operations in American waters U-boat numbers had increased sufficiently to make this more difficult and Britain had to attack and make an attempt at sinking U-boats. She was greatly helped by a considerable increase in escorts, anti-submarine vessels, aircraft, better weapons and much improved technology. Technology certainly played a vital role in the subsequent rounds of the convoy battles. Firstly, High Frequency Direction Finders (HF/DF or 'Huff Duff') made it possible to detect the direction of the shortest radio signals, even if the operator failed to grasp the message. Furthermore this device could focus on short-wave transmissions, something German technologists held as impossible. Determining the source of radio signals had become part of naval life before the war when U-boats used radio direction finders with great success, but it was necessary for two or more stations to get a bearing on a signal long enough for them to identify, in order to pinpoint its source by triangulation. Early in 1940 Germany thought she had frustrated this by introducing the so-called 'Short Signal', which was considered as having been too quick for direction finders. The British invention of HF/DF, which could determine the approximate direction of even short signals on short wave, remained unknown to the German High Command throughout the whole war despite a Royal Navy officer having been careless enough to mention this method in a radio message which was deciphered by the Germans, but luckily passed unnoticed at the time. Perhaps this vital clue might not have slipped through if the German Navy had put more emphasis on intelligence gathering.

Higher naval commanders were also faced with a fantastic amount of paperwork, so much that many found it impossible to read everything which appeared on their desks. Consequently they had to be selective and could well have missed vital information because there was no time to absorb it.

It appears as if HF/DF produced considerable errors of up to 30%, but that was not important because the Admiralty did not rely on it to pinpoint U-boats at sea, because Enigma produced good results. Escort commanders used their sets to find out when attacks were to be expected, which was possible because U-boats usually radioed home to announce the start of their run-in. Error or not, HF/DF did tell escorts the direction of an attack and the number of broadcasts indicated how many U-boats to expect, thus the Germans had lost the terrific advantage of surprise and defences could be established to intercept U-boats before they reached the merchant ships.

Once U-boats were closing in, radar could be used to detect them on the surface and after they had been forced under, Asdic located them for depth charge attacks. The story of German radar, or the next link in the chain of defeat, started around the time when Hitler came to power in 1933. A year later on 20 March, such equipment was already being tested on the balcony of what is now the water police headquarters on the Kiel waterfront by the Blücher Brücke. A modified version of this apparatus was installed on top of the forward artillery control tower of the light cruiser *Königsberg*, then an artillery training ship. It produced quite accurate results against aircraft at ranges of about 10km, but the delicate mechanism was upset by the terrific vibrations it received every time a salvo was fired. Consequently it failed to function until adjustments and minor repairs were made and this deficiency was emphasised by people who were in favour of improving optical range finders. Thinking their radio detection equipment could only work as far as the line of sight, Germany was looking for an artillery range finder to be used during poor visibility as an alternative to optical equipment after the target had been visually sighted. Parallel British research was more concerned with the creation of a search device.

The *Königsberg* was used as headquarters for Dönitz's staff during the autumn manoeuvres of 1938 and after the exercises, OL Otto Köhler (First Radio Officer and Adjutant), who had served as liaison officer between the ship's company and the U-boat staff, was invited to a farewell party in the admiral's mess. Dönitz asked Köhler what he thought of the U-boats' performances and suggested he should join the U-boat Arm. Köhler replied that he had watched with great interest, but had learned that future successes depended on U-boats remaining undetected while they closed in on the surface. Dönitz nodded in agreement, having just demonstrated that the principle worked very well. Köhler went on to say that the radar equipment three decks above them would soon be used to show up every buoy when they passed through the narrow channel towards the locks in Wilhelmshaven and it could therefore also be used to determine the positions of surfaced submarines, making future night attacks most difficult or even impossible. There followed an ice cold silence. Then slowly the bustle built up again, with people arguing in the U-boats' favour. Sensing he was outnumbered in a tense atmosphere, Köhler decided to withdraw to seek the cooler, fresher air of the open deck.

I have known about the *Königsberg* conversation since the late 1960s when Otto Köhler and Helmuth Giessler (communications expert and author) helped me to write the first edition of this book and the details printed above were included in the original manuscript. Gd Adm Karl Dönitz took the trouble to go through those pages before they went to press and passed most favourable comments, but asked for the passage relating to the *Königsberg* conversation to be deleted. After considerable mind searching, I acquiesced and the information was not published. Dönitz kindly lent me a thick file on the subject and made the following remarks:

It is necessary to mention that since 1936 I had been deeply concerned with movements of U-boats on the surface and had pressed for boats with faster speeds. To this end, I supported Prof Hellmuth Walter and his high speed hydrogen peroxide submarine.

I have no clear recollections of the conversation aboard *Königsberg* and cannot quite see its significance. Are there suggestions that I should have abandoned wolf pack tactics, which had served us so well until the summer of 1943, because Köhler mentioned the possibility of some futuristic device detecting boats on

Above:
The waterfront in Kiel before the war. A rebuilt version of the Blücher Brücke is still there, but the signal tower from which this photo was taken has been demolished and not replaced. Most of the small buildings have gone as well, but the house indicated by an arrow is now occupied by the water police. It is of interest because Germany's first radar experiments were conducted on the balcony hidden behind the tree. To the left of the pier is *U27*, to the right *U34*, and next to the tender *U33*. They were all Type VIIA. The unique feature of this type, an above-water torpedo tube, can clearly be seen on *U33*. A rescue buoy, known as *Spatz* (Sparrow), is also visible forward of the 88mm gun and just aft of the conning tower. In the background on the right is *U26*, a Type IA. *Imperial War Museum (IWM)*

Left:
U862 (KK Heinrich Timm), a very long range Type IXD2 with modified AA armament. The left conning tower wall accommodates the bedstead-like *Hohentwiel* radar aerial and the circular hole for the periscopic rod aerial. To the right, next to this hole, is the torpedo aimer with special binoculars clipped in position. The navigation or sky periscope, with the larger head, is towards the front of the boat and the attack periscope towards the rear (nearer the camera) with a circular dipole radar detection aerial between them. The circular containers on the lower platform are for ammunition storage. The upper platform has two large containers to accommodate parts of the Bachstelze, the gliding helicopter. The launching platform at the top of the rails and the drum housing the winding gear on the other side can also be seen.

the surface? What should I have done in 1938? What other tactics should I have employed to equal or better our successes?

One cannot demand that a commander throws reality overboard because of a futuristic comment about a technical invention which will require time to develop and might be capable of detecting submarines on the surface. If this was the case, present day historians will say, 'If Dönitz had not lost his nerve in 1938, he could have fought a successful offensive until radar cut him off in 1943.' It would have been wrong to abandon wolf pack tactics in 1938. Had we been able to put more U-boats into the Atlantic before 1943, we would have achieved much greater successes and the Battle of the Atlantic would have had other results, with considerably different strategic consequences.

The *Königsberg* conversation should not have influenced submarine tactics then being developed by the still young U-boat flotillas, but German prewar radar developments should have made military leaders more perceptive to the influence of electronic inventions. A good number of the better U-boat officers displayed a significant ignorance in technical fields, with some of the aces even demonstrating a failure to understand the limitations of their relatively simple sound detection apparatus.

Almost four years after the *Königsberg* conversation during February 1942, Köhler called on Adm Hans-Georg von Friedeburg (C-in-C of the U-boat Arm's Organisation Department and 2nd Admiral for U-boats) aboard the depot ship *Erwin Wassner* to report that he had just commissioned *U377*. There he was greeted by Claus Korth (*U57* and *U93* and then on von Friedeburg's staff), who referred to the earlier conversation, saying men continued to laugh at Köhler's remarks for a long time after he had left! The last twist to the story only came out in August 1985, when I met Claus Korth in the U-boat Archive at the Federal German Naval Air School on the Island of Sylt and read him the notes for this revised edition. He agreed with my text, but on checking his career discovered that he had not been aboard the *Königsberg* at the time because he was on leave in southern Germany and did not return until several weeks after the event.

Therefore, he must have heard about the conversation from someone else and it must have been significant enough for him to have remembered it for almost four years. This would suggest that Köhler's opinion had been expressed more strongly than a mere comment, and it is a pity for the many who died that men laughed instead of paying attention to the 'futuristic invention' aboard the *Königsberg*.

Hitler's order shortly after the outbreak of the war to stop research into technical fields which could not be completed within a year has often been quoted as a reason why the navy lost so much ground in the radar development race, but this argument fails to explain why the Luftwaffe made so much progress. The air force was also working in the field of radar to aid night fighters and to allow for accurate bombing through clouds. This work was still at a comparatively primitive level when the war started and an intensification in activity led to the production of some reasonably sophisticated equipment. In fact the British Royal Parachute Regiment earned its first honours early in 1942, in a remarkable raid on radar installations at Bruneval on Cap d'Antifer, just north of Le Havre, where they dismantled important parts of German radar equipment.

This shows that not all German technological research had been abandoned at the start of the war and one gets an impression of the navy having been a little too unprepared when radio detection was used against German units. However, the blame for this lack of development cannot be laid at Dönitz's door. After all he was only a commander of a small unit when the war broke out, but it does appear strange that there was not a naval department with technological experts to at least keep abreast of developments. In retrospect it appears unfair to Hans Meckel that the vital work of trying to establish the role of radar at sea fell upon him, an ex-U-boat commander who hardly had the highly technical background for such a specialised task.

Some U-boat men suspected radar to have been used against them since the summer of 1941, but analysis of their claims usually attributed sudden attacks to either inexperience or negligence. At about the same time experiments were carried out to establish telephone links between Dönitz and his commanders at sea. KL Waldemar Seidel (Director of the Naval Dock yard at Lorient and Wolfgang Hirschfeld (radio operator of *U109* under KL 'Ajax' Bleichrodt) proved the principle could work. The idea was for Dönitz to dictate his question directly into a coding machine (*Schlüsselmaschine M*) and for the morse signal to be sent the moment it illuminated above the keyboard. With little need for further development, it was possible for him to quiz commanders at sea by using the telephone on his desk.

The first operational radio-telephone conversation was held on 17 June 1941 with Johann Mohr (*U124*) to ask whether there were any indications of *U124* having been detected by radar. Mohr replied that he had been forced to take evasive action on seven occasions, but was attacked only once. Destroyers had closed in at fast speeds but almost certainly had not seen the U-boat because they did not give chase when evasive action was taken. He guessed the approaches were coincidental during normal zig-zagging procedures. Similar reports which continued to flood in throughout 1941 were a direct result of radar's weak link of only working over relatively long distances. When the radar set came too close to the target, the echo merged with the transmission signal and this happened roughly at the time when a surface ship came into view of the lookouts on the U-boat. Thus the escort was running blind during the last minutes of the attack and had to find the target by visual sighting, something which proved most difficult on dark nights against Atlantic waves. The problem was later overcome by leaving the radar equipment near the convoy and directing the hunters through the newly introduced VHF radio, which carried speech instead of morse.

It was not until the start of 1942 when U-boats were concentrated around Gibraltar, that reports of aircraft attacks increased sufficiently for the U-boat Command to question again whether radar might be playing a role. The experts from Berlin were most sceptical, saying it would be virtually impossible to obtain a response from such a small target as a surfaced submarine and the question was not clarified until a few months later, in June 1942, after KA Ludgwig Stummel (Head of the Navy's Communication Department) arrived in France for tests. His investigations showed airborne radar to be in use in the Bay of Biscay and he suggested a radar detection device to bridge the gap until more positive measures could be taken.

Aircraft had been experiencing the same problem as surface ships, with the loss of radar contact for the last stage of the attack. This blackout was overcome by the introduc-

tion of the 'Leigh Light', named after its inventor Sqn Ldr Humphrey de Verde Leigh. Fitted under the aircraft, the light provided a short period of powerful illumination during this critical time when radar contact was lost. It gave U-boats such a devastating battering in the Bay of Biscay that on 24 June 1942 they were ordered to travel underwater in this dangerous area, thus greatly increasing the time needed to pass between the Atlantic and the French bases. Improvised AA armament in the form of light machine guns were hastily fitted to U-boats, but these only served as morale boosters, since they were too small to be of much use against the large, fast aircraft employed by the RAF.

The local Luftwaffe commander was asked for fighter cover and Dönitz paid a personal visit to Göring's headquarters, but despite a slight increase in support very little was done to help. Even damaged boats could not be assisted and had to crawl home through the dangerous 'Black Pit of Biscay' on their own. *U71* (KL Walter Flachsenberg) was hit by aircraft on 5 June 1942, some 100 miles west of Bordeaux and *U105* (KK Heinrich Schuch) was crippled off Cape Finisterre at around the same time. Neither of the boats could be given air cover for the dangerous crossing of what had suddenly become the RAF's own shooting range. Dönitz remarked in his diary that the situation was deplorable, with no defence against the new fast aircraft. The RAF could do as it pleased right in front of Germany's front door and he thought the Luftwaffe should be able to provide some protection, at least for damaged boats. Dönitz concluded his report by saying the situation of knowing that U-boats were effectively without support must be most demoralising to the crews.

It was not easy to meet KA Stummel's recommendations of equipping boats with radar detectors, although the *Nachrichtenmittelversuchskommando* (Communication Equipment Test Command) had developed a suitable receiver to pick up such impulses. German industry was working to capacity and could not accommodate extra production lines, but the French firms of Metox and Grandin helped with the construction of the first sets. The urgency of the problem was emphasised by the loss of three experienced boats to Bay air patrols. (*U502* KL Jürgen von Rosenstiel, *U578* KK Ernst-August Rehwinkel and *U751* KL Gerhard Bigalk) and the U-boat Command's only consolation was that this new receiver had been successfully tested by *U107* (KL Harald Gelhaus) one

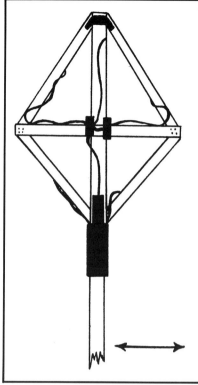

Above:
U758 (KL Helmut Manseck) signalling to *U591* (KL Hans-Jürgen Zetsche). Note the rod aerial on the left and the 'Biscay Cross', the first makeshift radar detection aerial, on the right.

Above right:
The first Metox Radar Detection Aerial — The 'Biscay Cross'. Some of these were made from packing case timber and the outside frame was often missing, in which case wires were just wrapped around the cross structure. The arrow indicates the approximate width of a man's head.

Right:
U645 (OL Otto Ferro) with rigid radar attached to the conning tower. This could only locate objects ahead and slightly to the side of the boat and it was necessary to sail in a complete circle for all-round coverage. The commander is holding a megaphone and there are more than the usual lookouts on the bridge, which suggests something of interest is happening, perhaps a meeting with a supply boat.

week before *U578*, the last of the three, went down on 10 August 1942.

Initial supply could not keep up with demand and boats leaving France had to dismantle the equipment to hand it over to incoming boats; this was not too complicated since nothing was bolted to the boat. The apparatus consisted of an aerial made from a rough wooden cross with a wire trailing down to the receiver, which later became known as the 'Biscay Cross' and 'Metox', although the official German names were Radar Detection Aerial 2 'Honduras' and R600A. It had a stunning effect at the battlefront by giving 95% of U-boats in the Bay of Biscay an opportunity to dive before the RAF could get within range and virtually changed the serious situation overnight, despite the primitive nature of the aerial which had to be thrown down the hatch every time the boat dived.

The Biscay Cross was superseded by a more sophisticated, circular pressure-resistant aerial, which had the additional advantage of detecting radar impulses at ranges exceeding 100km. At the early stage both the clumsy cross and the circular dipole aerial were used together to put the crew on alert once a contact was picked up on the long-range antenna. The boat did not dive until these signals were also received on the Biscay Cross, indicating the aeroplane was only 30km away. The main problem with the Metox receiver was that it did not always respond in the same way. Sometimes it would buzz and at other times give hair raising whistles, all of which played so much on the crews' nerves that some commanders are reputed to have switched the irritating device off.

The Air to Surface Vessel Radar (ASV) which the Allies were using was similar to the German DT Apparatus, mentioned earlier as having been installed aboard light cruiser *Königsberg*, and was afterwards also fitted to several other surface ships. It was not rendered completely useless as the Germans had hoped, because the RAF quickly noticed the dramatic change in their targets' behaviour and merely introduced a different attacking technique. Aeroplanes would cruise at high altitude with the ASV switched on and upon making contact, the transmitter would be cut off and the pilot informed of the approximate position in order to manoeuvre into a favourable attacking position, whilst losing height for his last run-in. If visibility was good, he could attack without further use of radar, although at night the ASV might be switched on for an occasional sweep to check whether the aeroplane was still running on the right path.

The next chapter in the radar and U-boats story began to unfold on 12 February 1943, when German AA batteries shot down a British bomber near Rotterdam in Holland. Following the usual standing orders, Luftwaffe personnel located the wreck for a routine exmination and this search revealed something new in the form of a blood-encrusted box with the words 'Experimental 6' written in pencil on the side. The rest of the story is now well known and one only needs to mention that this Rotterdam apparatus (as it became known) was a new type of radar working on a centimetre instead of decimetre wavelength, something which German experts had believed to be impossible. It explained numerous earlier reports from U-boat commanders, who insisted they had been attacked by aircraft although their Metox receiver failed to give a warning. These claims were initially put down to negligence and the widespread knowledge that Metox sets were switched off because of the whistles and shrieks which emanated from them, caused interrogators to treat such reports with scepticism. By that time, when the news of the centimetric radar as used in the Rotterdam Apparatus became known, there was very little Germany could do. Research was hopelessly behind, having been stopped before the war when experts convinced naval officials that the effect of radar signals diminished as the wavelengths got smaller and centimetric apparatus could not work at all.

Radar foxers were tried as well, with two types having come into fairly widespread use: *Thetis* was a three-dimensional cross with wires strung between wooden supports which could float on water to reflect radar signals, while *Aphrodite* consisted of a lighter-than-air balloon attached by a 60m length of wire to a float, which the balloon could not lift clear of the water while strips of metal foil acted as radar reflectors. However, all these introductions did nothing to help swing the U-boat campaign back to the offensive and merely served as a means of survival for U-boat crews.

Above:
U995 at Laboe near Kiel showing the conning tower with 37mm and twin 20mm AA guns. The *Hohentwiel* aerial can be seen on the left. It carried a variety of radar and radar detection aerials, usually with both types, one on either side of the frame.

Right:
U245 (KK Friedrich Schumann-Hindenberg) with makeshift radar detection aerials fitted inside the radio direction finder. On the right is Type *Fliege* (Fly) and on the left Type *Mücke* (Mosquito).

8

A Summary of U-boat Types

Type	Remarks
I	Operational.
II	Operational.
III	Not put into production. At first this design was similar to Type I, with an additional section to hold mines or torpedoes just aft of the bow compartment. This project was scrapped and the existing Type VII re-numbered to III. This re-numbered design was also based on Type I, with an additional part to hold mines aft of the engine compartment. Later, a pressurised hangar for accommodating two midget motor torpedo boats was added to the rear of the conning tower.
IV	Not put into production. A large (about 2,500 tons) supply boat with workshop facilities to allow self-contained U-boat flotillas to operate in distant seas with pocket battleships. The idea was for this type to be stationed in South Polar Seas as a repair base.
V	Originally a 300-ton boat with a special Walter propulsion unit for operating with the High Seas Fleet. The plans were scaled down and an experimental craft of about 80 tons was laid down at Germania Werft in Kiel. Launched on 19 April 1940, she was identified as *V80* and used for trials until the end of 1942. She was sunk off Hela in 1945. *V300*, identified by the original tonnage specification, was developed from *V80*, but the displacement of 300 tons dictated by the Naval Command in 1933/34

Type	Remarks
	proved impractical and the boat was enlarged to about twice this size. One boat, designated as *U791*, was due to have been laid down at Germania Werft in Kiel during 1942, but the project was abandoned in favour of smaller experimental vessels. The Naval Command identified this modification as Type XVII while Prof-Walter used 'W', the next letter of the alphabet after 'V', the Roman numeral for Type Five. (Also see Type XVII.)
VI	Not put into production. This boat was based on the hull shape of Type I and propelled by a closed-circuit steam engine. Such an idea had been put forward before World War 1, but it did not progress beyond the initial design stage.
VII	Early in the 1930s, when Germany was not permitted to build submarines, this had been a variation of Type I with a hangar to hold a midget motor torpedo boat. This was re-numbered as Type III and number VII used to identify the Atlantic boats of World War 2.
VIII	Not put into production. Very little is known about Type VIII, although I have seen a reference that this was supposed to have had apparatus for extracting oxygen from seawater, but have not managed to verify it.
IX	Operational.
XA	Not put into production. A large ocean-going submarine designed

Type	Remarks	Type	Remarks
	in 1936/37, but there were no definite plans to build it. Instead the project was modified into a minelayer of Type XB.	**XIV**	Operational supply boat.
X B	Operational minelayer.	**XV**	Not put into production. The supply boat of Type XIV was modified and version XIVB, of almost 2,000 tons designed, but this was abandoned in favour of a larger 2,500-ton boat with additional workshop space, known as Type XV. The project did not progress beyond the initial design stage.
XI	Not put into production. Contracts for four boats, numbered *U112* to *U115*, were negotiated in January 1936 with Deschimag of Bremen and cancelled in 1939 before the keels were laid down. This type was a 3,150/3,950-ton submarine cruiser with six torpedo tubes and two turrets containing 127mm guns. The crew would have comprised well over 100 men.	**XVI**	Not put into production. A supply boat with extensive workshop facilities of about 5,000 tons.
XII	Not put into production. A 2,000-ton version of the successful Type IX, interest in which was reviewed during the war when large transporters were required for making submerged voyages to the Far East. About 10 were due to have been built at Deschimag in Bremen, but the project was never fully developed and the keels were not laid down.	**XVII**	Experimental project. This was a modification of the Type V Walter Boat. A large number of variations were under consideration when this improved design was conceived and two slightly different types were laid down simultaneously at Blohm und Voss in Hamburg and at Germania Werft in Kiel. The following boats were commissioned: Project Wa201 in Hamburg: *U792* (OL Horst Heitz) on 16 November 1943 and *U793* (OL Günther Schauenburg) on 24 April 1944; Project Wk202 in Kiel: *U794* (OL Werner Klug) on 14 November 1943 and *U795* (OL Horst Selle) on 22 April 1944.
XIII	Not put into production. A small coastal submarine based on Type II with four bow torpedo tubes and increased speed and range.		

Right:
There were no clothing regulations for U-boats at sea and men usually wore anything they fancied, even Luftwaffe headgear, as seen on the right. The grid on the left is the top of a ventilation shaft and one of the 20mm twin AA guns can also be seen. The hole behind the man with the binoculars accommodates the attack periscope.

Type	Remarks
XVII B	Experimental project. Another variation of the Walter Principle built by Blohm und Voss in Hamburg. The following boats were commissioned: *U1405* (OL Wilhelm Rex) on 21 December 1944; *U1406* (KL Walter Klug) on 8 February 1945, and *U1407* (OL Horst Reitz) on 13 March 1945. *U1408* and *U1409* were almost completed but damaged during air raids and scrapped on the building site after the war.
XVII C to XVII J XVII J to XVII K	It has already been mentioned that a large number of variations of this theme were under consideration. Variation G was due to have been laid down at Germania Werft. The contract was scrapped before work could begin. Another variation of the Walter principle. An experimental boat, *U798* was started at Germania Werft but not completed. The boat was scrapped after the war.
XVIII	*U796* and *U797*, with Walter Propulsion Units, were due to have been built at Deutsche Werke in Kiel but abandoned before the keels were laid.
XIX	Not put into production. A freight-carrying submarine developed from the minelayer Type X B. Abandoned in favour of Type XX.
XX	Not put into production. A modification of Type XIX, which was due to have been built at Deutsche Werft in Hamburg and at Vegesacker Werft in Bremen-Vegesack. Some of the work was taken over by Germania Werft in Kiel. It seems highly likely that the actual construction did not start. This was a transport submarine with propulsion similar to Type VIIC, which was out-of-date by the time it was required.
XXI	Operational electro-boats. At least six variations, numbered XXI B onwards, were considered but none were laid down,

Type	Remarks
	although detailed drawings exist.
XXII	Not put into production. A small coastal boat with closed-circuit propulsion unit. Plans scrapped during the autumn of 1943 in favour of Type XXIII.
XXIII	Operational. Coastal electro-boats.
XXIV	Not put into production. An ocean-going boat of almost 2,000 tons with Walter Turbines as the main propulsion unit.
XXV	Not put into production. A small boat of less than 200 tons with only electric motors and no means of charging batteries without external help.
XXVI	Building not completed. Construction may have started at Blohm und Voss in Hamburg but individual sections were almost certainly not assembled. A 1,000-ton submarine.
XXVII A	A midget submarine, also known as Type *Hecht*. About 60 were completed but there appears to be very little information about their careers.
XXVII B	A modification of *Hecht*. Also known as Type *Seehund*. About 150 were completed.

None of the following projects were put into production and most only reached the initial design stage.

Type	Remarks
XXXI	A 1,200-ton boat.
XXXII	A 20-30-ton midget submarine project.
XXXIII	A 400-ton boat with closed-circuit propulsion.
XXXIV	A 90-ton project with an engine which was boosted by injecting oxygen.
XXXV	A larger version of XXXVI.
XXXVI	Similar to XXXV.

9

The Boats

The term U-boat tends to conjure up visions of highly efficient ultra-modern craft, and some of them, especially those under construction towards the end of the war, were certainly years ahead of their time. However, the boats which actually did the fighting during World War 2 were not much better than their predecessors of 1918. Three types of World War 2, Types II, VII and IX, were based on earlier models, making it easy to compare the progress:

Further noteworthy modifications introduced for World War 2 and not shown in the table were as follows:
(a) Both the diesel engines and the electric motors were more reliable and could operate with less noise, making life easier for the crews but making it more difficult for an enemy to detect boats by acoustic means.
(b) Batteries were more efficient, making it possible to remain submerged for longer periods.
(c) Torpedoes could be shot without expelling compressed air to the exterior, meaning there were no tell-tale bubbles on the surface to give away the position of a submerged boat.

(d) Electric torpedoes which did not leave a wake, had been developed by the start of World War 2, but the older compressed air variety was still in widespread use.

On the deficit side, however, one must take into account that individual valves on German boats had to be shut manually. Hydraulic systems for vents, as used by the Royal Navy, did not feature in them.

Types

Different U-boat types were identified by numbers, usually written as Roman numerals, later modifications being given letters after the number, eg: Type II, IIB, IIC and so on. The original design was suffixed with the letter 'A' as soon as further variations were under consideration. The type numbers were allocated at the drawing board stage and not all were put into production.

The individual number of each boat, always prefixed by the letter 'U', was usually allocated when the building plans were handed over to the ship yard. At this stage there could still be a considerable amount of work in planning the actual production

Type	Displacement ↑	Displacement ↓	Top speed ↑	Top speed ↓	Range ↑	Range ↓	Deepest Diving Depth	Armament
UB II (1915)	274t	303t	9.2kt	5.8kt	5kt/6,450sm	4kt/45sm	50m	2 Torpedo tubes/ 1×88mm gun
UF (1918)	364t	381t	11kt	7kt	7kt/3,500sm	4kt/35sm	75m	5 Torpedo tubes/ 1×88mm gun
IIA (1935)	254t	381t	13kt	6.9kt	8kt/1,600sm	4kt/35sm	150m	3 Torpedo tubes 1 or 2×20mm AA guns later increased to 4
IID (1940)	314t	460t	12.7kt	7.4kt	8kt/5,650sm	4kt/56sm	150m	As II A
UB III (1915/1916) (latest type)	c555t	c684t	13.5kt	7.5kt	6kt/7,120sm	4kt/50sm	75m	5 Torpedo tubes/ 1×105mm
VII A (1936)	626t	915t	17.0kt	8.0kt	10kt/6,200sm	4kt/94sm	200m	5 Torpedo tubes/ 1×88mm+AA guns
VII C (1940)	769t	1,070t	17.0(+)kt	7.6kt	10kt/8,500sm	4kt/80sm	200m	5 Torpedo tubes 1×88mm+AA guns
U 81 (1915)	808t	946t	16.8kt	9.1kt	8kt/11,220sm	5kt/56sm	50m	6 Torpedo tubes/ Guns variable
IX A (1935)	1,032t	1,408t	18.2kt	7.7kt	10kt/10,500sm	4kt/78sm	200m	6 Torpedo tubes/ Guns variable
IX C (1940)	1,120t	1,540t	18.3kt	7.3kt	10kt/13,450sm	4kt/63sm	200m	6 Torpedo tubes/ Guns variable

Notes

↑ = On surface   ↓ = Submerged

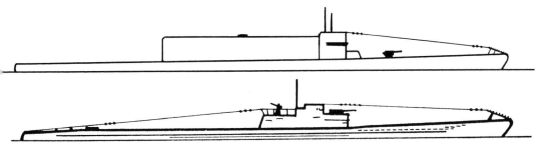

Top:
Type III
Designed in 1933, but never put into production. This boat was designed to carry two motor torpedo boats in a hangar behind the conning tower. The idea being that the submarine would partly submerge enabling the boats to float in and out, but this could only be performed in very calm weather.

Above:
UA
This was a conventional ocean going submarine orginally built for Turkey as *Batiray*, but never handed over. It was completed during March 1939 and then commissioned into the German Navy on 20 September 1939.

---

process and in finishing design details, especially in the case of new projects. Keels were not laid until after a construction contract was issued and a number of projects never got to that stage, being delayed or scrapped in the time between the yard being awarded the project and actually finalising the formalities. Thus boats were not launched in numerical order and quite a few numbers are missing. To confuse the issue further still, a number of boats launched before the war were re-numbered for administrative purposes and therefore had two numbers. In addition to this, ship building yards also used a construction number, which differed to the one prefixed by the letter 'U', but this hardly features outside construction yard documents.

Type I

IA	Based on prewar designs prepared by the German Submarine Construction Bureau in Holland. (2) *U25* and *U26*.
IB	and onwards were not put into production.

* The figure in brackets indicates the total number of boats launched and this is followed by the U-boat numbers.

This was one of the early designs as the type number suggests. In fact, this design was conceived in 1932 when the shackles of the Versailles diktat prevented such activities in Germany. The idea first went into production in Spain, where one boat later known as *Gür*, was launched. The basic plans were modified and eventually *U25* and *U26* were launched in 1936 at Deschimag in Bremen. Both boats had the annoying feature of not responding well to the controls. It was difficult to keep them at periscope depth, they would easily overshoot when diving too fast, they had an irritating roll in rough weather, and their conning towers tended to be wetter than anticipated. Consequently, they were banished to the submarine schools, but the shortage of ocean-going boats meant they returned to operational duties once the war started. It is interesting to note that both Eberhard Godt (Chief of the Operations Department, which was later renamed U-boat Command) and Hans-Georg von Friedeburg (C-in-C of the Organisation Department and 2nd Admiral for U-boats) served for short periods as commanders of *U25*.

Type II *(Nicknamed Dugout Canoes)*

IIA	Based on Type UB II (1915), UF (1918) and the Finnish *Vesikko*. (6)	*U1* to *U6*.
IIB	(20)	*U7* to *U24*, *U120* and *U121*.
IIC	(8)	*U56* to *U63*.
IID	(16)	*U137* to *U152*.

Later modifications, ie series 'B' onwards, were variations on the same theme to make the design more battleworthy by incorporating larger fuel bunkers. Engines were not enlarged to compensate for the extra displacement and consequently there was a slight loss of performance, but this was so little as to be hardly noticeable. Despite this, the boats could only remain at sea for about three to four weeks because the endurance

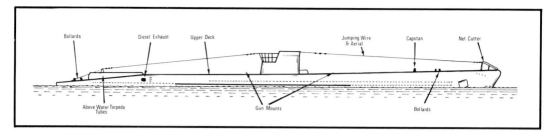

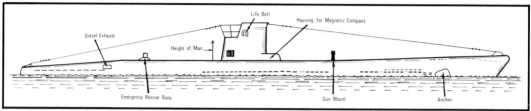

Top:

Type VII A U32

Above:

Type II C U57

---

was determined by the quantities of food and water carried. However, once the war started it was the lack of torpedoes which usually forced them back to port and a number of the 'dugouts' were employed as minelayers instead. They could carry some 18 mines instead of five torpedoes, and their small size coupled with good manoeuvrability made them particularly suitable for approaching close to British harbours. In 1940, when action was focussed on the North Channel (between Ireland and Scotland), U-boats were also employed as reconnaissance craft to discover convoy routes in British waters.

From the end of 1939 onwards these small boats were withdrawn from operational flotillas and moved into the Baltic to serve with U-boat schools, although a number were later sent as far as the French bases. Six Type II boats were moved to the Black Sea, as has been described earlier. There were two 'odd' types: *U120* and *U121* were originally built for China, but the war started before they could be delivered. These two had standard Type IIB hulls with a different conning tower design which proved unsuitable in rough weather and was therefore not further adopted.

Type VII

VII A   Based on the UB III (1915). Prototype: Finnish *Vetehinen*.
(10) *U27* to *U36*.

VII B   Improved version of Type VII A.
(24) *U45* to *U55*,
       U73 to *U76*,
       U83 to *U87*,
       U99 to *U102*.

VII C   Further improvement of versions A and B.
(Over 600)

U69 to *U72*,	*U825* to *U828*,
U77 to *U82*,	*U901* to *U908*,
U88 to *U98*,	*U921* to *U930*,
U132 to *U136*,	*U951* to *U1032*
U201 to *U212*,	*U1051* to *U1058*,
U221 to *U232*,	*U1063* to *U1065*,
U235 to *U329*,	*U1101* to *U1110*,
U331 to *U458*,	*U1131* to *U1132*,
U465 to *U486*,	*U1161* to *U1172*,
U551 to *U683*,	*U1191* to *U1210*,
U701 to *U722*,	*U1271* to *U1279*,
U731 to *U779*,	*U1301* to *U1308*.
U821 to *U822*,	

VII C/41 Numbers included with VII C.
An improvement of version C with stronger pressure hull for deeper diving to about 250m. The conning tower carried more armour as well as a number of other minor modifications.

VII D   Similar to version C, but with an additional section to hold mines just aft of the conning tower.
(6) *U213* to *U218*.

VII E   Not put into production. Similar to Type VIIC, but with a 12-cylinder two-stroke diesel engine to save weight.

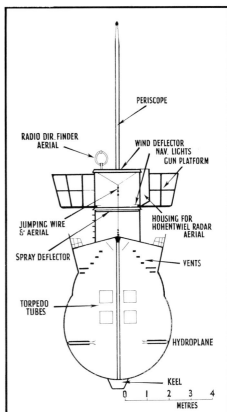

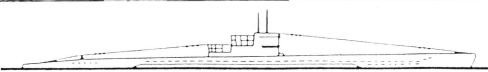

VII F Similar to version D, but the section just aft of the conning tower was designed as cargo space instead of containing mine shafts.
(4) *U1059* to *U1062*.

Type VII not only formed the backbone of the German Navy but represented by far the largest class of submarine ever built. The first, *U27*, was launched during June 1936, 12 months after *U1* appeared with a further 10 boats being completed before the close of that year. From then on they continued in production until the very end of the war and were still being laid down long after they proved to have been obsolete, at a time when the new generation of electro-boats were already under construction. The Type VII proved to be exceptionally seaworthy and easily manoeuvrable, even under the most difficult conditions. Various teething prob-

Top left:
The long, sleek distinctive cigar shape of the Type VIIC. The boat on the right is probably *U405* with her galley hatch just aft of the conning tower open.

Top right:
Type VII C, as seen from the front.

Above:
Type VII C. 1944 with additional AA gun platform behind the conning tower.

lems were sorted out and a completely modified version launched only two years after the first Type VII. The new Type VII B boats were thought to be Germany's best design and it was believed that they would be

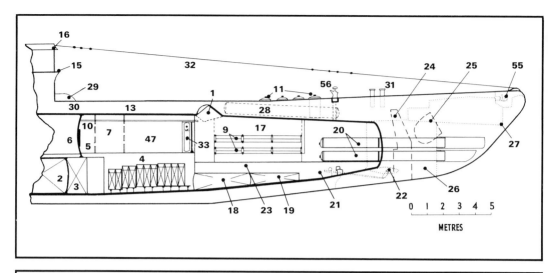

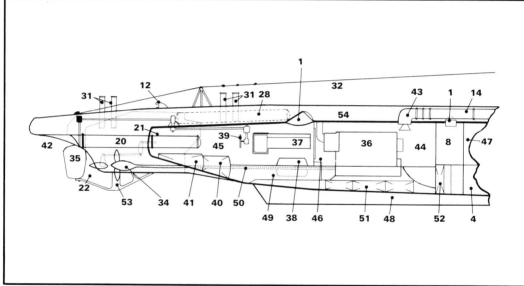

Top:
Section through the bows of a Type VII C with Atlantic bows
1 Hatch; 2 Diving tank III; 3 Oil tank; 4 Battery room;
5 Circular pressurised door; 6 Control room;
7 Commander's 'cabin'; 9 Bunks. These could also be used for storing torpedoes; 10 Pressurised walls;
11 Pressurised containers for inflatable life rafts;
13 Pressure hull wall; 15 Wave or spray deflector;
16 Wind deflector; 17 Bow torpedo room with accommodation for crew; 18 Torpedo tank; 19 Trim tank; 20 Torpedo tube; 21 Manual hydroplane control (only used in emergencies); 22 Hydroplane; 23 Storage space for torpedoes; 24 Anchor chain locker;
25 Anchor hawse; 26 Position of diving tank II;
27 Stabilising tank; 28 Storage space for torpedoes;
29 Magnetic compass; 30 Storage space for rigid schnorkel; 31 Bollard; 32 Jumping wire and aerial (prevents boat being caught in nets); 33 Toilet;
47 Accommodation; 55 Hook and tow rope; 56 Winch.

Above:
Section through the stern of a Type VII C
1 Hatch; 4 Battery room; 8 Galley (kitchen); 12 Light;
14 Air duct; 20 Torpedo tube; 21 Manual hydroplane control (only used in emergencies); 22 Hydroplane;
28 Storage space for torpedoes; 31 Bollard;
32 Jumping wire; 34 Propeller; 35 Rudder; 36 Diesel engine; 37 Control panel; 38 Electric motor;
39 Emergency steering wheel; 40 Torpedo tank;
41 Trim tank; 42 Position of diving tank I; 43 Air inlet into engine room; 44 Diesel engine room; 45 Rear torpedo and electro control room; 46 Door;
47 Accommodation; 48 Keel; 49 Storage space for torpedoes; 50 Propeller shaft (clutches not shown);
51 Various oil tanks; 52 Position of tanks for drinking water and used water tanks; 53 Propeller guard and bottom bracket for rudder; 54 Diesel exhaust.

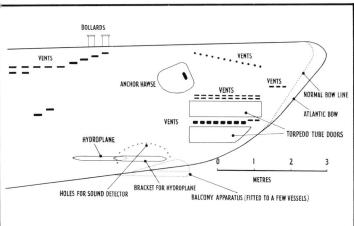

Above:
Launching *U218*, a Type VIID, which was the only type with mineshafts just aft of the conning tower. The commander, KL Richard Becker, and the majority of the crew had already been appointed and participated in the launching. Their emblem of three black fishes can be seen on the bows of the boat, a short distance forward of the row of circular vents.

Left:
Bows of a Type VII C

Below:
Type VIIC Conning Tower
After 1943 with enlarged gun platform, as seen from the top.

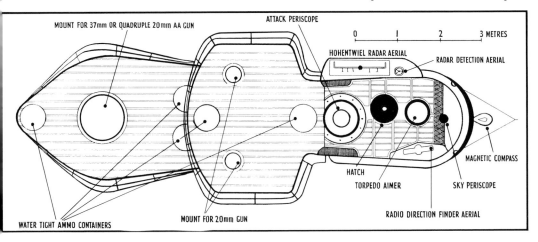

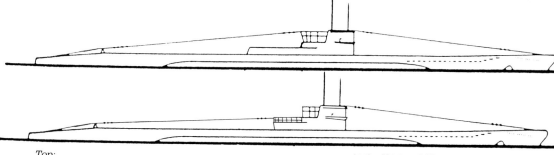

Top:

Type VII D. Similar to Type VII C except there was an additional section to carry 15 mines aft of the conning tower.

Above:

Type VII F. Similar to Type VII C except there was an additional section to carry torpedoes or general cargo forward of the conning tower.

responsible for bearing the brunt of the war at sea. However, a few modifications were drawn up just before the start of the war to give rise to the 'C' series, which came off the production lines in 1940.

The Type VII C boats were used for a wide variety of different tasks and consequently they also received a great deal of individual modification, both for operational and experimental purposes. So although these boats may have belonged to the same type, there were enormous variations in individual fittings and each building yard also produced numerous minor variations. It would be impossible to list all the differences, but noteworthy variations, which might be spotted on photographs are as follows:

1. Schnorkels, with a variety of head valves were fitted from the late autumn of 1943 onwards and the first ones appeared at the front early in 1944.
2. Special *Atlantic* bows were fitted to some boats.
3. Some VII C boats were without a rear torpedo tube and others only had two bow tubes. (Without rear tube: *U203*, *U331*, *U351*, *U401*, *U431*, *U651*; with two bow tubes: *U72*, *U78*, *U80*, *U554*, *U555*. *U93* was launched with a rear tube, but this was damaged early in the war and the rear torpedo door was welded shut.)
4. Conning towers, especially the AA armament and radar aerials, differed considerably.

Type IX

IX A   Developed from *U81* (1915)
  (8)   *U37* to *U44*.

IX B   Improved IX A

(14)   *U64* and *U65*,
    U103 to *U111*,
    U122 to *U124*.

IX C   Improved IX B
(143)   *U66* to *U68*,   *U841* to *U846*,
    U125 to *U131*,   *U853* to *U858*,
    U153 to *U176*,   *U865* to *U870*,
    U183 to *U194*,   *U877* to *U881*,
    U501 to *U550*,   *U889* to *U891*,
    U801 to *U806*,   *U1221* to *U1235*.

IX C/40   This type had slight modifications, which are given in the tables of technical data. There still appears to be some dispute about which boats belonged to this group and they hav all been listed under IX C above. It is probable that the following boats were built with the C/40 modifications.
    U167 to *U170*,   *U853* to *U858*,
    U183 to *U194*,   *U865* to *U870*,
    U525 to *U550*,   *U877* to *U881*,
    U801 to *U806*,   *U1221* to *U1235*.
    U841 to *U846*,

Below:
U196 (KK Eitel-Friedrich Kentrat), a very long range Type IXD2 boat, leaving La Pallice on 16 March 1944 for a voyage to Penang. Kentrat remained in Japan as Chief of the Naval Base at Kobe and he worked on the staff of the Naval Attache in Tokyo. OL Werner Striegler who had reached Japan as commander of *UIT25*, took over, but his luck did not hold: *U196* was lost in the Sunda Strait towards the end of November 1944; the exact reason for the loss has never been clarified.

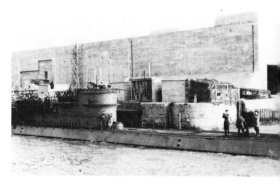

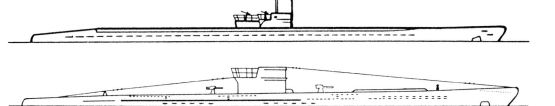

IX D1 A long dista..ce transporter based on IX C
(2) *U180* and *U195*

IX D2 An armed version of IX D1
(30) *U177* to *U179*,   *U859* to *U864*,
    U181 and *U182*,   *U871* to *U876*,
    U196 to *U200*,   *U883* and *U884*.
    U847 to *U852*,

Nicknamed *Seekuh* (Sea Cow) and Type IX D
Überseekuh (Overseas Cow). The origins of
this design stem from two contrasting
demands: firstly, to have a long-distance
submarine, and secondly to build a larger
boat for tactical commanders at sea. The
concept of a submarine operations room on
land, as was used by the U-boat Command
throughout the war, was considered impractical before the war. It was then thought
highly likely that battles would be led by
commanders at sea and large submarines, to
accommodate the additional staff with extra
equipment, were built to allow for such
eventualities. The need for flagships with
staffs at sea diminished as the war progressed and the idea was totally abandoned
during the autumn of 1940 because experience had shown that land-based officers
could do the work more efficiently. The
following boats were specially equipped with
extra communications equipment: *U66* to
U68, *U103* and *U104*, *U124* to *U131* and
U153 to *U158*. Type IX boats were not so
manoeuvrable as the smaller Type VII, but
still proved to be excellent for use in the
Atlantic. The problem of having a slightly
longer diving time became critical towards
the end of the war and some of the boats were
modified to have narrower bows to permit
quicker flooding. This feature is most useful
for helping to identify old photographs and
applies to the following Type IXC: *U170*,
U190, *U516*, *U530*, *U539*, *U804*, *U805*, *U858*,
U866 to *U868*, *U1232*, *U1233* and to the
following Type IX D2: *U195*, *U864*, *U873* to
U875 and *U883*.
    A small number of boats (*U183*, *U184*,
U185 and *U187*) were fitted with a special
type of dominant radio/reconnaissance mast

Top:
Type IX D1
1943, shown with hinged schnorkel.

Above:
Minelayer Type X B. U 119
The raised section in front of the conning tower
contained six shafts, each with three mines. There
were also four sets of six mineshafts on the side of the
boat. The two starboard sets are shown on the
diagram, but the lids were flush fitting, so on a
photograph one would probably only spot them when
looking down on to the boat. *Easy identification
feature.* This was the only type which had that raised
section on the deck in front of the conning tower.

on the port side of the conning tower, which
was removed shortly after its introduction,
but features prominently in some photographs. The first Type IX boats were fitted
with two periscopes in the conning tower
room, from where the commander would
have led a submerged attack, and a third
periscope in the central control room below.
This last mentioned device, which had a thick
head lens, was called a sky or navigation
periscope. However, it was subsequently
removed from later boats as it did not feature
on the majority Type IXC or IXD before
schnorkels were installed.
    Type IXD was designed as an underwater
transporter and built without torpedo tubes.
Only two were launched before construction
switched to IX D2, which was an armed
version of the original.
    The variations listed under Type VII also
apply to Type IX.

Type X B
X B   Developed from Type I A (1936) and from
        the design of X A, which was never put
        into production.
        (8) *U116* to *U119*,
            UU219 and *U220*,
            UU233 and *U234*.

This large minelayer, which was unsuitable
for convoy battles because it was armed with
only two stern torpedo tubes, was too clumsy
and took too long to dive in an emergency.

The bows had six special mine shafts to hold 18 mines and in addition to this there were another 24 mine shafts on the sides of the pressure hull, holding two mines each. The Type X B was also used to replenish front boats, sometimes going out for a mining operation and then remaining at sea in the role of supply boat. Consequently, they suffered a similar fate to the Type XIV. These minelayers could not be introduced into service straight away because the mine which was specially developed for them was not produced on time and torpedo mines, used by other U-boats, did not fit into the X B mineshafts.

Type XIV

XIV   (10) *U459* to *U464*,
            U487 to *U490*.

These boats were specially designed to supply fighting boats with basic necessities such as ammunition, fuel, water and food, to enable them to operate further afield. They were not commissioned until after surface supply ships had proved obsolete for the task and at a time when the Royal Navy could understand a large proportion of the German radio code and dispatched submarines, warships or aircraft to the secret refuelling positions in lonely parts of the oceans. Consequently, all Type XIV vessels suffered from similar problems of having their locations broadcast to the enemy and they were sunk in quick succession.

Weapons

In 1939, the main weapons for submarines were torpedoes or mines, as indicated in the table of technical data. Larger boats also had an 88mm or 105mm gun forward of the conning tower and light AA armament, usually in the form of a single 20mm weapon on the gun platform just aft of the tower, but other combinations also existed. Whilst these weapons were suitable for use against defenceless merchant ships or primitive aircraft, none of them could deal with fast moving warships of the type used as escorts or as submarine chasers.

Before the war, there was certainly no shortage of ideas about dealing with the threat of attacking destroyers. Werner Fürbringer (one of the first instructors at the Anti-Submarine School in Kiel where U-boat men were being secretly trained before 1935) and Karl Dönitz (then Flag Officer for U-boats) considered a number of alternatives.

Fürbringer was most concerned with the possibility of a potential enemy finding a successful underwater detection device and thus neutralising the submarine's great advantage of remaining unseen below the surface. Not knowing exactly how such an invention might develop, he concentrated on the next link of the attack process. Arguing that the enemy would be most vulnerable at the moment of closing in to drop depth charges, he suggested that positive buoyancy bombs be developed, the idea being for them to work in reverse of depth charges by being jettisoned from a submerged position to float to the surface. The proposition did not make much progress and was rejected as early as 1936 on the grounds that there was no evidence of a potential enemy finding a method of detecting the presence of submerged submarines.

The 50 year-old Fürbringer who had seen service in World War 1, made further suggestions in 1938 when he dismissed the development of the acoustic torpedo, saying it could be frustrated too easily by the enemy either towing a noise maker or ejecting noise making apparatus. As an alternative, Fürbringer suggested a radio-controlled torpedo, which was by no means a new idea since such equipment had been tested before the start of World War 1. Fürbringer also modified the idea by suggesting a wire controlled device which could not be interfered with by the enemy. Rocket-propelled torpedoes with hydrogen peroxide propulsion units working on the Walter Principle, and special anti-submarine chaser mines were also considered, but none of these came to fruition before the war. Once the conflict was under way, the necessity for anti-submarine chaser weapons diminished because Asdic, the underwater detection apparatus, did not play a major role in the opening moves and, like Radar, the threat was pushed into the background and not fully investigated until it was too late.

Metamorphosis

It has often been said that the U-boat offensive collapsed during that fateful May of 1943, but on examining war statistics it is apparent that this change had already started by the first quarter of 1941. The U-boat Command made a significant move to create new weapons as early as September 1942, when a detailed report of disturbing new trends in the Atlantic were laid before Gd Adm Erich Raeder (Supreme C-in-C of the

Navy). Because of the urgency of the situation, Dönitz was called to a meeting with Hitler on the same day as his document was delivered to the Supreme Naval Command. Following a heated discussion, Hitler agreed to the following four points: to start planning the production of the new Walter boats with higher underwater speeds; to modify boats already in production to increase the diving depth; to develop new weapons for U-boats and to improve AA armament. Much of the immediate development was devoted to designing and planning new ideas and virtually nothing appeared to alleviate the thrashing which the men at the front were receiving, especially from the new menace of large, fast aircraft. The black picture of the U-boat offensive improved a little during March 1943, when over 100 U-boats were at sea to fight the largest convoy battle of the war against Convoys HX229 and SC122. Yet despite this apparent climax, the average sinkings per U-boat at sea had dropped dramatically and only one month later came the 'Crisis Convoy', when the escorts of HX231 under the command of Peter Gretton, managed to drive off *every* attacking U-boat. What happened next is well known today: in May, U-boat sinkings rose to such catastrophic proportions that Dönitz evacuated boats from the convoy routes to the North Atlantic. It was clear that new defensive measures which people had been talking about since before the start of the war, had to be introduced if U-boats were going to survive.

Conning Tower Conversions

Despite the initial steps to increase AA armament having been taken as early as June 1942, it was autumn before the first conversion of two 15mm automatics (instead of the single 20mm) was tested on *U553* (KK Karl Thurmann). This proved unsatisfactory because the additional bulk made the boat unstable and difficult to keep at periscope depth. The armament was also considered insufficient to penetrate into large fast-flying aircraft, so the design was changed to accommodate two 20mm automatics, one in the position of the original gun and the other on a new platform a little lower and to the rear of the conning tower. This was tried out on several boats, including *U758* (KL Helmut Manseck) during November 1942. Further experiments continued and it was eventually the fourth conversion which was universally adopted. This was to enlarge the existing gun platform, the so-called 'Wintergarden', to

hold two 20mm twins and the new, lower platform to be fitted with something larger. Two versions were due to have been tested during April 1943, but the 37mm gun was not yet ready and therefore only the newly developed 20mm quadruple was tried out. This was used in battle for the first time on 8 June 1943 by *U758* (KL Helmut Manseck) against Avenger and Wildcat aircraft. Despite only inflicting little damage, the U-boat Command considered the design to be promising, but in the long run it proved unsatisfactory. It was eventually replaced by a 37mm quick-firing gun, especially adapted for submarines, until the new 37mm automatic came into service during October 1943. Other types of guns and different combinations in their arrangement can be seen in old photographs, but were not universally adopted.

Meanwhile, the large 88mm or 105mm quick-firing gun forward of the conning tower was no longer of use in the Atlantic and was removed from the end of April 1943 onwards, although commanders could retain it if they so wished. This gun remained on some boats serving in the Arctic and in the Mediterranean, and was later reinstated on boats operating in the Baltic.

Bridge conversion plans continued throughout 1943 and three boats, *U362* (OL Ludwig Franz), *U673* (KL Haelbich and *U973* (OL Klaus Paepenmöller), were equipped with a third gun platform forward of the conning tower for another 20mm quadruple, but this addition made them rather unstable and was quickly abandoned. Further ideas such as accommodating four 37mm guns were considered, but never adopted. However, the suggestion of the third platform forward of the conning tower was used to modify seven U-boats as special aircraft 'Flak-Traps', to operate in the Bay of Biscay from May 1943 onwards. This proved unsuitable against the modern aircraft employed by the RAF and the conversions were dismantled during November 1943. The seven Flak-Traps were: *U211* (KL Karl Hause), *U256* (OL Wilhelm Brauel), *U263* (KL Kurt Nölke), *U271* (KL Curt Barleben), *U441* (KL Götz von Hartmann [May to August] and KL Klaus Hartmann [August 1943 to June 1944]), *U621* (OL Max Kruschka) and *U953* (OL Karl-Heinz Marbach).

The increasing number of air attacks also resulted in more men being injured by shrapnel so conning towers were changed in an attempt to overcome this problem. Consequently both tower walls and guns were

Right:
U377 in October 1943 with Conning Tower Conversion Type IV: two twin 20mm guns on the upper platform and one quadruple 20mm AA gun on the lower one. OL Gerhard Kluth (commander) is on the left of the bridge and Ernst-August Gerke (1WO) on the upper deck (extreme right, bottom).

Below:
U377 early in 1942 showing a typical Type VIIC conning tower before the major refit of 1943. A=Gyrocompass; B=Engine telegraph dial; C=Speaking tube with whistle; D=Torpedo aiming device; E=Rod aerial which could be withdrawn into the conning tower wall or raised almost as high as the periscope; F=Commander's flag pole; G=The ends of the ventilation shafts, covered with a grid; H=Magnetic compass, covered by a coat; I=Attack periscope. Also note the slot for the radio direction finder to the right of the speaking tube.

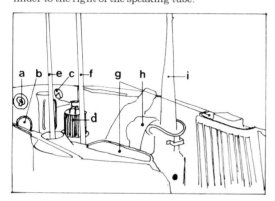

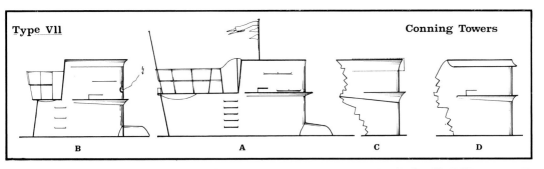

Type VII   **Conning Towers**

B   A   C   D

Top:
The fronts of early conning towers were straight.
U-boat designer Christoph Aschmoneit tried to create
something similar to the condition on the upper
platform of the Naval Memorial at Laboe near Kiel,
which is considerably less windy than the slightly
lower lookout base. To achieve such wind still
conditions, he suggested a collar be fitted half way up
the conning tower, as shown in **A**. This was later
modified by adding another collar at the top, as shown
in **B**. The upper collar was later changed as is shown
in **C**. This proved more successful and became a
standard fitting as shown in **D**.

Above:
The commissioning of *U365* (OL Heimar Wedemeyer)
on 8 June 1943 in Flensburg. This was one of the first
boats to be built with the new conning tower design
and shows a Type 1 Conning Tower Conversion: two
platforms, each with a single 20mm AA gun.

Above right:
U73 with an unusual AA gun platform. Note the
Biscay Cross, the first home-made radar detection
aerial on the top of the conning tower.

Right:
The 37mm gun of *U181* (KK Kurt Freiwald), seen here
en route to Penang.

Right:
Two different schnorkels on Type VIIC boats, *U826* (KL Olaf Lübcke) is in the foreground. The attack periscope (on the right with the smaller head lens) terminated in the commander's control room inside the conning tower, while the sky or navigation periscope (on the left with a larger lens) was operated from inside the central control room. The latter was below the conning tower room and therefore the sky periscope could not be raised as high as the other one, which can clearly be seen in this photo, showing both periscopes fully raised. The periscopes have been covered with hoods to prevent the crew looking out. Periscopic rod aerials, located inside conning tower walls, can also be seen.

Top right:
U516 (OL Friedrich Petran) of Type IXC40. Note the circular dipole aerials of the radar detection apparatus on top of the schnorkel. The sky or navigation periscope, with large head lens, is on the left and the attack periscope on the right.

Right:
U1058 (OL Hermann Bruder) on the left and *U1109* (OL Friedrich van Riesen) with white conning tower on the right, in Loch Foyle shortly after the war. The electro-pneumatic hinged schnorkel, with its recess in the upper deck, can be seen. The ventilation shaft runs down both sides of the rear edge of the conning tower and some boats had an external pipe from the schnorkel to this duct, as can be seen on *U1058*. Other boats, such as *U1109*, had this connection lower down and out of sight. The deck planking sticking up on the left is the cover to the forward torpedo hatch.

equipped with armoured shields. Cupboard-like structures consisting of two steel doors with a lid on top, were provided as shelter for the duty watch but this turned out to be impractical and most were removed again during November and December 1943.

The enlarged AA armament necessitated more men to be up top to man the guns, and this meant it would take longer to dive in an emergency. This battle of seconds could well have contributed to U-boat losses especially among inexperienced crews. Liberators, Sunderlands or Catalinas needed about 40 to 50 seconds for their final run-in to kill the U-boat. Yet the fastest time for a Type VII C to leave the surface, with the Wintergarden fully manned, was 30 to 40 seconds and this could only be achieved with a highly trained crew. Therefore, the margin between survival and death was very narrow, making it highly likely that a large number of boats were sunk during this critical battle of the seconds. Once down below, the additional weight helped to make the boat more unstable and the larger bulk increased drag and reduced the already slow underwater speed.

Schnorkels

Germany's U-boats spent most of their time on the surface and only dived to evade the enemy or for occasional submerged attacks. The events of 1943 made it quite clear that a new generation of submarine for full-time submerged operation was essential to keep pace with modern trends. This would take some time to produce and a stop-gap measure had to be introduced. The idea of providing submerged boats with breathing pipes, had been suggested before 1881, and the first device was probably fitted to the American *Argonaut I* in 1897. The Royal Netherlands Navy developed the concept during the 1930s, with a view to not only supplying fresh air to the crew, but also to run diesel engines below the surface. Kptlt J. J. Wichers worked on this principle, which was installed on the Dutch submarines *O19* and *O20* during 1938 and improved versions were later placed in *O21* to *O23*. Some of these air masts fell into German hands after the invasion of Holland and *O21* made her way to Britain to operate under the White Ensign of the Royal Navy. Neither Germany nor Britain had a use for the Dutch schnorkel and they were removed from operational boats. J. F. van Dulm (commander of *O21*) regretted this because although the pipe could not be used in the rough waters of the North Atlantic for what it had been designed, it proved most useful as a means of ventilating the boat during storms because the pipe helped to prevent water from being washed in and thus kept the interior much dryer.

In Germany, Hellmuth Walter had suggested a schnorkel as early as 1933, but this was not taken up by the Naval Command and it was to be the summer of 1943 before serious research started. A hastily made shaft was tried out with *U57* (OL Walter Zenker) and *U58* (OL Horst Willner). Having proved quite successful, pressure was put on the Naval Arsenal in Kiel and on the Naval Dockyard in Wilhelmshaven to produce more models in larger quantities. However, this new device did not generate much interest, especially as the first operational boat to have a schnorkel fitted, *U264* (KL Hartwig Looks), was lost in February 1944 during the first attempt to use it.

The schnorkel certainly did nothing to revert the U-boats' role from the defensive to the offensive. Instead it appeared to have presented more problems than it solved and at best only provided the difference between death and mere survival. It enabled boats to remain submerged while charging batteries, but the top schnorkeling speed under the most favourable conditions, was reduced to an absolute maximum of 7kt. For most of the time progress was much slower, which meant it was taking much longer to get into the operations area of the mid-Atlantic. In addition to this, it was most difficult to pursue convoys.

Schnorkeling was also a highly uncomfortable and dangerous undertaking. At times waves would wash over the top of the headvalve, meaning air would be sucked from the interior of the boat before the diesels stopped, to create an uncomfortable low pressure condition, which caused intense pain to the crew. *U1203* (OL Sigurd Seeger), tried schnorkeling for the first time in Oslo Fjord and two of the crew, who failed to adjust to the terrific differences, had to be taken off with damaged ear drums.

Operational boats usually dived at the point where the escorts through the coastal minefield left, and on return U-boats would surface there again, which meant that the men were confined to the inside of the narrow iron coffin for a long time, not even being able to go outside for the occasional breath of fresh air or for a smoke. While schnorkeling, movement inside the boat was also confined to prevent upsetting the trim. The engineering officer usually managed to compensate for this, but balance was most delicate when 'hanging on' the schnorkel, making even such relatively simple adjustments most difficult and men often had to ask permission before shifting their weight any distance. It might be interesting to add that the centre of gravity of a U-boat was some distance behind the conning tower. Therefore the bows pitched considerably more than the stern, and it was most difficult to keep the top of the schnorkel in the right place above the water in anything but the calmest of seas.

The cook could not throw gash overboard and more of his rotting waste had to be stored. Going to the toilet became a problem as well, because boats spent more time at greater depths where the pressure was too great to empty the contents and new high power thunder boxes had to be developed. In the meantime, men at the front had to improvise and use tins, which not only helped to make life more difficult, but also the living atmosphere more unpleasant.

New boats are planned

The years following Dönitz's appointment as Submarine Flotilla Commander saw the original six boats grow into what has been described as the Fourth Branch of the Armed Forces. (Army, Air Force, Navy and U-boats.) The development was so rapid that many people have taken the turn of events for granted, thinking growth followed an obvious path in reasonable harmony, while others, especially non-German writers, have labelled Dönitz as the master architect of the U-boat Arm.

Dönitz was sent to U-boat Flotilla *Weddingen* in 1935 because nobody else was available. He was left free to develop his own ideas because at the time there was no naval policy about the employment of submarines, and not because he was an expert in this field. This left him in amazing isolation where he could create the *Freikorps Dönitz* rather than co-ordinating submarines into an overall naval policy. This situation has led numerous people to conclude he was also responsible for the construction of submarines, which is not true. There was a special Submarine Construction Bureau within the Supreme Naval Command, which dealt with technical developments and although Dönitz bombarded them with numerous memoranda, very little attention was paid to his views. One can definitely say that he contributed virtually nothing to prewar submarine development.

This state of affairs changed on 8 September 1939 when G Adm Erich Raeder (Supreme C-in-C of the Navy) stated in a policy document that future U-boat types would be determined in consultation with the Flag Officer. Yet this change in attitude did not last very long and in November, shortly after Dönitz had been promoted to Konteradmiral, Raeder sent the U-boat Command a terse note saying, 'The Commander-in-Chief for U-boats is prohibited from occupying himself with technical problems and will confine his activities exclusively to conducting battles at sea'.

1941 was a year of frustration in the U-boat Command when it was most difficult to drive home attacks because Britain had started systematically to avoid wolf pack formations. Dönitz's diary often refers to inadequacies and some of his remarks were underlined by men in the Supreme Naval Command, who made marginal remarks like 'We don't want a submarine navy!'. It might have been obvious that the lack of success in 1941 and the heavy losses sustained later made it clear that a new generation of U-boat was needed, but the initial movements to get such plans under way were painfully slow.

There were no shortages of ideas: Prof Hellmuth Walter and Germania Werft in Kiel had even carried out experiments with a Type V boat which could do almost 30kt submerged and did not need air to run its engine. (30kt was faster than most Royal Navy ships could do on the surface.) The idea was by no means new, with single propulsion units having been considered before World War 1. The Walter Turbine had several drawbacks: firstly, two Type VII Cs could be built for the price of one Walter boat; secondly, the new fuel was highly concentrated hydrogen peroxide, which was consumed in such large quantities that the gauge was calibrated in tens of litres, rather than in units; thirdly, the fuel was a scarce chemical with no production line to manufacture it in the large quantities required by U-boats, and on top of this it was highly volatile. Yet despite these disadvantages, Walter did prove he could produce a completely new generation of submarine.

One of the first questions from the committee considering an alternative to the Type VII C was where was the professor intending to store such vast quanities of fuel? Walter had overcome this difficulty by designing a boat with two pressure hulls, one underneath the other, as in a figure '8'. The upper one was to contain the turbine and accommodation plus the usual controls, while the lower hull would be one large fuel tank. Someone on the committee suggested that a new fast underwater submarine could be produced more easily by fitting a conventional system in the upper hull and filling the lower compartment with batteries. The additional electric power would provide a much faster underwater speed.

It was decided to continue experiments with the Walter Principle and at the same time prepare the other idea for mass production. Two different types of 'electro boat' were thought to be required: a large version (Type XXI) to replace Type VII C, and a smaller version (Type XXIII), which could be produced faster and used for operations in British coastal waters. The responsibility for building these boats was given to Dr Albert Speer's Department of Military Armament; Speer concluded that it would be possible to produce about 20 Type XXI U-boats per month. However, the first of this type (*U2501* OL Otto Hübschen, launched on 12 May 1944) never saw active service because the war ended before trials could be completed.

Several major problems hampered production. Skilled labour in the ship yards had been reduced by about 70% because most of the men had been called up for service in the armed forces, and most of the highly demanding work was being done by men who had come out of retirement, by women, children and even prisoners of war. The situation was made worse by not scrapping the Type VII C. Instead, this obsolete boat was still being produced and its continuing construction tied up a large number of skilled workers. The difficult construction was being done at a time when the RAF was intensifying its campaign of terror bombing of civilians and housing. Large cities such as Hamburg and Bremen often received three to five separate waves of bombers per night, making it most difficult for the work on the boats to continue. The actual shipyards appear not to have been singled out as targets and suffered little damage until the final months of the war. It is incredible that the new boats were being produced at such an astonishingly fast rate, despite the bombing campaign against the homes of the workers. The electro boats were certainly years ahead of their time and it is a great credit to the German shipbuilding industry that it succeeded in producing this truly revolutionary project against such heavy odds and in an astonishingly short period of time.

Below:
Type XXI boats were built in sections and only needed to be assembled at the riverside yard. This is Blohm und Voss in Hamburg.

The Electro Boats — Types XXI and XXIII

XXI   A large ocean-going boat to replace
Type VII. The following were
commissioned:
U2501 to *U2552*
U3001 to *U3035*
U3037 to *U3041*
U3044
U3501 to *U3530*

XXIII   A small coastal boat.
The following boats were commissioned:
U2321 to *U2371*
U4701 to *U4707*
U4709 to *U4712*
The following boats left for operational
missions: *U2321*, *U2322*, *U2324*, *U2326*,
U2329, *U2336*.
A further 12 boats were lying in
Norwegian waters when the war ended,
awaiting orders to sail.

A new method adopted for building the
Type XXI was to produce them in sections
with different yards making different parts.
Each section took about three weeks to build
and moving them to the riverside yard took
about five days. Fitting the sections together
was often completed in under 18 days and
then merely 10 to 14 days more were needed
for fitting out. The unavoidable delays caused
by the war became so great that only four
Type XXI boats were ready by January 1945
and two boats, *U2511* (KK Adalbert Schnee)
and *U3008* (KL Helmuth Manseck), actually
left for operational patrols. *U2511* received
details of the capitulation and orders to stop
fighting while waiting for convoys to the
north of Britain. On his way home, Schnee,
who had learned to shoot in *U23* under Otto
Kretschmer, met a group of ships and tried
out a mock attack to see whether the old
methods still worked. He closed in until he
reached a favourable shooting position, and
then slipped away without being noticed.
However, he proved that the Type XXI could
have re-balanced the situation in the Atlantic
and had Germany started to produce these
boats earlier, the war might have lasted a
little longer, to have been terminated by an
American atomic blast in Europe instead of
Japan.

Type XXI boats were certainly far superior
to any existing operational submarine at the
time. In addition to the general performance
given in the *Table of Technical Data*,
provisions were made for a deep freezer,

ventilation plant, hydraulic torpedo loaders
which could re-load six tubes faster than men
could deal with one tube in a conventional
type. The Type XXIII had no machinery for
re-loading torpedoes at all. Instead the small,
cramped vessels only carried two which were
installed from an exterior cradle.

Armament — Torpedoes

At the start of the war there were two basic
types of torpedo in the naval armoury: G7a
and G7e. 'G' signified the diameter of 534mm.
'7' the length of 7m (the exact length was
7,086mm), 'a' was the first in the new series
developed after World War 1 and 'e' stood for
electric. The first mentioned was perfected
between the two wars and consisted of a
star-shaped, four-cylinder internal combus-
tion engine, which was driven by a mixture
of fuel, compressed air and water to create a
small amount of steam. Its main disadvan-
tage was that exhaust gasses and oil floated
to the surface, leaving a tell-tale wake and
making them unsuitable for daylight
attacks. G7e was fully electric and did not
leave such a wake, but the performance was
not so good and it needed more attention,
with batteries requiring constant re-
charging.

The approximate performance of these two
torpedoes was as follows:

G7a 30kt for 12.5km ⎫
40kt for 8.0km ⎬ Carrying a warhead
44kt for 6.0km ⎭ of about 380kg

G7e 30kt for just over 5km, but carrying
about 500kg of explosives.

At the start of the war there were two ways of
detonating torpedoes, either by contact or
magnetic pistol. The mode of detonation
could be set manually while the torpedo was
lying in the tube ready for firing. The torpedo
crisis of the first winter of the war is well
known today and resulted in the less effective
contact detonators being used at the beginning of the war.

Towards the end of 1942, a special
anti-convoy torpedo was produced. Known as
FAT, (*Federapperat-Torpedo* and sometimes
erroneously also called *Flächenabsuch-
Torpedo*), it travelled in a straight line for a
predetermined distance and then zig-zagged
to the right or left, depending on how it had
been adjusted. This concept was further
developed into LUT (*Lagenunabhängiger-
Torpedo*), which could be fired at depths of up

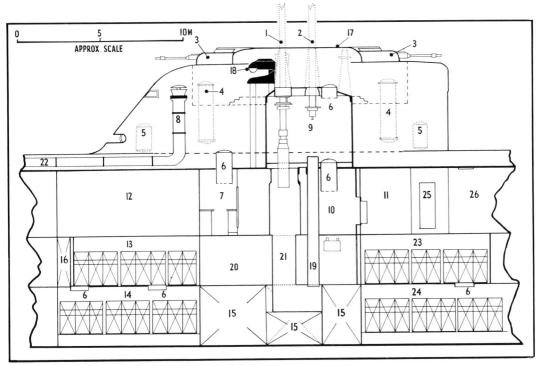

Left:

Conning tower section of a Type XXI

1 and **2** Periscopes; **3** Anti-aircraft guns; **4** Water-tight containers for AA ammunition; **5** Water-tight containers for rubber dinghies; **6** Hatch; **7** Galley (kitchen); **8** Air intake (when boat is on the surface); **9** Conning tower room; **10** Control room; **11** Commander's cabin; **12** Crew accommodation; **13** Battery room; **14** Battery room; **15** Tanks for various purposes; **16** Drinking water tank; **17** Position of radio direction finder aerial; **18** Schnorkel (periscopic); **19** Periscope well; **20** This section contained: munition room, potato room, deep freezer and tank for dirty water; **21** Periscope well; **22** Air duct to engine room; **23** Battery room; **24** Battery room; **25** Radio and listening room; **26** Accommodation.

Below:

Type XXI

This boat was supposed to have replaced the Type VII C in the battle for the Atlantic, but the war stopped after two had left port for operational patrols. The long rectangular box between the conning tower and bows contained rectractable hydroplanes.

Bottom:

A row of Type XXI boats seen shortly after the war. The place has been given both as Lisnahilly and Lisahally; the spelling on Ordnance Survey maps is Lissnahawley. The boat nearest the camera can be identified as *U2502* (KL Heinz Franke). Karl Wahnig, of *U802*, has a picture of the boats taken from the quayside and this shows *U3514* (OL Günther Fritze) to be next and then *U3017* (OL Rudolf Lindschau). The boat on the left has not yet been identified. It is interesting to note that the vents on the conning towers are different on every boat.

Right:
A type XXI boat in dry dock,
probably *U2502* (KL Heinz
Franke).

Below:
U2321 (OL Hans-Heinrich
Barschkis), a Type XXIII, seen in
dry dock. Increased anti-
submarine measures made
surfacing at sea virtually
impossible by the time these
boats were brought into service,
and consequently they were built
without an upper deck above the
pressure hull.

Left:
U826 (KL Olaf Lübcke) after the war in Scotland with a crewman holding the business end of a torpedo. At the front of the torpedo head is a small propeller which screwed the contacts of the detonator together, to ensure there would be no explosion until it had travelled through water for some distance. The two large prongs are part of the contact pistol. They were smaller than the radius of the torpedo, making it possible for the torpedo to hit a curved hull and slide under it without detonating. This fault was not noticed until the end of the war. *IWM*

Left:
Training torpedoes are loaded aboard *U586* in Kiel. Note the man working a hand-operated winch to raise the torpedo to the correct angle for lowering. This view shows the stern where three torpedoes could be stored: one in Tube 5, another below the floor between the electric motors, and the third in the upper deck storage container.

Below:
U377 (OL Gerhard Kluth) is seen here on a misty autumn day in 1943. The conning tower modifications are clearly visible.

to 50m; there was no need to use the periscope for aiming since it had a special detection device known as *Nibelung* or *S-Anlage*. LUT came to the front during February 1944, but the advanced *S-Anlage* was only installed in Types XXI and did not see operational service in the war.

The *Zaunkönig* or T5 was an acoustic torpedo introduced to operational boats during October 1943. It was conceived for use as an anti-destroyer weapon and it had only to be aimed in the general direction of the noise source and fired to find its own way. The system incorporated a device to prevent it being frustrated by a noise-making distraction, which could lure it from its real target. This worked because the torpedo could only 'hear' up to 30° either side of its forward path and once it detected noise of a certain intensity, the torpedo would swing to the left or right and travel in a circle until another noise source attracted the acoustic head. Whilst going round in a circle the torpedo could not respond to the noise which had originally caused it to circle because the sound head was shielded at the sides; but at one point it would probably face the ship which was towing the 'foxer' or had ejected a noise-making buoy, and head off towards it. A ship was too big to circumnavigate and sooner or later the torpedo would collide with the hull or be detonated by its magnetic field.

Unfortunately, some of the faults which caused the torpedo crisis of 1939/40 had not been recognised at the time and started to reappear when the T5 came into service. Consequently the German Navy suffered a torpedo catastrophe. Some 700 acoustic torpedoes were shot, but only produced 77 definite hits, meaning this highly rated anti-destroyer weapon had a miserable success rate. (The U-boat Command guessed there was a considerable discrepancy between actual sinkings and figures given by commanders, but their estimate was nowhere near these figures, which came to light much later during the 1970s, when Prof Dr Jürgen Rohwer researched the subject.)

Handling and overhauling torpedoes was one of the toughest jobs in a U-boat. On top of that, the centre of gravity of the boat was some distance aft of the conning tower and consequently the bows pitched considerably more than the stern. To make conditions even worse, many men were squeezed into the small bow torpedo compartment without washing facilities, and electric torpedoes required constant maintenance as has already been mentioned. One torpedo was

usually hauled partly out of the tube each day for an overhaul. Reloading was physically demanding work and could not be carried out on the surface if there was more than moderate seas or any danger of having to dive suddenly. To reload, men and bunks had to be moved out of the way, torpedoes unlashed from their storage position and then winched up with chains and finally manhandled into the tube. Trimming the boat slightly bow heavy made it easier to heave them downhill, but despite this, it still took a good half an hour to reload one. Therefore, it is not difficult to appreciate that a boat would have to remain submerged for more than an hour to reload three or four torpedoes, and this was long enough to lose an entire convoy at sea, meaning another spell of running on the surface at fast speed before getting into another favourable shooting position.

Torpedoes were usually brought to the boat in a barge or special electrically-driven truck and loaded under the supervision of the torpedo mechanic, who was the only NCO to sleep with the crew because he needed to be in the bow torpedo compartment. There were 'long and short rules' to be followed when loading: long rules meant that the entire torpedo received a detailed check before being allowed on board, while short rules allowed the mechanic to accept them after testing only a few vital points. Once on board, the serial numbers were recorded and signed for, and then they became part of the boat's expendable equipment, but had to be accounted for in the log book.

In a Type VIIC, torpedoes were accommodated as follows: five in the torpedo tubes, four below the floor in the bow compartment, two above the floor in the bow compartment, one between the electro motors in the stern, one torpedo in an external container above the bow compartment and another one in an external container on the stern. This made a total of 14. In the Atlantic, reloading from external containers became impractical once the threat from enemy aircraft became common, and from the end of 1942 VIICs usually only carried 12 torpedoes.

Armament — Mines

By the start of the war, Germany had developed a special mine for ejection through torpedo tubes. Known as TMA (Torpedo Mine Type A), it held about 215kg of explosives and was half the size of a standard torpedo, which meant it was possible to accommodate

Left:
Loading mines into *U117* (KK Hans-Werner Neumann), a Type XB boat. The mineshafts on both sides of the hull can clearly be seen.

Below left:
The bow torpedo room of *U995* looking forward from the torpedo tube doors. There are tubes on both sides and the special machine for adjusting *LUT* torpedoes can be seen at the back of the picture. (*LUT: Lagenunabhängiger Torpedo*, developed as an anti-convoy weapon.) Adjustments to torpedoes could be made whilst the 'eels' were lying in their tubes, waiting to be fired.

Below:
Bootsmaat Hermann of *U376* (KL Karl Friedrich Marks) in the bow torpedo compartment of this Type VIIC. The torpedo loading gear can be seen towards the left of the picture. The dials above Hermann's head are on the device which was used to make final adjustments in torpedo settings just before they were fired.

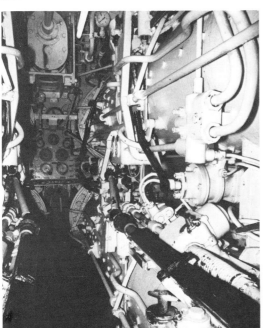

91

two at a time in one tube. However, tubes required a special modification to eject them and this was not fitted to all boats. On top of this the commander had to have special training to lay mines. Mines for the mine-layer U-boat of Type XB were specially designed during the war for the vertical shafts and were not ready for production until a considerable time after the first Type XB boats had been commissioned. Known as SMA (Shaft Mine Type A), they held about 350kg of explosives and weighed 1,600kg.

Armament — Artillery

Heavy Artillery The large guns fitted forward of conning towers were usually either 88mm or 105mm quick firing, as indicated in the *Table of Technical Data*, for use against surface targets. Theoretically they could have been trained against aircraft, but a U-boat was too unstable as a gun platform and there was no hope of hitting a small, fast-moving target. The ammunition was stored in a magazine situated under the floor of the interior and cartridges had to be carried up by hand and passed through the conning tower hatch. From there they had to be handed via the wintergarden to the gunners and this complicated path helped to make fast firing difficult. The hatches leading to the upper deck were usually not opened at sea because it would have taken too long to close them in an emergency.

AA 37mm Before the change in armament which started in 1942, Types IX and XIV had a quick-firing gun fitted to the upper deck, just aft of the conning tower. Later 37mm anti-aircraft (AA) guns were fixed to the lower wintergarden. The AA gun was semi-automatic in as much as a clip holding several cartridges could be attached manually and the weapon fired automatically. The cartridges for at least some of the quick-firing guns were considerably larger to hold more explosives and had to be fed singly into the breach.

AA 20mm Originally only single barrelled guns were fitted as AA guns and they were usually sited on the wintergarden of the conning tower, but some Type II and VII A had them fixed to the upper deck. A twin and quadruple barrelled version was introduced later during the war, as has already been mentioned.

Other Guns A few boats were equipped with 15mm AA guns for experimental purposes, but the penetrating power was not sufficient and the model was not adopted. From 1942 onwards, small machine guns were also provided for protection against

Right:
The 88mm gun is seen here on *U405* (KK Rolf-Heinrich Hopmann) runing into Narvik after the battle for Convoy PQ18. In front is a minesweeper escort. The 'L' shaped bracket at the top right of the gun is for holding the gun sight; this delicate optical device was usually stored inside the boat.

Left:
The gun crew of *U201* (KL Adalbert Schnee), trying out the 88mm quick firing gun. The insignia of a lion and sickle is the coat of arms of the town of Remscheid in the Ruhr. Later the boat carried a snowman (Schnee means snow) as insignia and this was given a Knights Cross when the commander gained the award.

Below:
The first gun drill on *U377*: operating this gun in heavy seas was difficult because of the unstable platform, yet despite this some men managed to achieve uncanny accuracy with this cumbersome weapon. Its use in an attack was not easy, especially if the target retaliated by running away; *U69* (KL Jost Metzler) had to shoot over 150 shells at the 2,918grt steamer *Robert L. Holt* before she went down.

Above:
The commissioning of *U480* (OL Hans-Joachim Förster) on 6 October 1943 at Deutsche Werke in Kiel with the new quadruple 20mm AA gun.

Above right:
A good view of the 88mm gun aboard *U405* with gun sight in position. The ball hanging from the net jumping wire indicates the boat to be lying at anchor.

Right:
U181 (KK Kurt Freiwald) showing the 37mm gun in action. Ammunition had to be clipped manually on to the gun and was then shot automatically, however the rate of fire was too slow for large fast-flying aircraft.

aircraft, but this was more for boosting morale since they were inadequate against large aircraft. The Naval Command also considered a variety of other weapons, including guns from aircraft, but none of these were adopted.

Hand Weapons U-boats were also equipped with a variety of hand weapons, depending on the mission in hand. The standard inventory usually consisted of six pistols, six rifles, some single and double barrelled signal pistols and demolition charges. A few boats which visited land weather stations or carried out similar assignments, were provided with more hand guns. It was usually maintained that men were not allowed to carry personal hand guns on patrol, but there were certainly exceptions to this rule. My father (*Stabsober-maschinist — Diesel, U377*) for example, is reputed to have always kept an automatic pistol to terminate his own life if the torture of war became unbearable.

Chance for Red? — The Toilet

Every U-boat, except midget craft, had a toilet, with the larger types even having two, but one of them was usually used as a larder and therefore could not accommodate the crew until they had passed the contents through the other one. All U-boats had a so-called 'upper deck toilet' as men just urinated over the side. Of course, this luxury could not be used when the boat was submerged and once deeper than about 25m

the interior toilet had to be closed as well because the water pressure outside the boat was too great to pump the contents out. This was hardly an imposition at the beginning of the war, but longer dives became the order of the day as the anti-U-boat measures became more ferocious, with boats in the Mediterranean and in American waters regularly remaining submerged for periods of 24 hours or so and special, high-pressure thunder boxes had to be installed. After all a functional 'head' could make all the difference between total and partial concentration.

The operation of this high-pressure toilet proved to be so difficult that men with a technical aptitude were specially trained to learn the intricacies of the new weapon. There was a delicate naval term for these men, and the term 'Toilet Graduate' will probably suffice in English. At least one boat, *U1206* (KL Karl-Adolf Schlitt), was lost as a direct result of mishandling this complicated 'thunder box'. Kptlt Schlitt tried the system for himself but the LI sent a toilet graduate to help, and somehow with two minds on the same job, the levers were pulled in the wrong order and the commander's offering plus a thick jet of salt water was squirted into their faces. Seeing what had happened, the LI took the boat up to relieve the pressure, but some of the inflowing water drained into the batteries below to produce poisonous chlorine gases (chlorine is produced when salt from sea water reacts with sulphuric acid in the batteries) and eventually, after an attack from aircraft, the boat had to be abandoned.

Left:
A man from *U181* (KK Kurt Freiwald) uses the upper deck, starboard toilet. The boat has suffered rather badly during storms, as can be seen by the missing deck sections.

10

Tables of Technical Data

This information has been provided to help compare the fighting capabilities of U-boats and many numbers have been rounded off to simplify reading. Attention is drawn to the new edition of Gröner and books by Rössler, which give detailed technical information.

Most of the performance figures are based on results obtained during trials. In some cases they were improved when machinery was driven harder under war conditions, but more often poor quality and battle damage reduced the performance.

Type	Description	Date first launched	Complement[1]	Displacement[2] Official	Su
IA	Ocean going/Conventional	1936	4/39	712t	
IIA	Coastal/Conventional	1935	3/22	250t	
IIB	Coastal/Conventional	1935	3/22	250t	
IIC	Coastal/Conventional	1938	3/22	250t	
IID	Coastal/Conventional	1940	3/22	—	
VIIA	Sea/Ocean going/Conventional	1936	4/40 to 56	500t	
VIIB	Sea/Ocean going/Conventional	1938	44 to 56	517t	
VIIC	XSea/Ocean going/Conventional	1940	44 to 56	—	c
VIID	As Type VIIC+Additional mine shafts	1941	4/40	—	
VIIF	As Type VIIC only with Additional section to carry freight	1943	4/42	—	1
IXA	Long distance Ocean going/Conventional	1938	4/44	740t	1
IXB	Long distance Ocean going/Conventional	1939	4/44	—	1
IXC		1940	4/44	—	1
IXC/40		1942	4/44	—	1
IXD$_1$	Ocean going/Conventional transporter	1941	4/51 inc MO	—	1
IXD$_2$	Ocean going/Conventional/long distance	1941	4/51 to 61 inc MO	—	1
XB	Ocean going minelayer/Could be used as supply boat	1941	5/47 inc MO	—	1
XIV	Ocean going Transporter 'Milkcow'	1941	6/47	—	1
XXI	Planned to replace Type VIIC	1944	5/52	—	1
XXIII	Similar to Type XXI only smaller coastal boat	1944	2/12	—	
V80	Experimental	1940	4	—	
XVIIA (W A201)	Experimental boats	1943	25	—	
XVIIA (W K202)	Experimental boats	1943	3/9	—	
XVIIB	Double hulled experimental	1944	3/16	—	
XVIIK (U798)	Experimental/Not completed	1945	3/16	—	
XIA	Double hulled U-cruiser	Not built	110 to 120	—	3
XVIIA	V300 (U 791) Experimental	Project cancelled	25	—	
XVIIG	Experimental	Project cancelled	3/16	—	
XVIII	Appearance similar to Type XXI	Project cancelled	4/47	—	1
XX	Long distance transporter	Project not developed	c55-60	—	c2
XXII	Coastal	Project not developed	2/10	—	
UA	Ocean going	1938	45	—	1
UB	Ex HMS Seal	1938	c47	—	1
UC1 and UC2	Ex Dutch Norwegian B5 and B6	1929	21-25	—	
UD1	Ex Dutch 08		c25	—	
UD2	Ex Dutch 012	1930(?)	34	—	
UD3, UD4, UD5	Ex Dutch O25 and O27	1940	45	—	
UF2	Ex French La Favorite	1940(?)	40	—	
UIT17	Ex Italian CM1	1943	8	—	
UIT21	Ex Italian Giuseppe Finzi	1935	72	—	1
UIT22 and UIT23	Ex Italian Alpino Bagnolini, Reginaldo Giuliani	1939	57	—	1
UIT24	Ex Italian Commandante Cappellini	1939	57	—	1
UIT25	Ex Italian Luigi Torelli	1940	57	—	1

Left:
A training flotilla of Type II boats coming alongside their tender.

...erged	Length Overall	Beam Maximum	Depth	Maximum speed		Radius of action		Diesel electric run
				Surfaced	Submerged	High speed	Cruising	
)t	72.4m	6.2m	4.3m	17.8kt	8.0(+)kt	17kt/3,300sm	12kt/6,700sm	10kt/8,100sm
0(+)t	40.9m	4.1m	3.8m	13.0kt	6.9kt	12kt/1,050sm	8kt/1,600sm	8kt/2,000sm
4t	42.7m	4.1m	3.9m	13.0(−)kt	7.0kt	12kt/1,800sm	8kt/3,100sm	8kt/3,900sm
5t	43.9m	4.1m	3.8m	12.0kt	7.0kt	12kt/1,900sm	8kt/3,800sm	8kt/4,200sm
0t	44m	4.9m	3.9m	12.7kt	7.4kt	12kt/3,450sm	8kt/5,650sm	8kt/5,650sm
5(−)t	64.5m	5.9m	4.4m	16.0(+)kt	8.0kt	16kt/2,900sm	10kt/6,200sm	10kt/6,800sm
0t	66.5m	6.2m	4.7m	17.0(+)kt	8.0kt	17kt/3,850sm	10kt/8,700sm	10kt/c9,500sm
0t	66.5m	6.2m	4.7m	17.0(+)kt	7.6kt	17kt/3,250sm	10kt/8,500sm	10kt/c9,500sm
5t	76.9m	6.4m	5.0m	16.0kt	7.3kt	16kt/5,050sm	10kt/11,200sm	10kt/13,000sm
5t	76.9m	7.3m	5.0m	17.0(+)kt	7.9kt	16kt/5,350sm	10kt/14,700sm	10kt/13,950sm
8t	76.5m	6.5m	4.7m	18.0(+)kt	7.7kt	18kt/3,800sm	10kt/10,500sm	10kt/11,350sm
0t	76.5m	6.8m	4.7m	18.5(−)kt	7.3kt	18kt/3,800sm	10kt/12,000sm	10kt/12,400sm
0t	76.4m	6.8m	4.7m	18.3kt	7.3kt	18kt/5,000sm	10kt/13,450sm	10kt/16,300sm
5t	76.8m	6.9m	4.7m	18.3kt	7.3kt	18kt/5,100sm	10kt/13,850sm	10kt/16,800sm
0t	87.6m	7.5m	5.4m	17.0(−)kt	7.0kt	15kt/5,600sm	10kt/12,750sm	10kt/13,000sm
0t	87.6m	7.5m	5.4m	19.0(+)kt	6.9kt	19kt/8,500sm	10kt/31,500sm	10kt/32,300sm
0t	89.8m	9.2m	4.7m	17.0kt	7.0kt	16kt/6,750sm	10kt/18,450sm	10kt/21,000sm
0t	67.1m	9.4m	6.5m	15.0kt	6.5kt	14kt/5,500sm	10kt/12,350sm	10kt/12,000sm
0t	76.7m	8.0m	6.3m	15.6kt	16.8kt	15kt/5,100sm	10kt/15,500sm	—
5t	34.5m	3.0m	3.7m	9.7kt	12.5kt	8kt/2,600sm	6kt/4,450sm	—
0t	22.0m	2.1m	3.2m	4.0kt	28.0kt	—	—	—
0t	34.1m	3.4m	4.6m	9.0kt	5.0kt	9kt/1,840sm	—	—
0t(?)	34.0m	3.4m	4.5m	9.0kt	26.0kt	9kt/1,140sm	—	—
5t	41.5m	4.5m	4.3m	8.8kt	25.0kt	8kt/3,000sm	—	—
5t	40.7m	4.5m	c4.9m	14.0kt	16.0kt	14kt/1,100sm	10kt/2,600sm	—
0t	115.0m	9.5m	6.2m	23.0kt	7.0kt	22kt/4,000sm	10kt/20,600sm	10kt/2,400sm
5t	52.1m	4.0m	5.5m	9.3kt	20.0(−)kt	9kt/33sm	5kt/500sm	—
5t	39.5m	4.5m	4.7m	8.5(+)kt	25.0kt(?)	8kt/3,000sm	—	—
5t(?)	71.5m	8.0m	6.4m	18.5kt	24.0kt	17kt/3,000sm	10kt/7,000sm	—
0t	c77.0m	c9.2m	c6.6m	12.0(+)kt	6.0(−)kt	12kt/11,00sm	10kt/18,900sm	—
5t	27.0(+)m	?	?	7.0kt	20.0kt	6kt/1,550sm	—	—
8t	86.7m	6.8m	4.1m	18.0kt	8.5kt	18kt/4,900sm	10kt/13,100sm	10kt/16,400sm
3t	89.3m	7.7m	5.2m	16.0kt	8.5(+)kt	14kt/4,950sm	10kt/6,500sm	—
4t	51.0m	3.7m(?)	3.5m	15.0(−)kt	10.0(+)kt	—	—	—
0t	44.7m	4.9m	3.9m	13.0kt	9.0(−)kt	13kt/c1,300sm	—	—
5t	60.5m	5.4m	3.6m	15.0kt	8.0kt	—	10kt/3,500sm	—
2	77.5m	6.6m	4.0m	20.3kt	8.0kt	19kt/2,500sm(n)	10kt/7,100sm(n)	—
8t	68.2m	5.3m	4.6m	14.0(+)kt	10.0kt	—	—	—
4t	33.0m	2.9m	—	14.0kt	6.0kt	—	10kt/2,000sm	—
0t	84.3m	7.7m	5.2m	17.0(+)kt	8.0(−)kt	—	8kt/11,400sm	—
5t	76.1m	7.1m	—	17.0(+)kt	8.5kt	—	8kt/13,000sm	—
3t	73.1m	8.2m	—	17.5kt	8.0kt	—	8kt/9,500sm	—
9t	76.4m	7.9m	4.7m	18.0kt	8.0kt	—	8kt/10,500sm	—

Type	Radius of action Submerged	Maximum Diving Depth	Diving Time[4] Stationary	Alarm moving	Approx Reserve Buoyancy	Oil Fuel Carried	Diesel Engines Number	HP
IA	4kt/90sm	200m	60(−)sec	30sec	120t	96t	2	3,000(+)
IIA	4kt/35sm	150m	45sec	30(−)sec	49t	12t	2	700
IIB	4kt/43sm	150m	35sec	30(−)sec	50t	21t	2	700
IIC	4kt/43sm	150m	25sec	25(−)sec	50t	23t	2	700
IID	4kt/56sm	150m	25sec	25(−)sec	50t	38t	2	700
VIIA	4kt/95sm	200m	50sec	30sec	119t	67t	2	2,300
VIIB	4kt/90sm	200m	50sec	30sec	104t	108t	2	2,800 to 3,2…
VIIC	4kt/80sm	250m[5]	50sec	30sec	102t	114t	2	2,800 to 3,2…
VIID	4kt/69sm	200m	50(−)sec	30(−)sec	115t	170t	2	2,800 to 3,2…
VIIF	4kt/75sm	200m	60(−)sec	30sec	97t	199t	2	2,800 to 3,2…
IXA	4kt/78sm	200m	?	35sec	121	154t	2	4,400
IXB	4kt/64sm	200m	?	35sec	127t	166t	2	4,400
IXC	4kt/63sm	200m	?	35sec	112t	208t	2	4,400
IXC/40	4kt/63sm	200m	?	35sec	103t	214t	2	4,400
IXD$_1$	4kt/115m	200m	50sec	35sec	189t	252t plus c200t as cargo	2	2,800 to 3,2…
IXD$_2$	4kt/57sm	200sm	50sec	35sec	188t	442t	2×9 cyl / 2×6 cyl	5,400
XB	4kt/95(−)sm	200m	?	c40(−)sec	414	368	2	4,800
XIV	4kt/55(−)sm	200m	?	?	368	203t+432t as cargo	2	3,200
XXI	10kt/110sm 5kt/365sm	250(+)m[7]	?	18sec	?	250t	2	4,000
XXIII	10kt/35sm 4kt/194sm	160m	?	10(−)sec	?	207t	1×6cyl	576 to 63…
V80	28kt/50sm	?	?	?	?	20t of H$_2$O$_2$	One Walter turbine developing 2,000BHP	
XVIAA (W A201)	2kt/76sm	?	?	?	?	40t perhydrol or Aurol 18t oil 14t oil	1×8cyl	230BHP
XVIIA (W K202)	26kt/80sm	?	?	?	?	40t perhydrol	Diesel and Electric 210B…	
XVIIB	15kt/163sm 25kt/123sm	150m	?	?			1×8cyl Diesel with provision for two	
XVIIK (U798)	6kt/30sm 4kt/50sm	150m	?	?		26t oil 55t Ingolin	1×20cyl	1,500BHP
XIA	2kt/140sm	200m	?	?				
XVIIA (U791)	19kt/205sm 10kt/450sm	?	?	?	?	24t Perhydrol 100t Aurol		300-330B…
XVIIG	25kt/123sm	150m	?	?			1×8cyl (2 were planned) ?	
XVII	24kt/200sm 16kt/350sm	?	?	?			Diesel engines/Electric m… and Walter turbine/4,000… 15,000BHP	
XX	4kt/50sm	c200m	?	?	?	470t+c700 as freight	2	2,800
XXII	20kt/100sm	?	?	?	?		Diesel engine/Electric mo… and Brückner & Kanis/W… turbine	210 to 1,7…
UA	3kt/130sm	200m			?	c200t	2	4,200 to 4,6…
UB		120m			?	140(−)t	2	3,300
UC1 and UC2		50m				20(−)t	2	900
UD1		50m				20(−)t	2	480
UD2	8kt/25sm	90(−)m			?	?	2	1,800
UD3, UD4								
UD5		c100m			?	?	2	c5,500
UF2		c100m				100t	2	3,000
UIT17	4kt/70sm						2	600
UIT21	4kt/80sm	200m			?	250(−)t	2	4,400
UIT22 and UIT23	4kt/108sm	100m			?	135t	2	3,500
UIT24	4kt/80sm	100m			?	110t(?)	2	3,000
UIT25	3kt/100(+)sm	100m			?	200(−)t	2	3,600

Notes

1 Either officers/men or total.
2 Official figures published before the war.
3 As designed.
4 Time to put 10m of water above the hull.
5 Many boats went much deeper
6 Some boats had two bow tubes and one stern tube. Others were without a stern tube.
7 Probably down to 500m.

8 U792-U793.
9 U794-U795.
10 The maximum number of mines carried gives a misleading figure because operational boats usually only carried 8-10 or 16-20 mines. Reloading during an operation was considered too risky.
11 Note that from 1943 torpedoes which were carried in external containers between the pressure hull and upper deck could not be transferred to the interior, thus reducing the total in Type VII by two and Type IX by four.

	Electric Motors		Torpedo tubes		Approximate T or M	
ber		HP	Bow	Stern	carried	Guns fitted
		1,000	4	2	14t or 42M	1×AA 20mm (2,000rds)/1×105mm (150rds)
		360	3	0	5T or 18M	None or 1 to 2×AA 20mm (850rds) After 1940 4×AA 20mm
		360	3	0	5T or 18M	Same as Type IIA
		410	3	0	5T or 18M	Same as Type IIA
		410	3	0	5T or 18M	Same as Type IIA
		750	4	1	11T or 33M	1×88mm (250rds) 1×AA 20mm (4,380rds)
		750	4	1	14T or 39M	Same as Type VIIA
		750	4 (usual)*	1	14T or 39M	Same as Type VIIA
		750	4	1	12T or 39M	1×88mm (250rds)/AA?
		750	4	1	14T and 21T (As freight)	1×AA 37mm (c2,000 rds)/2×AA 20mm (c4,400rds) 1×88mm (250rds)
		1,000	4	2	22T or 66M	1×105mm (180rds)1×AA 37mm (2,625rds)/4×AA20mm (8,500rds)
		1,000	4	2	22T or 66M	As Type IXA
		1,000	4	2	22T or 66M	As Type IXA
		1,000	4	2	22T or 66M	As Type IXA
		1,000	None/After re-fit same as Type 1XD$_2$		—	1×105mm (c200rds)/1×AA 37mm (575rds)/ 1 to 2 AA or Twin AA 20mm (8,000[+]rds)
ble		1,000	4	2	24T or 72m	As Type IXD$_1$
		1,100	0	2	15T or 22M plus 66M in special mine shafts	1×105mm (200rds)/1×AA 37mm (2,500rds)/ 1×AA 20mm (4,000rds)
		750	0	0	—	1 to 2×AA 37mm/2 to 4×AA 20mm
ble plus 2 double ow speed		4,200	6	0	24T or ?M	2×Twin AA 20mm (16,000rds) with provision for 2×Twin AA 37mm (4,188rds)
ble for fast speed plus gle for slow speed		580	2	0	2T	None
		?	None	None	—	This boat was only experimental and not planned to be put into operational service?
s 2 Walter/Germania nes developing 5,000BHP		?	None — Provision for 2 bow tubes		About 6	None
er/Germania turbine 0BHP			2	0	4	None
ctric motor and ackner & Kanis/Walter ne			None — Provision for 2 bow tubes		c4	None
		1,500BHP	None	—	—	—
			4	2	?	4×127mm (940rds)/2×AA 37mm (4,000rds)/ 1×AA 20mm (2,000rds) 1 small aircraft
		150-4,360 BHP	Provision made for 2 bow tubes		c6T	None
s Walter turbine		?	Provision made for 2 bow tubes		c4T	None
			6	0	c24T	2×AA 30 Twin (4,180rds)
		750	None	None	—	2×AA 20mm Twin (8,000rds)/1×AA 37mm Twin (3,000rds)
			2	0	c2	No conning tower or gun platform
		1,300	4	2	c24	1×105mm/2×AA 20mm
		1,630	6	0	Over 100 mines	1×102mm
		700(+)	2	2	6T(?)	
		300(+)	4	?	8T(?)	
		600	4	1	c10	2×40mm (c500rds). Later only 1×AA 20mm (c1,000rds)
		1,000	4	2+2 on deck	c14	Variable
		1,400	4 bow, 2 stern plus deck tubes			1×88mm/1×AA 20mm
		60	2	0		None (?)
		1,800	4	4	c16T	2×120mm/4×AA ?mm
		1,400	6	2	c21T	2×100mm
		1,300	6	2	c25(+)T	2×100mm
		1,250	6	2	c21T	2×100mm

Abbreviations used in these tables

(+)	More than.	H$_2$O$_2$	Hydrogen peroxide	m	Metre.
(-)	Less than.	(?)	After a statement means that the information has still not been verified.	mm	Millimetre.
	On surface.			T	Torpedo.
	Submerged.			M	Mine.
MO	Medical Officer.	(?)	In place of a statement means the information is not known.	rds	Rounds of ammunition.
c	Circa (about).			HP	Horse power.
sm	Sea miles.	t	Metric tons or cubic metres.	BHP	Brake horse power.
kt	Knot.	AA	Anti-aircraft.	Cyl	Cylinder.

11

Administration of the U-boat Arm

The Administrative Pattern

The establishment of a Submarine Defence School in Kiel on 1 October 1933 was the unofficial foundation of Germany's new U-boat Arm. Konteradmiral Arno Spindler (Submarine Adviser with the Imperial Naval Command) helped in setting it up and KK Kurt Slevogt was the first Chief of the School. Two submariners from World War 1, Werner Fürbringer and Walter Hülsmann and two younger men, Hans 'Harro' Rösing and Kurt Freiwald, who had been trained by the Submarine Construction Bureau, acted as instructors. The first course was attended by: Klaus Ewerth (killed as commander of *U850*), Hans-Günther Loof (killed as commander of *U122*), Hans Looschen, Hans Meckel (U-boat commander who later worked in U-boat Command), Hans Michahelles, Heinz Scheringer (commander of *U26* who became PoW when the boat was sunk), Werner von Schmidt, Hannes Weingärtner (killed as commander of *U851*) and about 50 NCOs and men.

The first six U-boats to be launched after 15 June 1935 went to the Submarine School, which was under the jurisdiction of the Torpedo Inspectorate and not the newly-formed submarine flotilla. On 27 September 1935, Karl Dönitz officially took over the first operational group as Flotilla Chief. At that time, the following U-boats existed:

U-boat Flotilla Weddigen
Base Kiel
Chief Karl Dönitz
U-boats U7 KL Kurt Freiwald
      U8 KL Harald Grosse
      U9 KL Hans-Günther Looff
      U10 OL Heinz Scheringer
      U11 KL Hans Rösing
      U12 OL Werner von Schmidt
        (commissioned on 30 Sept 1935)

U-boat School
Head of School and Chief of the Flotilla
FK Kurt Slevogt

U-boats U1 KL Klaus Ewerth
      U2 OL Hans Michahelles
      U3 OL Hans Meckel
      U4 OL Hannes Weingärtner
      U5 OL Rolf Dau
      U6 OL Ludwig Mathes

In addition to this T23, T156 and T158 as well as the new depot ship *Saar* were attached to serve as flag ships, tenders and also to help train new recruits.

The following development was not intended to build up a powerful fighting force, but to establish a large and widespread administration network. *Flotilla Weddigen* was kept small and another unit, *Flotilla Salzwedel*, added to serve the North Sea from Wilhelmshaven. During August 1939, just before the war, the U-boat Arm looked as follows:

U-boat Headquarters
Base Kiel aboard tender *Hai* (F6)
Führer der Unterseeboote (FdU) (Flag Officer for U-boats) KS & Kommodore Karl Dönitz
1st Staff Officer: KK Eberhard Godt
2nd Staff Officer: KL Hans-Gerrit von Stockhausen
3rd Staff Officer: KL Hans Cohausz
Chief Engineering Officer: FK(Ing) Otto Thedsen
U-boat Escort Ship: *Erwin Wassner* (KK Heinrich Bertram)

1st U-boat Flotilla *(Flotilla Weddigen) Founded September 1935*
Base Kiel
Chief KL Hans-Günther Looff
U-boats U9 KL Ludwig Mathes
      U13 KL Karl Daublebsky von
         Eichhain
      U15 KL Heinz Buchholz
      U17 KL Heinz von Reiche
      U19 KL Hans Meckel
      U21 KL Fritz Frauenheim
      U23 KL Otto Kretschmer
Other Units Escort ship *Donau* (KL Hans Kaack)
           Escort ship *Memel*

2nd U-boat Flotilla *(Flotilla Salzwedel) Founded September 1936*
Base Wilhelmshaven

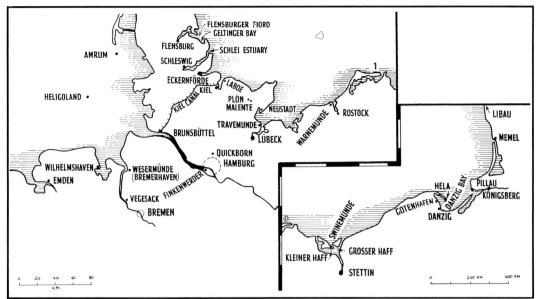

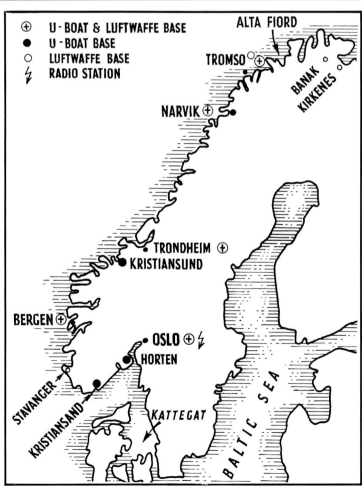

Above:
Map of Northern Germany
showing U-boat bases,
headquarters, teaching
establishments and other places
mentioned. Note the different
scale: **1** indicates the same spit of
land on both maps.

Right:
German bases in Norway.

⊕   U - BOAT & LUFTWAFFE BASE
●   U - BOAT BASE
○   LUFTWAFFE BASE
⚡   RADIO STATION

Above:
Gd Adm Karl Dönitz, C-in-C of U-boats, was promoted to Supreme C-in-C of the Navy in January 1943, at a time when the war was already lost. On the left is his last adjutant, KK Walter Lüdde-Neurath, who never served in U-boats. He was with torpedo boats at the start of the war and served in destroyers before being promoted to 1st Staff Officer of the Flag Officer for Destroyers. From that position he took over from KK Jan Hansen-Nootbaar as adjutant. *IWM*

Above right:
U14 (KL Victor Oehrn) of the Lohs Flotilla with Flotilla Chief (KL Hans Eckermann) on the left, KS and Kommodore Karl Dönitz, Flag Officer U-boats, in the middle. Next to him is KL Eberhard Godt, who later became chief of the Operations Department (known as the U-boat Command later in the war). Godt always preferred to remain in the background, and photographs of this important yet modest gentleman are rare.

Right:
U203 (KL Rolf Mützelburg), with her crew on the conning tower and upper deck, runs into France after her 6th cruise.

Chief KK Hans Ibbeken
U-boats U26 FK Oskar Schomburg
U27 KL Johannes Franz
U28 OL Günter Kuhnke
U29 KL Otto Schuhart
U30 OL Fritz-Julius Lemp
U31 OL Hans Habekost
U32 KL Paul Büchel,
later OL Hans Jenisch
U33 KL Hans-Wilhelm von Dresky
U34 KL Wilhelm Rollmann
U35 KL Werner Lott
Other Units Tender *Saar* (KL Ernst Bartsch)

3rd U-boat Flotilla (*Flotilla Lohs*) Founded October 1937
Base Kiel
Chief KL Hans Eckermann
U-boats U12 KL Dietrich von der Ropp
U14 KL Horst Wellner
U16 KL Hans Weingärtner
U18 KL Max-Hermann Bauer
U20 KL Karl-Heinz Moehle
U22 KL Werner Winter
U24 KL Udo Behrens
Other Units Tender *Weichsel* (KL Ernst Rapp)

4th U-boat Flotilla
This flotilla existed only on paper before the war. Some personnel had been allocated, but no boats.

5th U-boat Flotilla (*Flotilla Emsmann*) Founded November/December 1938
Base Kiel
Chief KL Hans Rösing
U-boats U56 KL Wilhelm Zahn
U57 OL Claus Korth
U58 OL Herbert Kuppisch
U59 OL Harald Jürst
U60 OL Georg Schewe
U61 OL Jürgen Oesten
Other Units U-boat escort ship *Lech* (OL Heinrich Brodda)

6th U-boat Flotilla (*Flotilla Hundius*) Founded October 1938
Base Wilhelmshaven
Chief KK Werner Hartmann
U-boats U37 KL Heinrich Schuch
U38 KL Heinrich Liebe
U39 KL Gerhard Glattes
U40 KL Werner von Schmidt
U41 OL Gustav August Mugler
U42 KL Rolf Dau
U43 KL Wilhelm Ambrosius
Other Units U-boat escort ship *Isar*

7th U-boat Flotilla (*Flotilla Wegener*) Founded June 1938
Base Kiel
Chief KL Ernst Sobe
U-boats U45 KL Alexander Gelhaar
U46 KL Herbert Sohler
U47 KL Günther Prien
U48 KL Herbert Schultze

U49 KL Kurt von Gossler
U51 OL Dietrich Knorr
U52 OL Wolfgang Barten
U53 KL Ernst-Günter Heinicke

U-boat School
Base Neustadt
Head of school KS Werner Scheer
Flotilla chief KL Heinz Beduhn
U-boats U1 Ol Jürgen Deecke
U2 OL Helmuth Rosenbaum
U3 KL Joachim Schepke
U4 OL Harro von Klot-Heydenfeldt
U5 KL Günther Kutschmann
U6 OL Joachim Matz
U7 OL Otto Salmann
U8 OL Georg Peters
U10 OL Wilhelm Schulz
U11 KL Viktor Schütze
U25 OL Georg-Heinz Michel
U36 KL Wilhelm Fröhlich

The U-boat School still came under the jurisdiction of the Torpedo Inspectorate, not Flag Officer for U-boats. *NB: U44, U50, U54 and U55* were not commissioned until after the start of the war.

The flotillas were named after famous submariners of World War 1:

Otto Weddigen, born 15 September 1880, destroyed three British cruisers on 25 April 1912 and was the first U-boat commander to be awarded the Pour le Merite.

Reinhold Saltzwedel, born 23 November 1889, was killed in the English Channel on 2 December 1917.

Bernd Wegener, born 22 May 1884, he was killed when the U-boat trap *Baralong* sank *U27*.

Hans Joachim Emsmann, born 20 June 1892 and killed when his boat was mined off Scapa Flow on 28 October 1918.

Johannes Lohs, born 24 June 1889 and killed when *UB 57* ran on to a mine on 14 August 1918.

Paul Hundius, born 2 February 1889 and killed in the English Channel on 16 September 1918.

The structure of the U-boat Arm underwent drastic reorganisation throughout the autumn of 1939 and a new pattern emerged, which remained in force until the fall of France in 1944 necessitated further changes. On 17 October, Dönitz, who had the title of *Führer der Unterseeboote — FdU* (Flag Officer for U-boats) and rank of Kapitän zur See und Kommodore, was promoted to Konteradmiral, with the new title of *Befehlshaber der Unterseeboote — BdU* (C-In-C for U-boats). At the same time the

U-boat administration was split into Operational and Organisational Divisions. Thus, Dönitz became *BdU Ops* and Hans-Georg von Friedeburg became *BdU Org*. His title was later changed to 2nd Admiral — U-boats and after that, to Commanding Admiral — U-boats. Initially all operational U-boat flotillas, personnel, supplies, training, weapons, communications, technical aspects, medical departments, administration and legal departments came under his jurisdiction. However, this became impractical once bases were established outside Germany and a different pattern was established to remove the care of operational boats from his extremely wide field of duty. Four new Flag Officers for U-boats (*FdU*) were appointed, each to be responsible for a specific operations area. Some regions were covered by so few boats that flotilla chiefs were left with the administration duties. It is necessary to emphasise that these *FdU* were only responsible for the organisational side and could only exercise operational control in their immediate coastal regions. Once at sea, U-boats were directed by the U-boat Command or relevant naval commanders.

Operations Area West

FdU headquarters	Paris/Angers
1st U-boat Flotilla:	Kiel/Brest
2nd U-boat Flotilla:	Wilhelmshaven/ La Rochelle
3rd U-boat Flotilla:	Kiel/La Pallice/ La Rochelle
6th U-boat Flotilla:	Danzig/St Nazaire
7th U-boat Flotilla:	St Nazaire
9th U-boat Flotilla:	Brest
10th U-boat Flotilla:	Lorient
12th U-boat Flotilla:	Bordeaux

The 2nd, 3rd and 7th Flotillas later moved to Norway.

Operations Area Norway and Arctic

FdU headquarters	Narvik
11th U-boat Flotilla:	Bergen
13th U-boat Flotilla:	Trondheim

Operations Area Mediterranean

FdU headquarters	Rome/Toulon/ Aix-en-Provence
23rd U-boat Flotilla:	Salamis
29th U-boat Flotilla:	La Spezia/Toulon/Pola/ Marseille/Salamis

Operations Area Central

This was founded during the early summer of 1942 with about 45 boats to prepare as a defence force for an anticipated Allied invasion of Europe.

Action Area: Black Sea
30th U-boat Flotilla: Constanca/Feodosia

Action area: Baltic
22nd U-boat Flotilla: Gotenhafen

Action area: Far East
No special flotilla operated in Far East Asia. Long-distance boats made journeys from France or Norway, and there was a German maintenance and administration department in Penang and later in other Asian ports.

On 30 January 1943, Gd Adm Erich Raeder resigned as Supreme C-in-C of the Navy, to be succeeded by Karl Dönitz, who also continued to hold the office of *EdU*. However, much of the day-to-day running of the U-boat Operations Department, which had become known as U-boat Command, was done under the leadership of Konteradmiral Eberhard Godt (promoted on 1 March 1943). In 1944, the U-boat Arm's role changed drastically and the administration had to be condensed as the Allies denied them the use of the French bases. Many men managed to leave France, either by using serviceable boats or by attempting the hazardous journey overland. Some bases, such as Brest, came under heavy attack and bitter battles were fought to prevent the advancing Allied armies from gaining access to materials or information which could help them to destroy U-boats at sea. Other ports, such as Lorient, were bypassed and remained in German hands, but cut off from the rest of the world until the end of the war in Europe.

The U-boat Command

As incredible as it may seem, the war against Britain (with the world's largest navy and largest merchant fleet) and the United States (with the second largest navy) was conducted by a very small group of men, known just as 'The U-boat Command'. Early on in the war it had the title of Operations Department and later it was officially known as *2. SKL BdU Op* (*2. Seekriegsleitung* [Naval War Staff]). It consisted of the following officers:

BdU Op (C-in-C of U-boats): Admiral (later Grand Admiral) Karl Dönitz
Head of Operations Department and later *BdU Op:* KS later KA Eberhard Godt

1st Staff Officer
Oct 39-May 40   KL Victor Oehrn
May 40-Nov 40   KK Werner Hartmann
Dec 40-Nov 41   KK Victor Oehrn
Nov 31-end   FK Günther Hessler

1st Staff Officer (Operations)
Oct 42-July 44   KL Adalbert Schnee

July 44-Dec 44 KL Heinrich Schroeteler
Mar 44-end   KK Ernst Hechler

2nd Staff Officer
Oct 39-Apr 40   KK Hans-Günter Looff
Apr 40-Jan 43   KL Karl Daublebsky
                v Eichhain
Feb 43-Apr 43   KL Peter (Ali) Cremer
Apr 43-end   KK Alfred Hoschatt

3rd Staff Officer
Sept 41-June 42 KL Herbert Kuppisch
June 42-end   KL Wilhelm Muhr

4th staff Officer
Oct 39-Dec 39   KL Hans-Gerrit
                v Stockhausen
Nov 39-June 44 KK Hans Meckel
June 44-Oct 44 KL Hermann Rasch
Oct 44-end   KK Waldemar Mehl

5th Staff Officer
Oct 39-July 41 KL Werner Winter
July 41-end   KK Dr Teufer

6th Staff Officer
June 42-Dec 42 KL Herbert Kuppisch
Dec 42-Mar 44   KK Herbert Schultze
Apr 44-Sept 44 KK Hans Witt
Oct 44-end   KL Kurt Neide

Engineering Officers
Nov 39-Oct 40   KL(Ing) Hans Looschen
Oct 40-Jan 43   KK(Ing) Karl Scheel
Feb 43-July 44 KL(Ing) Gerd Suhren
July 44-end   KL(Ing) Karl Heinz Weibe

U-boat Flotillas
1st U-Flotilla
Command Operational, FdU (West)
Base Kiel June 41-Sept 44 in Brest then dissolved
Boats In Kiel — Type II. In France — Types VII B,
C, D and X B
Number of boats 140
Commanding officer
Jan 40-Oct 40   KK Hans Eckermann
Nov 40-Feb 42   KK Hans Cohausz
Feb 42-July 42 KL Heinz Buchholz
July 42-end   KK Werner Winter

2nd U-Flotilla
Command Operational, FdU (West)
Base Wilhelmshaven and then also Lorient. From
summer 1941 only in Lorient
Boats Mainly Types IX
Number of boats 90
Commanding Officer
Jan 40-May 40   KK Werner Hartmann
June 40-Oct 40 KK Heinz Fischer
Oct 40-Jan 43   KK Viktor Schütze
Jan 43-end   KS Ernst Kals

3rd U-Flotilla
Command Operational, FdU (West)
Base La Pallice and La Rochelle
Boats Originally Type II, then Types VII B and C
Number of boats 110
Commanding Officer
Mar 41-July 41 KK Hans Rösing
July 41-Mar 42 KL Herbert Schultze
Mar 42-June 42 KL Heinz von Reiche
June 42-Oct 44 KK Richard Zapp

4th U-Flotilla
Command Operational, FdU (East). This flotilla

Left:
The crew of *U405* demonstrate
that the upper deck of the boat
also served as a dining room.

was set up especially for final fitting out of new boats and funnelling them on to front flotillas

Base Stettin

Boats Boats passed through this flotilla before going on to an operational group

Number of boats 281

Commanding Officer

May 41-July 41 KL Werner Jacobsen

July 41-Aug 41 KL Fritz Frauenheim

Aug 41 to end FK Heinz Fischer

5th U-Flotilla

Command Operational, FdU (East). This flotilla was set up especially for the final fitting out of new boats and funnelling them on to front flotillas

Base Kiel

Boats *

Number of boats 340

Commanding Officer

Jun 41-end KK Karl-Heinz Moehle

6th U-Flotilla

Command Operational and training FdU (West)

Base Originally Danzig, then St Nazaire

Boats VII B and C

Number of boats 93

Commanding Officer

From Aug 41 KK Fritz Frauenheim, but he did not take up the appointment

Sept 41-Oct 43 KK Wilhelm Schulz

Oct 43-Aug 44 KL Carl Emmermann

7th U-Flotilla

Command Operational, FdU (West)

Base First Kiel, then also in St Nazaire and from June 41 only in France. Boats later moved to Norway

Boats Mainly Type VII

Number of boats 114

Commanding Officer

Jan 40-May 40 KK Hans Rösing

May 40-Feb 44 KK Herbert Sohler

Feb 44-Mar 44 KK Adolf Piening

8th U-Flotilla

Command Training, FdU (East)

Base Eastern Baltic ports

Boats *

Number of boats 256

Commanding Officer

Oct 41-Jan 42 KL Wilhelm Schulz

Jan 42-Jan 43 KK Hans Eckermann

Jan 43-Apr 44 KK Werner von Schmidt

Apr 44-Jan 45 FK Hans Pauckstadt

9th U-Flotilla

Command Operational FdU (West)

Base Brest

Boats Types VII C and D

Number of boats 85

Commanding Officer

Nov 41-Mar 42 KL Jürgen Oesten

Mar 42-Aug 44 KK Heinrich Lehmann-Willenbrock

10th U-Flotilla

Command Operational, FdU (West)

Base Lorient

Boats Mainly IX C and X B

Number of boats 81

Commanding Officer

Jan 42-Oct 44 KK Günter Kuhnke

11th U-Flotilla

Command Operational, FdU (Norway)

Base Bergen

Boats VII C

Number of boats 189

Commanding Officer

May 42-Jan 45 FK Hans Cohausz

12th U-Flotilla

Command Operational, FdU (West)

Base Bordeaux

Boats IX D1, D2, XB, XIV and others

Number of boats 48

Commanding Officer

Oct 42-Aug 44 KK Klaus Scholtz

13th U-Flotilla

Command Operational, FdU (Norway)

Base Trondheim

Boats VII C

Number of boats 55

Commanding Officer

June 43-end FK Rolf Rüggeberg

14th U-Flotilla

Command Operational, FdU (Norway)

Base Narvik

Boats VII C

Number of boats 6

Commanding Officer

Dec 44-end KK Helmut Möhlmann

15th U-Flotilla

Command FdU (West — Bergen)

Base Norway

Boats None

Number of boats 0

Commanding Officer

KK Ernst Mengersen had been appointed, but the Flotilla did not become operational

16th U-Flotilla

Command Not operational

17th U-Flotilla

Command Not operational

18th U-Flotilla

Command Probably operational in Baltic shortly before end of war

19th U-Flotilla

Command Training flotilla

Base Pillau and just before the end of the war in Kiel

Commanding Officer

KK Jost Metzler

Function The flotilla specialised in training lookouts and teaching boat movements in ports

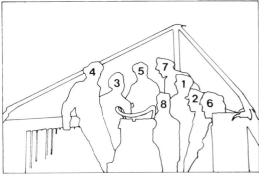

Above:
U377 in Norway during the summer of 1942. **1** KK
Otto Köhler (commander); **2** OL Karl-Heinz Nitschke
(LI); **3** *Stabobermaschinist* (Diesel) Jak Mallman;
4 LT Bruno Langenberg (II WO and later commander
of *U366*); **5** *Obersteuermann* Martin Weidmann;
6 *Elektro-Obermaschinist* Rienecker; **7** OL Walter
Pietschmann (1 WO and later commander of *U712* and
U762); **8** *Bootsmann* Albert Jungclaus. The periscope
housing can be seen in the foreground and the scaffold
is part of the torpedo loading gear.

Right:
U377's commander (KK Otto Köhler) and 1 WO (OL
Walter Pietschmann). The *Eins WO* is resting his hand
on the torpedo aiming device, which would have had
special binoculars clipped on top when in use. The first
officer was responsible for aiming and shooting
torpedoes during surface attacks.

as well as docking techniques. It also conducted courses for new commanders in boat handling

20th U-Flotilla
Command Training flotilla
Base Pillau from June 1943 and abandoned in February 1945
Commanding Officer
KK Ernst Mengersen
Function Flotilla established to specialise in initial tactical training.

21st U-Flotilla
Command 1st Ubootslehrdivision
Base Originally Neustadt, then moved to Pillau. This was the flotilla which was attached to the U-boat School before the war
Commanding Officer
to Mar 40   KL Heinz Beduhn
Mar 40-June 43 KK Paul Büchel
June 43-Sept 44 KK Otto Schuhart
Sept 44-Mar 45 KL Herwig Collmann
Function School flotilla

22nd U-Flotilla
Command 2nd Ubootslehrdivision
Base Gottenhafen, towards the end of the war in Wilhelmshaven
Commanding Officer
Jan 41-Jan 44   KK Wilhelm Ambrosius
Jan 41-July 44 KK Wolfgang Lüth
July 44-end   KK Heinrich Bleichrodt
Functon School flotilla

23rd U-Flotilla
Command Training flotilla
Base Danzig August 1943 to March 1945
Commanding Officer
Aug 43-Mar 45 KK Otto von Bülow
Function Specially set up to teach commanders how to shoot torpedoes from submerged positions

24th U-Flotilla
Command Training flotilla
Base First Danzig, then Trondheim, Memel, Gotenhafen and Eckernförde
Commanding Officer
Nov 39-July 42 KK Hannes Weinärtner
July 42-Jan 43 KS Rudolf Peters
Apr 43-Mar 45 FK Karl-Friedrich Merten
Function Taught commanders how to shoot torpedoes from submerged position and later specialised in underwater detection methods

25th U-Flotilla
Command Training flotilla
Base Danzig, then Trondheim, Memel, Libau, Gotenhafen and Travemünde
Commanding Officer
Apr 40-Dec 41 KK Ernst Hashagen
Dec 41-Aug 43 KK Karl Jasper
Aug 43-Dec 43 FK Karl Neitzel
Dec 43-Apr 45 KK Robert Gysae
Apr 45-end   KK Wilhelm Schultz
Function To teach shooting

26th U-Flotilla
Command Training flotilla
Base Pillau and later Warnemünde
Commanding Officer
Apr 41-Jan 43   KK Hans-Gerrit v Stockhausen
Jan 43-Apr 43   KK Karl-Friedrich Merten
Apr 43-Mar 45 FK Helmut Brümmer-Patzig
Mar 45-end   KK Ernst Bauer
Function To teach shooting

27th U-Flotilla
Command Training flotilla
Base Gotenhafen
Commanding Officer
Jan 40-Dec 41   KK Ernst Sobe
Jan 42-Oct 42   FK Werner Hartmann
Oct 42-July 44 KL Ernst Bauer
Function Tactical training for new boats

28th U-Flotilla
Command Probably not operational

29th U-Flotilla
Command Operational — FdU Mediterranean
Base La Spezia, also Toulon, Pola, Marseilles and Salamis
Commanding Officer
Dec 41-May 42 KK Franz Becker
June 42-July 43 KK Fritz Frauenheim
Aug 43-Sept 44 KK Günter Jahn
Number of boats 54

30th U-Flotilla
Command Operational — Black Sea
Base Constanza and Feodosia
Commanding Officer
Oct 42-May 44 KL Helmut Rosenbaum
June 44-Oct 44 KL Klaus Petersen
Oct 44-Oct 44   KL Clemens Schöler
Number of boats 6

31st U-Flotilla
Command Training — FdU East
Base Hamburg then Wilhelmshaven and Weser-münde
Commanding Officer
Sept 43-Apr 45 KS Bruno Mahn
Apr 45-end   KK Carl Emmermann
Function Initial U-boat training

32nd U-Flotilla
Command Training — FdU East
Base Königsberg then Hamburg
Commanding Officer
Apr 44-Mar 45 FK Hermann Rigele
Mar 45-end   KK Ulrich Heyse
Function Initial U-boat training

33rd U-Flotilla
Command Operational — FdU West
Base Flensburg and ports in Asia
Commanding Officer
Sept 44-Oct 44 KK Georg Schewe
Nov 44-end   KK Günther Kuhnke
Number of boats 75

The Men

The campaign to draw German boys and men into the recruiting offices was similar to the British approach and did not show the horrors of submarine warfare. The image of a magnificent life was especially perpetuated by a band of war correspondents who profited from photographing men in action. Some of these correspondents had a free hand to utilise information which even boat commanders were prohibited from discussing in public and their privilege to ensure a continuous queue at naval recruiting offices. Whilst many courageous correspondents worked under the same harsh military discipline as the men they reported on, there was a small despicable number who apparently used their position for maximum advantage to themselves and their special privileges for personal gain.

It has often been said that only volunteers were considered for U-boats, which is not quite true because some men volunteered for other branches of the navy and were later posted to submarines, without being allowed a say in the matter. Whether transferring from surface ships or having newly joined, men faced a medical examination to check if they could withstand the rigours of sub-

marine life. A new recruit then received a free travel warrant to one of the naval training establishments (*Schiffstammdivision*, known earlier as *Marine Inspektion* and later as *Schiffsstammregiment*), where he went through approximately three months of initial training. This was given to all newcomers no matter what unit they wished to join; it consisted of land-based naval infantry training to teach military discipline and to acquaint men with their new way of life. Some basic survival training was given and the course was usually concluded with a full scale manoeuvre. Afterwards the groups of men were split up to be sent to specialised training establishments where they learned a trade. The length of time they remained at this school depended on the nature of their chosen career.

The next step was to visit one of the U-boat schools to be taught the basics about submarines, which usually included an experience in a diving tank to practise escaping from submerged boats. At this stage, some men (or perhaps boys might be a better term) were sent off to join the crews of operational boats to face the enemy for the first time. The vast majority of men passed on

Left:
Aboard *U73* (KL Helmut Rosenbaum), *Torpedomaat* Hölscher is selling duty-free cigarettes and spirits to the torpedo mechanic, the commander and to *Electro-Obersmaschinist* Karl Keller on the right. One does not usually associate duty-free goods with warships, but many boats had a small shop.

Right:
KK Wolfgang Lüth seen here at a farewell party when he left *U181* to hand over to Kurt Freiwald. Lüth commanded *U9* at the start of the war and was awarded the highest degree of the Knights Cross: Knights Cross with Oakleaves, Swords and Diamonds. The only other person in the navy to receive this award was KK Albrecht Brandi, also a U-boat commander. Lüth was Chief of the Naval Officers' School in Mürwick (Flensburg) when the war ended, and where he was shot by his own guard after failing to respond to a challenge on a dark night.

Below:
U462 (OL Bruno Vowe), a purpose-built supply boat of Type XIV, with an unusual bridge modification.

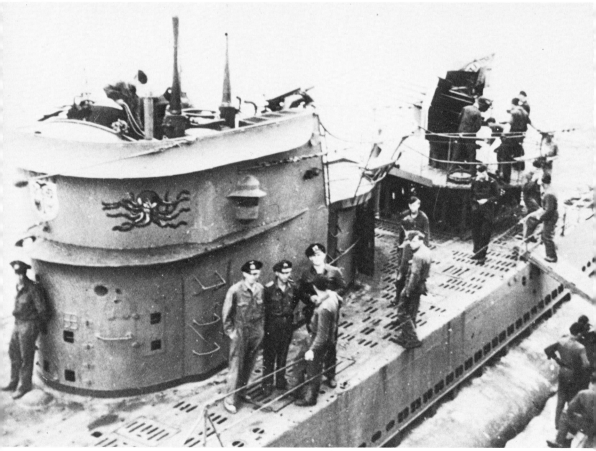

to brand new boats, and another period of training and preparation followed. Those who had been considered good enough to go to the front usually did so as additional 'ballast' and they would have spent their first voyage as an apprentice to a more experienced man. The time between finishing training and being posted was often cushioned by attendance at an establishment like the *Uboots-Ausbildungabteilung* (U-boat Training Department) in Plön, which acted as a personnel pool, to funnel men into appropriate vacancies.

High ranking officers and technical staff were often dispatched to the building yard one to three months before the boat was completed to get to know each other and to study the internal layout of their boat. A number of men also attended special technical courses organised by the building teams. Once commissioned, the U-boat passed through the U-boat Acceptance Command (*Unterseebootsabnahmekommando — UAK*) under KS Robert Bräutigam and later KS Walter Hülsmann. The headquarters were in Kiel, but branches existed close to the main ship-building centres. The aim of this command was twofold: firstly, to test that the machinery was functioning correctly; secondly, to check that the crew could handle the boat. These procedures usually took two to three weeks. Sometimes new boats were commissioned with experienced crews to be pushed through very quickly, while some crews were given a few weeks leave because the boat required further attention in dock.

There were no hard and fast rules about the exact sequence of events after leaving the Acceptance Command. The following is only an outline of the type of experiences the boats passed through before attending a graduation course at the Technical Education Group for Front Boats (*Technische Ausbildungsgruppe für Frontunterseeboote — also* known as *Agru Front*). This was under the command of KK(Ing) Hans Müller for most of the war and under KS(Ing) Kurt Heintz for the last 12 months of the conflict. Usually new boats would go from the Acceptance Command to a technical training flotilla, where an instructor would put the crew through a variety of situations which they might meet in action, such as coping with machinery failure. The men also passed through a 'shooting flotilla' to learn the skills of aiming torpedoes at moving targets. The torpedoes were used over and over again and consequently looked rather battered. On photographs these practice torpedoes can be

identified by a number of white rings or stripes painted around the dummy warhead, some even incorporated a lamp to observe progress at night. Boats also participated in deep diving, silent running tests, and occasional brief periods in a pressure dock. Deep diving was usually carried out in a trench in the sea floor to the west of the Danish island of Bornholm.

The German Navy seemed to have had some strange ideas about testing their hardware and today it is difficult to establish how far boats were actually tested before being put into action. Even before the war, serious testing did not seem to come high in the order of priorities. For example, the Flag

Below:
Men of *U586* loading the first practice G7e torpedoes into the bow compartment. Practice torpedoes can be identified by the white bands around the head. The upper deck torpedo storage container can be seen in front of the torpedo.

Officer for U-boats had to impose standing orders prohibiting boats from going deeper than 50m, although their designed depth was 200m. Deeper dives became the order of the day once the war started and then it was discovered that an engine room vent which in some boats closed against water pressure, could be broken by depth charges exploding close by or by diving too deep. Consequently boats had to be modified. The catastrophic sequence of events with torpedo development between the two wars is also well known today and in retrospect rather difficult to explain. Apparently the new torpedoes developed after World War 1 were only tested twice and failed to function properly on both occasions, yet despite this they were declared as 'operational'.

The period of training was concluded with a grand tactical manoeuvre at the *Agru Front*, which consisted of boats attacking a small convoy in the Baltic. In 1973, KK Hans Müller (ex-Chief of the *Agru Front*) wrote: 'The U-boat schools and training flotillas certainly did not earn their laurels. Practical U-boat experiences were first gathered at the *Agru Front* . . . What U-boat men did *not* know and could *not* do was horrifying'. After the war, a number of well experienced Chief Petty Officers stated that they were very happy *not* to have served under officers who left their boat to become commanders. Many were fanatical, ignorant young men without any understanding or feeling for the job they were expected to do, and they certainly could not shoulder the responsibilities of a commander. Perhaps this contributed towards the U-boat Command introducing a pre-tactical training session in 1943. This was set up by KL Claus Korth, a well experienced U-boat commander who had seen considerable action in *U57* and *U93*. However, the additional training lasted only about 10 days and Korth was of similar opinion to Hans Müller in saying this was a most harrowing time in his life. Boats usually arrived in groups of 10 to 12 and often he would have liked to have failed all of them, but he had strict orders that not more than two boats could be kept behind for a re-run of the training exercises. The C-in-C demanded them at the front, and to the front they went. Korth said that it was depressing to work with the crews and only to learn later that they had been killed during their first or second operational tour. To make matters worse he could not convey his views to anyone in higher authority, other than Adm Hans-Georg von Friedeburg, who shared his

opinion and could do nothing to stem the pressure which forced the inexperienced men to the front. The vast distances between training establishments in the eastern Baltic and the U-boat Command in France (and later Berlin), made any direct communication almost impossible and all the instructors could do was to obey orders to push more boats through the training network.

Once through the *Agru Front*, boats passed on to one of two special 'kitting out' flotillas, the 4th U-Flotilla in Stettin or the 5th in Kiel, to be loaded for their first war cruise. By early 1943, this period between commissioning the boat and leaving for the first war cruise could be as little as just over three months, but the majority of boats required five, six or seven months. This was an incredibly short time and some of it was taken up by a variety of non-training activities, as can best be illustrated by some specific examples: *U128* (KL Ulrich Heyse) was commissioned in Bremen on 12 May 1941 and had to spend almost four weeks at the Oderwerke in Stettin for finishing off before attending the *Agru Front* in Oslo Fiord (the *Agru Front* had temporarily moved out of the eastern Baltic to avoid conflict with Operation 'Barbarossa', the invasion of Russia), where the bottom of the boat was torn open by an uncharted rock. Emergency repairs were carried out in Horten before *U128* went to Kiel for repairs. Finally, after attending the *Agru Front* for a second time, the boat went back to Stettin for further mechanical adjustments and sailed for her first patrol on 8 December 1941, only seven months after her commissioning; *U512* (KL Wolfgang Schultze), commissioned on 20 December 1941, went down too steeply during deep diving trials, bumped the propellers on the bottom and had to go to the Oderwerke in Stettin for repairs. Following this, the boat was frozen in until the thaw in April 1942. The boat plunged out of control during her next diving tests, but was lucky in having the well experienced KL(Ing) Gerhard Suhren on board. (Suhren was Flotilla Engineering Officer, one of the few engineering officers to have been awarded the Knights Cross of the Iron Cross and brother of 'Teddy' Suhren, the famous U-boat commander.) *U512* returned to the surface, but had to go to Stettin for repairs. While practising to shoot torpedoes, *U512* was rammed by another U-boat and had to return to dock for more repairs. Final fitting out was carried out at the Schichau Werft in Danzig. Shortly after leaving, a clutch defect was

Far left:
Fähnrich zur See Otto Giese in his walking-out uniform. He was awarded the Iron Cross 2nd Class when he arrived in France as Second Officer of the blockade breaker *Anneliese Essberger*. Below the U-boat Badge is the Blockade Breaker Badge.

Left:
A bearded Otto Giese keeps lookout aboard *U181*.

Far left:
My father, Jak Mallmann, wearing the NCO's walking-out uniform.

Left:
KS Kurt Freiwald of *U181*, wearing tropical kit in Penang during the latter part of 1944. The badges are from left to right: the Spanish Cross with Swords (on the right breast pocket), the Distinguished Service Medal (*Kriegsverdienstkreuz*), Iron Cross First Class, and the U-boat Badge. Freiwald was one of the original core of U-boat men and the first commander of an operational U-boat (*U7*) after World War 1. He also had the distinction of having served as Adjutant to two Supreme C-in-Cs of the Navy, holding this office from 1938 to 1943.

Above:
Oberfunkmeister Wolfgang
Hirschfeld, wearing a reefer
jacket. Hirschfeld was radio
operator on *U109* under
Heinrich 'Ajax' Bleichrodt and
U234 under Hans Fehler.
Hirschfeld and KS Waldemar
Seidel were the first to prove that
the radio-telephone link could
work. This made it possible for
Dönitz to talk to commanders at
sea from the telephone on his
desk. Hirschfeld also kept a
secret diary which has been
published in Germany and is an
important contribution to naval
history.

Above right:
KL Fritz Frauenheim (*U121*,
U101, U-Flotilla Chief and other
posts) and KL Engelbert Endrass
(*U46* and *U567*). Endrass was
First Watch Officer of *U47* under
the famous Günther Prien and it
was him who shot the torpedoes
which sank the battleship HMS
Royal Oak in Scapa Flow.

Right:
Two U-boat commanders in full
dress uniform. KL Heinrich
'Ajax' Bleichrodt (*U48*, *U67* and
U109) (left), and KL Engelbert
Endrass (*U46* and *U567*). Both
men are wearing the Knights
Cross of the Iron Cross and
Endrass had just been awarded
the Oakleaves to this award,
which can be seen above the
cross.

discovered just before *U512* was rammed again, this time by a small fishing boat. The submarine was ordered to the Oderwerke in Stettin before finally setting out for the first cruise on 15 August 1942; *U164* (KK Otto Fechner) was commissioned on 28 November 1941 and went straight from the Acceptance Command to Deutsche Werke in Kiel to repair a serious diesel defect. Fine sand was discovered in the oil. Earlier, men had noticed the slogan 'sabotage U-boats' painted on a wall at Deschimag Works in Seebeck (Wesermünde) where the boat was built, and presumed they had been victims of a deliberate attempt to slow their passage to the front. Later the boat ran aground but managed to pull herself free, then while travelling through the Kiel Canal, *U164* collided with a steamer. There was no noteworthy damage on either occasion and the boat left for her first patrol some eight months after commissioning.

The important posts in a U-boat were as follows:

Commander: The commander was *not* responsible for shooting during surface attacks; instead, he had overall control of the boat and instructed which target to aim at. The work of actually getting the boat into a favourable position, aiming and shooting was done by the first watch officer. For this reason Heinrich 'Ajax' Bleichrodt (commander of *U48*) refused to wear the Knights Cross of the Iron Cross unless such an award was also given to Reinhard 'Teddy' Suhren. He had sunk more ships than anyone else, having been in action with Herbert 'Vaddi' Schultze and Hans 'Harro' Rösing. Finally Dönitz gave in to Bleichrodt's blackmail and deviated from the original policy of only awarding the Knights Cross to commanders by also awarding one to Suhren. When attacking from a submerged position, the commander was located at the attack periscope in the conning tower control room. Regulations to close the hatch leading down to the central control room were often ignored and many commanders kept in contact by shouting their instructions to the crew below through the opening rather than use the voice pipe.

IWO: *Erster Wach Offizier* — (pronounced Eins WO) — First Watch Officer and IIWO: *Zweiter Wach Offizier* — (pronounced Zwei WO) — Second Watch Officer. These posts were usually filled by men who were due to become commanders at a later date, but not all commanders were watch officers before taking on their own boat.

LI: *Leitender Ingenieur* (Chief Engineering Officer).

Obersteuermann: (Chief Helmsman) and also responsible for provisions and most official paperwork. This senior post, held by an NCO, carried considerable responsibility and in the Royal Navy the work was usually done by an officer. The term helmsman hardly describes the office since the man hardly sat at the wheel, but was responsible for navigation. He usually had a *Zentralemaat* (Central Control Room Mate) as assistant.

Diesel Obermaschinist: (Chief Diesel Mechanic). He was supported by a *Dieselmaat* (Diesel Mate) and two men.

Elektro Obermaschinist: (Chief Electro Mechanic). Also supported by a mate and two men.

Funker: (Wireless Operator). He was responsible for transmitting and receiving radio messages and working the code writer. He also operated the underwater sound detection gear and played records when required. Wireless Operators were usually excluded from manual work and not called upon to carry out other duties.

Torpedo Mechanic: The only NCO to live with the men in the bow torpedo compartment. He had a mate and several men of lower rank to assist him in his work. Two Torpedo Mates would have been located in the aft torpedo compartment.

Smut or *Smutje:* (Cook). The cook did not usually participate in normal duties; he had to prepare food in a tiny galley no matter what conditions prevailed.

Other positions such as keeping look out, steering and working hydroplanes were done by a number of the men, although when at action stations commanders often had specially appointed men in key locations. Under normal conditions the look out watch consisted of an officer, a petty officer and two to three men. If there was a danger of air attack more men were detailed to stand by the gun. Each man had a 90° sector to search for ships and aircraft. In dangerous situations such as sunrise, sunset, or in areas where aircraft were expected, the lookouts were increased. Each man was usually equipped with binoculars of 7×50 magnification for use in daylight, and in some cases special night glasses of lesser magnification but greater power were provided. Men who normally wore spectacles had special frames which fitted tight to their faces like goggles

Above:
Stabsobermaschinist Jak Mallman, wearing his white mess jacket. These were worn on land and in surface ships but not in U-boats. The anchor with cog on his sleeve signifies that he is in the technical division.

Above right:
My mother and father, showing an NCO's coat with dagger and the case for the Agfa box camera with which many of the photographs in this book were taken.

Right:
OL Ernst-August 'Jumbo' Gerke (1 WO) of *U377* wearing 'Large Rain Gear', which was also known as 'The Big Seal'.

Above:
Activity on the upper deck of *U181* (KK Kurt Freiwald) during a drying out session after a storm on her way to the Far East. Photographs tend to show U-boats trimmed for quick diving and this is interesting because it demonstrates how far the upper deck could be raised above the water when the tanks were fully blown. The life raft is not part of U-boat equipment, but had been fished out of the water; some of the crew have gone in for a swim to refresh themselves. Several men are wearing *Dräger Lungs* (escape apparatus) instead of life jackets, probably because *U181* did not carry such jackets.

Left:
The men of *U704* are demonstrating here that the upper deck could also be used as a bathroom.

with a flat front against which they could support the binoculars. Such glasses were also provided with a variety of optical filters for special effects: yellow for bright cloudy weather, amber for looking into the sun and green for clear, sunny days. It is quite interesting that the Royal Navy actually interrogated prisoners with a view of finding out for how long men kept look out, to determine when they were likely to be least alert. During this process, it was calculated that men spent three and a half hours out of four looking through their binoculars because they frequently stopped to clean the lenses and this added up to 30min in one normal watch.

Accommodation in German submarines was generally poor with little regard having been paid to the comfort of the crew. The commander had a small cabin, which in reality was part of the corridor by the central control room and could only be shut off from the rest of the boat by a heavy curtain. Officers, NCOs and some of the men enjoyed the privilege of sleeping in bunks, but there were not enough for the whole of the crew and many slept in hammocks or on the floor. Senior members of the crew were allowed a small amount of personal belongings, but the

majority were limited to a few spare sets of underwear. Washing facilities were more or less non-existent and water was rationed on long cruises. Boats often carried salt water soap and eau de cologne, which hardly removed the deeply ingrained grime acquired in the dirty, sweaty conditions. The men just had to cultivate an indifference to not being able to wash properly. 'Tar your clothes — the white is showing', was a common phrase. Some commanders were quite particular about the appearance of their crew, while many of the stronger characters did not mind how they or their crew looked. As a result, one can see a variety of fancy clothing in old photographs.

Below left:
Hermann Patzke emerging from the galley hatch, situated just aft of the conning tower. The pole in the middle of the picture and the bars at the side are part of the torpedo loading gear.

Below:
Watch Officer and *Obersteuermann* (Chief Helmsman) Hannes Limbach of *U181* in January 1945. Limbach, a holder of the Knights Cross, is seen emerging from the conning tower hatch to take his turn of duty on the bridge.

13

U-boat Bunkers

The need to provide concrete protection in port where U-boats were most vulnerable, was given serious consideration in the summer of 1940 after German hopes of a negotiated peace subsided and air attacks became an ever increasing threat. Plans were made to provide wet and dry accommodation, together with a few facilities for hauling boats out of the water in the French Atlantic bases and the first phase at Lorient and La Pallice was completed by the end of 1941. Shelters in St Nazaire and Brest were finished during the following summer, but construction at Bordeaux was delayed because its location further south was thought to make it less prone to attack.

The construction of the French bunkers was directed by the Todt Organisation, but later in Germany, much of the work was done by civil engineering firms. Because they consumed vast quantities of steel, cement, sand and coarse aggregates, designers looked around for local suppliers. Banks of high quality sand posed a constant problem for shipping in the rivers Elbe and Weser, making it easy to dredge or excavate it close to the building sites, but suitably sized pebbles did not occur naturally in large enough quantities close by. While planners looked for suitable transport to bring this from further away, it was suggested to use ash and slag as a substitute. Such substances were easier to obtain because they were produced in significant volumes as waste products by heavy industrial plants in Hamburg and Bremen. Although considerably less dense than natural pebbles, the resulting mix was thought to be good enough for bunkers and the use of these substitutes helped to alleviate difficult wartime transport problems. Many years after the war, when concrete structures in Britain started to show signs of deterioration shortly after being built and eventually had to be demolished before they were even 30 years old, German bunkers were still going strong, showing very little signs of crumbling. Research into the British concrete building scandal showed the German emergency wartime mix to be considerably stronger than conventional concrete because slag and flyash acted as excellent strengthening agents. The power of the bond can be illustrated by the demolition of the bunkers in Hamburg. *Fink II* in Finkenwerder was blown up by British forces after the war using the entire stock of Luftwaffe bombs in the vicinity. There appear to have been no large quantities of explosives left to deal with *Elbe II* in Vulkanhafen and its demolition was put out to private tender. At least three firms went bankrupt during the process of trying to remove it, and despite a concerted effort the bunker is still there. Only the centre wall has been blown out of true to bring the roof down.

Plans for concrete shelters did not run according to original schedules and several of the completed buildings were used for different purposes to which they had been planned. In 1944, the increase in terror bombing by the RAF shifted the emphasis towards the home front and projects in Germany were given priority over others already under construction in foreign countries. It was thought important to provide some protection for the building industry. Critical stages of U-boat production, such as the fitting out of launched boats and the assembly of Type XXI sections, were to be completed in bomb-proof bunkers.

Most bunkers were built on wet sites with flimsy metal shuttering, supported by an earthen embankment to keep water out and constant pumping was necessary to prevent the sites from flooding. It seems strange that Britain showed no interest in these most vulnerable targets and made no significant effort to disrupt the building process. Once the concrete had set hard, the RAF appeared in ever-increasing numbers to bomb the pens, but did very little damage to the U-boat campaign. One of the first raids on Lorient devastated housing in the harbour's vicinity and killed 150 French people, but the bunkers remained untouched and personnel was hardly affected because the men lived some distance out of the town. The bombing continued on an ever-increasing scale, creating vast areas of ruins around the target.

Britain stepped up the intensity of air attacks as well as the size of the bombs and the first heavy attacks with 5.5-ton 'earthquake' bombs in 1944 produced interesting results. The bunker in Bordeaux received 26 direct hits during one raid, but suffered only superficial damage. The detonations caused concrete dust to drop from the ceiling and men inside had their soup spoiled with grit. Brest, which at that time had a roof of only 5.6m in thickness without the burster course, fared worse: one bomb penetrated the roof and blasted a 10m wide hole. Two other direct hits exploded immediately above a dividing wall to cause only slight damage. This bunker was so well constructed that the bomb which penetrated the roof and exploded inside hardly damaged boats or equipment in adjoining bays. However, these raids made it quite clear that the additional 3.5m of concrete on the roof was going to be essential for future comfort and protection. It was also decided to strengthen walls from 2m to 4m. The majority of the U-boat building yards were without protection and suffered little damage until the very end of the war, when the U-boat campaign had ceased to be a problem. However, Britain seemed to have acquired a fascination for breaking bunkers and continued to bomb them. The heavy bombs were designed by Barnes Wallis, the same person who had created the bouncing bomb used to breach the Eder and Möhne Dams during the famous 'Dam Buster' raid in May 1943. Ten-ton Grand Slam bombs were aimed at U-boat pens with dramatic impact. In *Fink II* (Hamburg) they sliced through concrete roofs to explode in the bay below, devastating everything within it and completely turning over *U677* (OL Gerhard Ady) and *U747* (OL Günter Zahnow). However, this raid took place on 9 April 1945, with the attack to put the large *Valentin* bunker on the river Weser out of action having preceded it by less than two weeks. The fantastic effort which must have gone into these raids still seems to be out of all proportion to what they achieved, especially as the war was almost over. The First Lord of the Admiralty, The Rt Hon Albert Alexander, faced the House of Commons in February 1945 and justified the intensification of bombing the U-boat bunkers by saying that Germany was making a great effort in renewing her U-boat offensive on a grand scale. However, when the massive raids against Bremen took place, the British Army was almost within reach of the target and overran it just a few days later. These raids with massive bombs did demonstrate that a heavy explosion in front of a bunker blowing in the doors, could have made the concrete box a death trap had the war lasted longer and the bombing offensive intensified.

In France, there were bunkers at Brest, La Pallice, Lorient, Bordeaux and St Nazaire. The last mentioned was sited in a non-tidal harbour and boats had to pass through locks to reach the pens. However, the lock gates were destroyed by the famous British Commando raid in 1942 and the interior of the bunkers remained tidal for the rest of the war. Some of the pens were designed to provide only safe moorings. Others had lock gates and water could be pumped out to provide dry dock facilities. The roofs were high enough to pull periscopes from their housings and a variety of different types of doors were provided for the entrances. The simplest form was an iron curtain arrangement about 125cm thick, hung from the roof to end just above the water. Booms were sometimes provided to prevent aerial torpedo attacks from the front and U-boat commanders usually had instructions not to run diesel engines in the bunker approaches to prevent acoustic mines, possibly dropped during air raids, from being detonated. Norway had a bunker in Bergen named *Bruno*, and another one, *Dora I*, in Trondheim; *Dora II* was under construction, but never completed. Defences from air attack were less of a problem because both locations were considerably further from Britain than those in France. The bunkers in France and Norway were designed for repairing operational boats and there was only a limited amount of accommodation and canteen facilities required inside them since most of the crew were taken out of the port to special rest areas. As far as possible, men were given opportunities to relax away from their boats and sometimes, when more serious damage ensured longer confinement in port, they were sent home to Germany. Additional bunkers for personnel were constructed in critical areas to accommodate those people not in the main bunker. The special naval hotels away from the towns suffered very little interruption from air raids throughout the war.

The first shelter on home ground started before the war was *Nordsee III* on Heligoland, followed by *Fink II* at Hamburg-Finkenwerder and *Elbe II* at Europakai in the Hamburg-Vulkanhafen. The first phase of a two-bay bunker was completed by early 1942, but work on *Fink II* continued to add another three sections. *Fink II* was located at

Left:
The *Elbe II* Bunker in Hamburg, showing the rear door on the western side which consisted of an iron box filled with concrete.

Below:
The U-boat bunker at St Nazaire in France. The roofs were designed to be 3-5m thick and, with their iron reinforcement, could withstand any air attack until they were bombed by Avro Lancasters of No 617 Squadron RAF, with Barnes Wallis's special earthquake bombs. The Germans thought these were rocket-propelled bombs and set about to increase the thickness of the roofs to 8m. This new light-coloured concrete can be seen above the darker, original roof. *IWM*

Bottom:
The U-boats' lair: the bunker at St Nazaire.

Above:
The first U-boat bunker in Trondheim. *Dora I*, during 1942/43.

Right:
The U-boat bunker *Dora II* under construction in Trondheim during 1944.

Below:
U510 (KL Alfred Eick) inside the U-boat bunker at St Nazaire. *IWM*

Left:
Some bunkers were tidal, but others were fitted with lock gates and could be pumped out to serve as a dry dock. This is one of the gates of *Dora II* in Trondheim, Norway, photographed during the spring of 1985.

Above:
Closing the huge door of the floating submarine pressure dock in Kiel. This was used for tests on submarines, usually without men inside the boat. The dock had been built by Flender Werke of Lübeck and shows the second variant, the first one having been scrapped under the terms of the Versailles Treaty.

Below:
Looking out of *Dora I*, the U-boat bunker in Trondheim. On the left, *U861* (KL Jürgen Oesten) and *U995* (OL Hans-Georg Hess) on the right. In the background above *U995's* tower, is a circular air raid shelter for personnel. *IWM*

Deutsche Werft and *Elbe II* at Howaldts Werke and intended for the final fitting-out stages of U-boat construction.

Bunker construction in Kiel was thought to be not so vital because it was farther for bombers to fly and with a highly active naval dockyard in the vicinity, had considerably more AA guns. In 1943 when the RAF intensified its bombing campaign against German cities, the need for protection became more pressing. The buildings at Krupp Germaniawerft in Kiel and U-boat construction slips elsewhere had stood up comparatively well to bombing. It was thought that the iron girder construction with flimsy sides and glass roofs prevented explosions being contained within the buildings and most of the blast went upwards, causing little damage to essential machinery. Early in 1942 work started in Kiel to place a concrete cover over the existing dry dock No 3 at Deutsche Werke in the Construction Harbour, which was later commissioned under the name of *Konrad* and used for building midget submarines of Type *Seehund*. It was

extensively photographed shortly after British Forces arrived in the area and consequently a good number of interesting photographs of the interior exist. The other bunker in Kiel, named *Killian*, was situated at Dietrichsdorf to the north of the small Schwentine river. The remains are still easily identifiable from the western side of the Kielerförde.

There were also two bunkers on the river Weser, but neither of them came into use before the end of the war. *Hornisse* at Bremer Vulkan Works in Vegesack was abandoned at the end of the war with much of the roof still not having been laid and *Valentin* at Farge was nearly finished when it was attacked by the RAF with a dozen 10-ton Grand Slam bombs and a few of the smaller Tallboys. Two bombs penetrated the roof and destroyed the positions where sections of the new Type XXI were due to have been assembled.

There were plans for a number of other bunkers, but none of them were completed and it seems highly likely that foundations were not even laid.

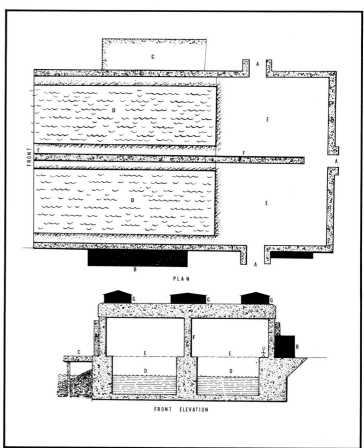

Right:
Elbe 2: U-boat bunker in Vulkan Hafen (Hamburg)
A Gates at rear of bunker;
B Store; **C** Thick concrete apron: large enough to accommodate U-boat, supported on concrete pillars, but stones underneath;
D Fitting-out basin — water level, tidal; **E** Workshop area at road/railway level; **F** Centre walls, with several doorways;
G Stone-built hut like buildings. Used either as offices, workshops or camouflage; ♀ Approximate size of a man.

14

Death with Dignity

There were never any illusions in German naval circles that the Third Reich could win a war at sea. In fact, Gd Adm Dr Erich Raeder (Supreme C-in-C of the Navy) told Hitler that their numbers were insignificant and in the event of a major conflict with Britain, the Navy could only show the world how to die with dignity. On 3 September 1939, he ordered his staff into action by saying, 'Britain has declared war and we have no alternative. Total engagement. Die decently'.

Less than two weeks later *U39* (KK Gerhard Glattes) sank with dignity because torpedoes failed in an attack against the aircraft carrier HMS *Ark Royal*. Thereafter, more boats were helped to their doom by faulty torpedoes. Karl Dönitz (C-in-C of U-boats) described the cause as criminal negligence, yet despite a court of inquiry, the 'Torpedo Fiasco' of 1939-40 developed into a catastrophe towards the end of the war. This has been outlined in *The German Navy in World War Two* and there is no need to reiterate the story here, but it is important to remember this sad episode in German naval history.

Everybody aboard *U31* (KL Hans Habekost) died a dignified death on 11 March 1940, when RAF Bomber Command scored its first victory against a U-boat. *U31* clearly demonstrated the vulnerability of the treacherous Schillig Roads in the approaches to Wilhelmshaven: the shallow water prevented the boat from diving to a safe depth, evasive action was made impossible by the narrow coastal channel and the AA armament was not powerful enough to cope with a bomber. The U-boat Command asked for escorts through coastal waters, but no assistance was given and the problem of dying on their own doorstep continued to plague boats throughout the war. Later, in the Bay of Biscay, there were several instances when it was even impossible to provide cover for damaged boats limping back to their bases.

Shortly after the war, Günther Hessler (commander of *U107*, U-boat Command Staff Officer and Dönitz's son-in-law) and Alfred Hoschatt (commander of *U378* and U-boat Command Staff Officer) compiled a monograph about the role U-boats had played between 1939-45. This magnificent study, for limited naval circulation, has never been published and has now all but vanished into obscurity. It reveals the most interesting fact that Dönitz frequently predicted events of the war long before they happened, but also that he failed to recognise these changes once they became reality. Let us take the move into American waters as an example. In December 1942, while the U-boat Command was preparing orders for the first thrust, Dönitz stressed the importance of getting in and hitting hard before the United States had time to organise her defences. He made it clear to his staff that successes could only be expected during the initial attack, and sinking figures were bound to tail off very quickly once retaliation started. Yet, four months later he appeared to have forgotten his own warning. Failing to accept that the second 'Happy Time' had come to an end, he tried and tried again to employ the same combination of tactics in different areas, hoping U-boats would find a weakness in the defences where the old techniques could still bring results.

Dönitz was unquestionably a brilliant leader and therefore one must ask why he failed to recognise his own predictions when they became reality? There are a number of similar questions with the same intrigue, which I have discussed with U-boat personalities who served under him, but a satisfactory answer has not yet been found. Instead, the deeper one looks for solutions, the more enigmas are discovered, and at times I have been under the impression that the search for every answer produces 10 new problems. For example, why did he put such great emphasis on training and then send out so many boats after only a brief practice period in the Baltic? In view of the complexity, it is impractical to examine the philosophy of the men who commanded the U-boat Arm, but it is important to remember that such points are significant elements when considering the defeat of the U-boat war.

In retrospect, it is easy to condemn Dönitz for some of his orders, and for this reason it is vital to make some attempt to establish the extent to which decisions made within the U-boat Command were governed by outside influences. Many writers have certainly overestimated the U-boat Command's sphere of power. Many decisions attributed to Dönitz were orders which had originated from higher up in the chain of command and he was only instrumental in carrying them out. There had been a noticeable chasm between Dönitz and the naval leadership. In fact, there were several occasions when his staff persuaded him not to go for a raging show-down with the admirals at the Supreme Naval Command because they felt such confrontation would only lead to more stringent restrictions on the U-boat Command.

Dönitz's power increased as time went on, and in January 1943 he was made Supreme C-in-C of the Navy. Inevitably, he became isolated from the vast majority of 'ordinary' people and this change from private individual to public figure placed him in a predicament because it meant that he lost the privilege of expressing his personal views in public. His high office made it necessary for him to support the government's line, although this is not to say that he became a puppet. Dönitz was one of the few who could, dared, and did, argue with Hitler, but only in the privacy of four walls.

When considering the U-boat's defeat, one tends to look to the Atlantic, yet it appears highly probable that a significant blow was struck from quite unsuspecting quarters, such as the British Commando raid on the dry dock in St Nazaire. The assault took place during the night of 27/28 March 1942, just a few weeks after Hitler had personally ordered all headquarters to be relocated in safe places away from fronts and out of reach of the enemy. Dönitz had no intention of quitting his waterfront command post at Kernevel (near Lorient) and played for time by asking for clarification of the terms 'front' and 'safe location'. A few days later, during the early hours of the morning, the telephone woke him with news of the St Nazaire landings. Realising that he could be the subject of the next attack, Dönitz ordered Kernevel to be evacuated. In doing so, he broke his own, specially-created strong tradition of keeping the finger on the pulse by being close to his men.

Radio, telephone and telex communications kept running and it usually took less than 10min to relay messages to the new headquarters in Paris. This was considered satisfactory by the U-boat Command. The later move to Berlin was also thought not to have been detrimental because the Operations Room remained in direct radio contact with the boats at sea. Dönitz regarded the later move to Berlin as vital because it brought him close to Hitler's headquarters and thus enabled him to keep up-to-date with the latest news of the rapidly changing fronts. However, there was a considerable lack of communication between the people who gave the orders and those who carried them out. The significance of this was probably not fully appreciated at the time and today one wonders how it influenced the men at the front. Some incidents certainly impaired their fighting spirit. For example, *U128* (KL Herman Steinert) was fitted with a new radio detection device and sent into the Bay of Biscay to check whether the RAF was using radar. The crew were not told about their mission and thought they were testing new radar equipment. Some men were under the impression that they had to test this against the enemy because the Luftwaffe refused to supply aircraft for the experiment. The incident depressed a number of the crew and one wonders how far similar incidents contributed to lethargic attitudes.

In May 1943, U-boats were destroyed in staggering numbers, and Dönitz described these events as 'unimaginable, even in my wildest dreams.' Consequently, this month has often been considered as one of the blackest in the annals of the German Navy. Yet, when the losses are calculated as a percentage of the number of boats at sea, May 1943 tends to lose significance compared to the summer of 1944: 36% of the boats at sea were sunk in May 1943, while a year later the figure rocketted further still. Accepting that there is a difference between the collapse of the offensive and the moment when U-boats started to die, one must look to the Allied invasion of France as the period of greatest slaughter. Not only did the invasion take a heavy toll in U-boats, but it also caused the entire organisation to withdraw to Norway or even to within the confines of the Reich.

An anti-invasion force had been designed earlier when one of Hitler's hunches led him to conclude that there would be an attack on the European mainland. Despite this, a specific force had not been established when the Allies pounced on Normandy in June

Above:
With the engines running slow astern, *U377* (OL Gerhard Kluth) backs out of the massive U-boat bunker in Brest.

Left:
Nine days before Christmas 1943: *U377* (OL Gerhard Kluth) leaves for her 13th and very last mission. A few weeks later she was sunk in the North Atlantic by a German torpedo. Above the bunker, towards the right, is the French Naval College used as headquarters for the 1st U-boat Flotilla.

Right:
KK Herbert 'Vaddi' Shultze, Commander of *U48*, with his hands in a muffler, and OL Erich Zürn (LI). *U48* was the most successful boat of World War 2. Both men were holders of the Knights Cross of the Iron Cross.

Below:
U586 (KL Dietrich von der Esch) showing the early conning tower layout. The 20mm AA gun is missing, but the attack periscope with magnetic compass attached to the support and the main hatch are clearly visible. To the right of the hatch is the torpedo aimer, and the slot which houses the circular radio direction finder can also be identified.

Left:

U405 (KK Rolf-Heinrich Hopman) was launched at Danziger Werft almost a year after *U73* and shows a similar deck structure. The men can be seen checking the torpedo in the external container between the pressure hull and upper deck. This pressure-resistant tube provided storage accommodation for one torpedo, which had to be manhandled into the boat before it could be fired. The rope running from the conning tower to the bows was known as a net deflector and also served as a radio aerial. A safety harness could be clipped on to it if there was a danger of men being washed off the deck.

1944. However, the dangers of an Allied bridgehead anywhere on the European continent were blatantly obvious and consequently Dönitz made every effort to frustrate this. During the morning of 6 June, he ordered every available boat into the English Channel to operate 'regardless of cost'. During the briefing for this drastic order, some U-boat commanders suggested they use their boats for ramming worthwhile targets, once torpedoes had been expended. The more level-headed men considered this futile since a worthwhile target would probably not even notice a submarine running into it and little could be achieved by such costly action. It must be emphasised that this idea of suicide attacks was suggested by U-boat commanders themselves. It was neither an order, nor was there any suggestion from high authority that it might be considered.

In the end, 14 boats left from St Nazaire, two came from Lorient, four from La Pallice and 18 from Brest. Unfortunately for these men, they had no support from any other service, a factor which had also plagued them in the past, only now there was a great difference: they were not going out to find one of several convoys in the vastness of the Atlantic, instead they were pitched against the invasion force. The Allies knew just as well as the Germans what the success or

failure of the first few days of the Normandy landing depended upon. So the Allies took positive steps to organise special anti-U-boat patrols. Operation 'Cork' was designed to 'cork off' the Western Approaches to the English Channel and prevent U-boats getting into the vital supply route to France.

Making matters even worse for the Germans, U-boat men were under the impression that the new T5 Acoustic Torpedo could reliably deal with small, fast warships. In June 1944 the U-boat Command thought that 128 destroyers had been sunk with acoustic torpedoes since their introduction in the autumn of 1943. (Germany often did not differentiate between different types of convoy escorts and classed all of them as 'destroyer'.) Another 23 ships were classified as probable sinkings. The men did not know that even the last two digits of 128, '28 destroyers sunk', was already a gross over estimation of reality. The more accurate total is probably around 20! The reason for this discrepancy is that a fault left over from the torpedo crisis of 1940 had not been recognised and now caused premature explosions. U-boats were instructed to dive for 10 to 15min after firing an acoustic torpedo, to prevent the deadly load from homing in on the U-boat. As a result, the men did not observe the sinking and only heard the detonation. The explosion caused too much disturbance to follow the target with the excellent sound detection apparatus, and when U-boats resurfaced they found the situation had changed enough for them not to detect that their target had not in fact sunk. That is, if they were lucky enough to surface again! Acoustic torpedoes had an arming distance of only 400m because the vast majority were shot on short ranges against fast approaching ships, which had already located the U-boat with radar or HF/DF. This meant that there was little time to dive to deeper and safer depths if the torpedo failed to stop the attacker.

The massacre of the boats thrown against the invasion was horrific and nobody came out of the ordeal unscathed. The few boats which put out of Brest on or shortly after D-Day serve to illustrate the extent of this massacre. Six of them had definitely been fitted with schnorkels, these were (in order of sailing): *U621* (OL Hermann Stuckmann), *U441* (KL Klaus Hartmann), *U984* (OL Heinz Sieder), *U764* (OL Hans-Kurt von Bremen), *U275* (OL Helmut Bork) and *U269* (OL Georg Uhl). Four were sunk before the end of August 1944. *U275* was mined off Beachy Head in Sussex during March 1945 and only *U764* survived to be sunk after the war during Operation 'Deadlight'. The boats without schnorkels were: *U989* (KL Hardo Rodler von Roithberg) sunk in February 1945, *U821* (OL Ulrich Knackfuss) sunk off the Lizard in Cornwall on 10 June, *U423* (OL Dietrich Sachse) sunk in the Channel on 20 August, *U740* (KL Günther Stark) sunk on 9 June off the Isles of Scilly, *U963* (OL Karl Boddenberg) survived the war and was scuttled off Oporto in Portugal on 20 May 1945, *U629* (OL Hans-Helmuth Bugs) sunk in the Channel on 8 June, *U415* (OL Herbert Werner) mined in Brest on 14 July. *U953* (OL Karl-Heinz Marbach) returned damaged to Brest and Marbach went to Berlin to receive the Knights Cross of the Iron Cross. Herbert Werner, who survived the sinking of *U415*, took *U953* on an epic voyage to La Pallice and then from there to Norway. Despite considerable damage, *U256* (OL Wilhelm Brauel) managed to limp back to Brest and in September, the commanding officer of the 9th U-Flotilla, KK Heinrich Lehmann-Willenbrock, used the boat to sail to Norway. Three different routes have been given for this attempt and on checking with the U-boat Command's log, I found the details in the first edition of this book to have been wrong as well. It appears that the boat sailed around

Ireland and then headed across the north of Scotland.

Operations from the French bases did not continue for very long because Atlantic ports were either taken or surrounded by Allied armies. The U-boat Command had already vacated the headquarters in Paris during March 1943 and was well out of reach of this turmoil. Originally, the men moved into temporary accommodation in Steinplatz (Berlin-Charlottenburg) until a new bunker was ready in Bernau (near Berlin, code named *Koralle*). Part of the Naval Command remained there until April 1945 and only left 30min before the first Russians appeared.

The withdrawal and contraction of every front has led to the impression that Germany was making some vague attempt at harassing British forces before finally dying a slow death. This is not so because the *Kriegsmarine's* biggest battle, the evacuation of the eastern provinces, only started during the last weeks of 1944 and continued until after the ceasefire in May 1945. Much of this activity has gone unreported and exact details will probably never be known because

---

Below:
KK Otto Köhler, *U377's* first commander. His opening speech to the crew during the commissioning ceremony was concluded with, ' . . . and above all I hope to bring you all back alive.' He had the good fortune of being able to do so. The *Ubootsabzeichen* (U-boat Badge) is below the Iron Cross First Class on his pocket; this was usually awarded after the men had participated in two or more operational patrols.

the chaotic situation prevented the keeping of detailed records. Some of the losses inflicted on the Germans were out of all proportion to what had been experienced in the Atlantic during both World Wars. For example, 6,500 people lost their lives when the passenger ship *Goya* was torpedoed on 16 April 1945. 5,100 people were killed when *Wilhelm Gustloff* went down on 30 January, 2,700 died in *General von Steuben* and so the list goes on. These almost unbelievably high figures represent only about 2% of the total who took part in the hazardous trek to the west, which gives some idea of the scale of operations. For a long time it had been thought that this massive evacuation was carried out over land or by surface ships. Only recently it came to light that U-boats also made a noteworthy contribution, and it will be another few years before Horst Bredow of the U-boat Archive on Sylt can complete this research.

Here is just one example. In March 1945, the 22nd U-Flotilla under KK Heinrich 'Ajax' Bleichrodt attempted and succeeded in reaching the west from East Prussia. Originally, Bleichrodt had orders to scuttle his U-boats, hand the crews over to the land defences and then sail without them to Kiel in the depot ship *Weichsel*. However, Bleichrodt argued that his men were neither trained for such warfare nor did they have any weapons, and he required escorts. So he announced that the entire flotilla would head west, taking with it parents, wives, children and fiancées. His superiors told him that submarines were useless as escorts, to which Bleichrodt replied, 'In an emergency the devil will eat flies! My men are coming with me!'. The problem of not having many provisions was overcome by taking a farmer friend with his pigs. The animals were herded to the quayside, butchered and the carcasses laid in the life boats. Temperatures were well below freezing, so there was little danger of the meat rotting. The chances of getting through were slim, but the flotilla had over 140 AA guns and it was decided to use these to frighten any attackers. The density of tracer shells was considerably increased and orders given to start shooting only after Bleichrodt had personally given the order. On command, every barrel was to fire as rapidly as possible. The trick worked. Despite being attacked several times, the enemy aborted every effort before coming within bomb-dropping range.

It is a little difficult to reconstruct how many U-boats took part in the evacuation, but the following are thought to have been present: *U8* (OL Jürgen Kriegshammer), *U11* (OL Günther Dobenecker), *U14* (OL Hans-Joachim Dierks), *U17* (commander for this voyage not known), *U30* (OL Günther Schimmel), *U71* (OL Emil Ranzau), *U96* (OL Robert Rix), *U137* (OL Hans-Joachim Dierks), *U143* (OL Walter Kasperek), perhaps *U145* (OL Friedrich-Karl Göner), *U146* (OL Karl Schauroth), *U149* (OL Helmut Plohr), *U150* (OL Hans-Helmuth Anschütz), *U339* (OL Werner Remus), *U350* (OL Erich Niester), *U351* (OL Hans-Jügen Schley), *U369* (KL Ludwig Schaafhausen), *U552* (OL Günther Lube), *U554* (KL Ernst-Wolfgang Rave), *U560* (OL Paul Jacobs), *U721* (OL Ludwig Fabricius), *U924* (OL Hans-Jürg Schild), *U1101* (OL Rudolf Dübler), *U1103* (KL Wilhelm Eisele or Jürgen Iversen), *U1167* (OL Karl-Hermann Bortfeldt) and *U1194* (OL Herbert Zeissler).

The voyage saw a remarkable birth. The wife of Ludwig Fabricius (*U721*) was taken off *Wilhelm Gustloff* shortly before the liner sailed and taken aboard the *Weichsel*, where Bleichrodt's wife, Carla (a gynaecologist), and the flotilla doctor helped to deliver a baby girl during heavy seas en-route to Kiel.

As the Allied armies crushed Germany, more and more refugees poured into the shrinking remains of the Third Reich. Many people knew the fighting could only continue for a short time and then everything which remained would fall into enemy hands. In Wilhelmshaven, it was decided to empty the entire dockyard. Men living in the town were told to take home anything they might need and the rest was thrown onto the street for people to pick up. Curtains, table cloths, blankets, furniture, tools, cutlery, everything not needed for immediate living went, before the advancing British troops could lay their hands on it. Then the dockyard was locked and the guards told not to let anyone in while the men waited. A few days later a jeep, with Lt-Cdr Peter Bartlett RN arrived. The war was over!

Shortly after this, British forces allowed a number of U-boats into Wilhelmshaven and when the crews had assembled on the side of the naval dockyard, 'Ajax' Bleichrodt, the senior German U-boat Officer, climbed onto a huge bollard placed there to hold the Kaiser's biggest battleships. He faced his men and said, 'We have survived a grim battle and now we have reached the bottom of an abyss. Conditions cannot get any worse. Things have got to get better. So hold your head up high and let us rebuild our Germany.'

Right:
The conning tower of *U405* near Narvik in Norway. The tanker in the background is probably *Kärnten*.

Below:
The photograph was taken in Bergen, Norway, just before the end of the war and shows (left to right): KK Adalbert Schnee (*U2511*); KK Jürgen Oesten (*U861*); KL Rolf Thomsen (*U1202*), and Heinrich Lehmann-Willenbrock (*U978*), in discussion shortly before *U2511* left for an operational mission. She was a Type XXI and only two of these boats saw operational service.

15

U-boats in Service

Abbreviations shown on page 141.

Vessel	Com	De-com/ sunk	Ships sunk	Months in active service	Vessel	Com	De-com/ sunk	Ships sunk	Months in active service
U001	29/07/35	15/04/40	0S	8	U053	24/06/39	23/02/40	8	6
U002	25/07/35	08/04/44	S	56	U054	23/09/39	??/02/40	0	5
U003	06/08/35	01/08/44	2S	60	U055	21/11/39	30/01/40	4	2
U004	17/08/35	01/08/44	3S	60	U056	26/11/38	28/04/45	7	65
U005	31/08/35	19/03/43	3S	43	U057	29/12/38	03/05/45	12	65
U006	07/09/35	07/08/44	S	59	U058	04/02/39	??/04/45	10	68
U007	18/07/35	18/02/44	S	54	U059	04/03/39	??/04/45	16	68
U008	05/08/35	02/05/45	0	69	U060	22/07/39	??/03/45	4	67
U009	21/08/35	20/08/44	7	60	U061	12/08/39	??/03/45	7	67
U010	09/09/35	01/08/44	2	59	U062	21/12/39	??/03/45	1	63
U011	21/09/35	14/12/44	0	63	U063	18/01/40	25/02/40	3	1
U012	11/09/35	08/10/39	0	63	U064	16/12/39	13/04/40	0	4
U013	30/11/35	31/05/40	10	6	U065	15/02/40	28/04/41	14	14
U014	18/01/36	03/03/45	10	67	U066	02/01/41	06/05/44	29	40
U015	07/03/36	31/01/40	1	5	U067	22/01/43	16/07/43	17	30
U016	16/05/36	24/10/39	1	5	U068	11/02/41	10/04/44	27	38
U017	03/12/35	02/05/45	2	65	U069	02/11/40	17/02/43	22	27
U018	04/01/36	25/08/44	1	60	U070	23/11/40	07/03/41	5	4
U019	16/01/36	10/09/44	14	61	U071	14/12/40	??/02/45	6	50
U020	01/02/36	10/09/44	9	61	U072	04/01/41	30/03/45	S	50
U021	03/08/36	05/08/44	7	60	U073	30/09/40	16/12/43	M	39
U022	20/08/36	??/03/40	4	7	U074	31/10/40	02/05/42	6	19
U023	24/09/36	10/09/44	6	60	U075	19/12/40	28/12/41	4	12
U024	10/10/36	25/08/44	1	58	U076	03/12/40	05/04/41	1	4
U025	06/04/36	03/08/40	9	12	U077	18/01/41	18/03/43	4M	26
U026	11/05/36	01/07/40	8	11	U078	15/02/41	16/04/45	S	50
U027	12/08/36	20/09/39	1	11	U079	13/03/41	23/12/41	3M	9
U028	12/09/36	17/03/44	15	54	U080	08/04/41	28/11/44	S	43
U029	16/11/36	17/04/44	12	53	U081	26/04/41	09/01/44	2M	33
U030	08/10/36	04/05/45	17	67	U082	14/05/41	07/02/42	4	9
U031	28/12/36	11/03/40	11	3	U083	08/02/41	09/03/43	2M	25
U032	05/04/37	30/10/40	23	14	U084	29/04/41	24/08/43	9	28
U033	25/07/36	12/02/40	6	6	U085	07/06/41	14/04/42	8	10
U034	12/09/36	05/08/43	16	47	U086	08/07/41	29/11/43	1	28
U035	03/11/36	29/11/39	4	47	U087	19/08/41	04/03/43	6	19
U036	16/12/36	04/12/39	2	47	U088	15/10/41	12/09/42	0	11
U037	04/08/38	08/05/45	45	69	U089	19/11/41	14/05/43	5	18
U038	24/10/38	05/05/45	40	67	U090	20/12/41	24/07/42	0	7
U039	10/12/38	14/09/39	0	67	U091	28/01/42	25/02/44	0	25
U040	11/02/39	13/10/39	0	67	U092	03/03/42	04/10/44	0	31
U041	22/04/39	05/02/40	6	6	U093	30/07/40	15/01/42	4	18
U042	15/07/39	13/10/39	1	6	U094	10/08/40	28/08/42	10	24
U043	26/08/39	30/07/43	22	47	U095	31/08/40	28/11/41	9	15
U044	04/11/39	20/03/40	8	4	U096	14/09/40	??/02/45	19	53
U045	25/06/38	14/10/39	3	4	U097	28/09/40	16/06/43	6M	33
U046	02/11/38	??/10/43	31	47	U098	12/10/40	19/11/42	0	25
U047	17/12/38	08/03/41	34	15	U099	18/04/40	17/03/41	35	11
U048	22/04/39	??/10/43	59	50	U100	30/05/40	17/03/41	27	10
U049	12/08/39	15/04/40	0	8	U101	11/03/40	21/10/43	4	43
U050	12/12/39	10/04/40	5	4	U102	27/04/40	30/06/40	0	2
U051	06/08/38	20/08/40	8	12	U103	05/07/40	??/01/44	31	42
U052	04/02/39	??/10/43	13	50	U104	19/08/40	21/11/40	0	3

Vessel	Com	De-com/ sunk	Ships sunk	Months in active service	Vessel	Com	De-com/ sunk	Ships sunk	Months in active service
U105	10/09/40	02/06/43	21	33	U150	27/11/40	05/05/45	S	54
U106	24/09/40	02/08/43	20	35	U151	15/01/41	—/05/45	S	52
U107	08/10/40	18/08/44	39	46	U152	29/01/41	02/05/45	S	52
U108	22/10/40	11/04/44	23	42	U153	19/07/41	13/07/42	3	12
U109	05/12/40	07/05/43	13	29	U154	02/08/41	03/07/44	13	35
U110	21/11/40	09/05/41	5	6	U155	23/08/41	05/05/45	18	45
U111	19/12/40	04/10/41	5	10	U156	04/09/41	08/03/43	22	18
U116	26/07/41	??/10/42	2XB	15	U157	15/09/41	13/06/42	1	9
U117	25/10/41	07/08/43	2XB	22	U158	25/09/41	30/06/42	18	9
U118	06/12/41	12/06/43	7XB	18	U159	04/10/41	15/07/43	14	21
U119	02/04/42	24/06/43	1XB	14	U160	16/10/41	14/07/43	19	21
U120	20/04/40	05/05/45	S	61	U161	18/07/41	27/09/43	19	26
U121	20/04/40	02/05/45	S	61	U162	09/09/41	03/09/42	3	12
U122	30/03/40	??/06/40	0	3	U163	21/10/41	15/03/43	4	17
U123	30/05/40	17/06/44	37	49	U164	28/11/41	06/01/43	1	14
U124	11/06/40	02/04/43	35	34	U165	03/02/42	27/09/42	5	7
U125	03/03/41	06/05/43	19	26	U166	23/03/42	01/08/42	4	5
U126	22/03/41	03/07/43	28	28	U167	04/07/42	06/04/43	2	9
U127	24/04/41	15/12/41	0	8	U168	10/09/42	06/10/44	1	25
U128	12/05/41	17/05/43	12	24	U169	16/11/42	27/03/43	0	4
U129	21/05/41	04/07/44	30	38	U170	19/01/43	05/05/45	1	28
U130	11/06/41	12/03/43	22	21	U171	25/10/41	09/10/42	2	12
U131	01/07/41	17/12/41	1	5	U172	05/11/41	12/12/43	20	25
U132	29/05/41	05/11/42	8	18	U173	15/11/41	16/11/42	3	12
U133	05/07/41	14/03/42	M	8	U174	26/11/41	27/04/43	4	17
U134	26/07/41	24/08/43	2	25	U175	05/12/41	17/04/43	5	16
U135	16/08/41	15/07/43	3	23	U176	15/12/41	15/15/43	2	27
U136	30/08/41	11/07/42	5	11	U177	14/03/42	06/02/44	0	23
U137	15/06/40	02/05/45	0	59	U178	14/02/42	20/08/44	0	30
U138	27/06/40	18/06/41	1	12	U179	07/03/42	08/10/42	0	7
U139	24/07/40	02/05/45	0	58	U180	16/05/42	22/08/44	0	27
U140	07/08/40	02/05/45	0	57	U181	09/05/42	05/05/45	2	36
U141	21/08/40	02/05/45	4	57	U182	30/06/42	16/05/43	2	11
U142	04/06/40	02/05/45	SU	59	U183	01/04/42	23/04/45	3	36
U143	18/09/40	05/05/45	2S	56	U184	29/05/42	20/11/42	2	6
U144	02/10/40	09/08/41	SU	10	U185	13/06/42	24/08/43	9	14
U145	16/10/40	05/05/45	S	55	U186	10/07/42	12/05/43	4	10
U146	30/10/40	02/05/45	1S	55	U187	23/07/42	04/02/43	0	7
U147	11/02/40	02/06/41	4	16	U188	05/08/42	20/08/44	1	24
U148	18/12/40	02/05/45	S	53	U189	15/08/42	24/04/43	0	8
U149	13/11/40	05/05/45	S	54	U190	24/09/42	14/05/45	2	32

Left:
Some 80% of the type VIIA boats produced are seen here in one of the sea locks of the 3rd harbour entrance at Wilhelmshaven, before the war.

Vessel	Com	De-com/ sunk	Ships sunk	Months in active service	Vessel	Com	De-com/ sunk	Ships sunk	Months in active service
U191	20/10/42	23/04/43	1	6	U253	21/10/41	23/09/42	0	11
U192	16/11/42	05/05/43	1	6	U254	08/11/41	08/12/42	2	13
U193	10/12/42	28/04/44	1	16	U255	29/11/41	05/05/45	0	42
U194	08/01/43	24/06/43	0	5	U256	18/12/41	23/10/43	0	22
U195	05/09/42	05/05/45	2	32	U257	14/01/42	24/02/44	0	25
U196	11/09/42	??/11/44	0	26	U258	04/02/42	21/05/43	2	15
U197	10/10/42	20/08/43	1	10	U259	18/02/42	15/11/42	M	9
U198	03/11/42	12/08/44	0	21	U260	14/03/42	12/03/45	4	36
U199	28/11/42	31/07/43	3	8	U261	28/03/42	15/09/42	0	6
U200	22/12/42	24/06/43	0	6	U262	15/04/42	01/04/45	8	36
U201	25/01/41	17/02/43	26	25	U263	06/05/42	20/01/44	2	20
U202	22/03/41	02/06/43	14	27	U264	22/05/42	19/02/44	4	1
U203	18/02/41	25/04/43	29	26	U265	06/06/42	03/02/43	0	8
U204	08/03/41	19/10/41	6	7	U266	24/06/42	14/05/43	4	11
U205	03/05/41	17/02/43	M	21	U267	11/07/42	04/05/45	0	34
U206	17/05/41	30/11/41	1	6	U268	29/07/42	19/02/43	1	7
U207	07/06/41	11/09/41	3	3	U269	16/08/42	25/06/44	0	22
U208	05/07/41	11/12/41	1	5	U270	05/09/42	12/08/44	3	23
U209	11/10/41	??/05/43	0	19	U271	23/09/42	28/01/44	0	16
U210	21/02/42	06/08/42	0	6	U272	07/10/42	12/11/42	C	1
U211	07/03/42	19/11/43	3	20	U273	21/10/42	19/05/43	0	7
U212	25/04/42	21/07/44	0	27	U274	07/11/42	23/10/43	2	11
U213	30/08/42	31/07/42	0	11	U275	25/11/42	10/03/45	0	28
U214	01/11/41	26/07/44	0	32	U276	09/12/42	29/09/44	0	21
U215	22/11/41	03/07/42	1	8	U277	21/12/42	01/05/44	0	17
U216	15/12/41	20/10/42	1	10	U278	16/01/43	05/05/45	0	28
U217	31/01/42	05/06/43	5	17	U279	03/02/43	04/10/43	0	8
U218	31/01/42	05/06/43	3	17	U280	13/02/43	16/11/43	0	9
U219	12/12/42	05/05/43	XB	29	U281	27/02/43	05/05/45	0	27
U220	27/03/43	27/10/43	2XB	7	U282	13/03/43	29/10/43	0	7
U221	09/05/42	27/09/43	12	16	U283	31/03/43	11/02/44	0	11
U222	23/05/42	02/09/42	~	4	U284	14/04/43	21/12/43	0	8
U223	06/06/42	30/03/44	4	21	U285	15/05/43	15/04/45	0	23
U224	20/06/42	13/01/43	3	7	U286	05/06/43	29/04/45	0	22
U225	11/07/42	21/02/43	5	7	U287	22/09/43	16/05/45	0	20
U226	01/08/42	06/11/43	1	15	U288	26/06/43	03/04/44	0	10
U227	22/08/42	30/04/43	0	8	U289	10/07/43	31/05/44	0	10
U228	12/09/42	04/10/44	2	25	U290	24/07/43	04/05/45	0	22
U229	03/10/42	22/09/43	6	11	U291	04/08/43	—/05/45	S	21
U230	24/10/42	21/08/44	2M	22	U292	25/08/43	27/05/44	0	9
U231	14/11/42	13/01/44	0	14	U293	08/09/43	05/05/45	0	20
U232	28/11/42	08/07/43	0	8	U294	06/10/43	05/05/45	0	19
U233	22/09/43	05/07/44	XB	10	U295	20/10/43	05/05/45	0	19
U234	02/03/44	16/05/45	XB	14	U206	03/11/43	22/03/45	0	16
U235	19/12/42	14/05/43	1	5	U297	17/11/43	06/12/44	0	13
U236	09/01/43	14/05/43	0	4	U298	01/12/43	—/05/45	S	17
U237	30/01/43	14/05/43	E	4	U299	15/12/43	05/05/45	0	17
U238	20/02/43	09/02/44	4	12	U300	29/12/43	22/02/45	5	14
U239	13/03/43	24/07/44	0	16	U301	09/05/42	21/01/43	0	8
U240	03/04/43	16/05/44	0	13	U302	16/06/42	06/04/44	2	22
U241	24/07/43	18/05/44	0	10	U303	07/07/42	21/05/43	1	10
U242	14/08/43	30/04/45	0	20	U304	05/08/42	28/05/43	0	9
U243	02/10/43	08/07/44	0	9	U305	17/09/42	17/01/44	4	16
U244	09/10/43	05/05/45	0	19	U306	21/10/42	31/10/43	3	12
U245	18/12/43	05/05/45	4	17	U307	18/11/42	29/04/45	0	29
U246	11/01/44	29/03/45	0	14	U308	23/12/42	04/06/43	0	6
U247	23/10/43	01/09/44	1	11	U309	27/01/43	16/02/45	0	25
U248	06/11/43	16/01/45	0	14	U310	24/02/43	05/05/45	0	27
U249	20/11/43	05/05/45	0	18	U311	23/03/43	24/04/44	1	13
U250	12/12/43	30/07/44	0	7	U312	21/04/43	05/05/45	0	25
U251	20/09/41	19/04/45	EU	43	U313	20/05/43	16/05/45	0	24
U252	04/10/41	14/04/42	1	6	U314	10/06/43	30/01/44	0	7

Vessel	Com	De-com/ sunk	Ships sunk	Months in active service	Vessel	Com	De-com/ sunk	Ships sunk	Months in active service
U315	10/07/43	05/05/45	1	22	U349	08/09/43	05/05/45	S	20
U316	05/08/43	02/05/45	S	21	U350	07/10/43	30/03/45	S	17
U317	23/10/43	26/06/44	0	8	U351	20/06/41	05/05/45	S	47
U318	13/11/43	05/05/45	0	18	U352	28/08/41	09/05/42	0	9
U319	04/12/43	15/07/44	0	7	U353	31/03/42	16/10/42	0	7
U320	30/12/43	08/05/45	0	17	U354	22/04/42	25/08/44	0	28
U321	20/01/44	02/04/45	0	15	U355	29/10/41	01/04/44	0	30
U322	05/02/44	25/11/44	0	9	U356	20/12/41	27/12/42	6	12
U324	05/04/44	05/05/45	0	13	U357	18/06/42	26/12/42	0	6
U325	06/05/44	30/04/45	0	11	U358	15/08/42	01/03/44	4	19
U326	06/06/44	??/04/45	0	10	U359	05/10/42	28/07/43	1	9
U327	18/07/44	27/02/45	0	7	U360	12/11/42	02/04/44	0	17
U328	19/09/44	05/05/45	0	8	U361	18/12/42	17/07/44	0	19
U329	??/10/44	30/03/45	0	5	U362	04/02/43	05/09/44	0	19
U331	31/03/41	17/11/42	M	20	U363	18/03/43	05/05/45	0	26
U332	07/06/41	02/05/43	9	23	U364	03/05/43	30/01/44	0	8
U333	25/08/41	31/07/44	10	35	U365	08/06/43	13/12/44	0	18
U334	09/10/41	14/06/43	0	20	U366	16/07/43	05/03/44	0	8
U335	17/12/41	03/08/42	0	8	U367	27/08/43	15/03/45	S	19
U336	14/02/42	04/10/43	1	20	U368	07/01/44	—/05/45	S	16
U337	06/05/42	15/01/43	0	8	U369	15/10/43	—/05/45	S	19
U338	25/06/42	20/09/43	5	15	U370	19/11/43	05/05/45	S	18
U339	25/08/42	??/02/45	SU	30	U371	15/03/41	04/05/44	3M	38
U340	16/10/42	01/11/43	0	13	U372	19/04/41	04/08/42	3M	16
U341	28/11/42	19/09/43	0	10	U373	22/05/41	08/06/44	4	37
U342	12/01/43	17/04/44	0	15	U374	21/06/41	12/01/42	1	7
U343	18/02/43	10/03/44	0	13	U375	19/07/41	30/07/43	M	24
U344	26/03/43	24/08/44	0	17	U376	21/08/41	10/04/43	0	20
U345	04/05/43	23/12/43	0	7	U377	02/10/41	15/01/44	1	27
U346	07/06/43	20/09/43	0	3	U378	30/10/41	20/10/43	1	24
U347	07/07/43	17/07/44	0	12	U379	29/11/41	08/08/42	0	9
U348	10/08/43	30/03/45	0	19	U380	22/12/41	11/03/44	2M	27
					U381	25/02/42	19/05/43	1	15
					U382	25/04/42	12/01/45	3	33
					U383	06/06/42	01/08/43	2	14
					U384	18/07/42	19/03/43	2	8
					U385	29/08/42	11/08/44	0	24
					U386	10/10/42	19/02/44	1	16
					U387	24/11/42	09/12/44	0	25
					U388	31/12/42	20/06/43	0	6
					U389	06/02/43	05/10/43	0	8
					U390	13/03/43	05/07/44	0	16
					U391	24/04/43	13/12/43	0	8
					U392	29/05/43	16/03/44	1	10
					U393	03/07/43	04/05/45	S	22
					U394	07/08/43	02/09/44	0	13
					U396	16/10/43	23/04/45	0	18
					U397	20/11/43	05/05/45	S	18
					U398	18/12/43	??/05/45	0	17
					U399	22/01/44	26/03/45	1	14
					U400	18/03/44	17/12/44	0	9
					U401	10/04/41	03/08/41	0	4
					U402	21/05/41	13/10/43	18	29
					U403	25/06/41	17/08/43	3	26
					U404	06/08/41	28/07/43	18	23
					U405	17/09/41	01/11/43	3	26
					U406	22/10/41	18/02/44	4	28
					U407	18/12/41	19/09/44	M	33
					U408	19/11/41	05/11/42	0	12
					U409	21/01/42	12/07/43	4M	18
					U410	23/02/42	11/03/44	3M	25
					U411	18/03/42	28/11/42	M	8

Below:

Dieselobermaschinist Jak Mallmann (left) and LI Karl-Heinz Nitschke taking a breather on the bridge of *U377*. Thick gloves were necessary for handling machinery, especially when it was running hot. The flag served as the *Kriegsmarine's* Ensign.

Vessel	Com	De-com/ sunk	Ships sunk	Months in active service	Vessel	Com	De-com/ sunk	Ships sunk	Months in active service
U412	29/04/42	22/10/42	0	6	U478	08/09/43	30/06/44	0	9
U413	03/06/42	20/08/44	4	26	U479	27/10/43	12/12/44	0	14
U414	01/07/42	25/05/43	0	10	U480	06/10/43	24/02/45	1	16
U415	05/08/42	14/07/44	4	23	U481	10/11/43	05/05/45	0	18
U416	04/11/42	30/03/43	SU	4	U482	01/12/43	16/01/45	5	13
U417	26/09/42	11/06/43	0	9	U483	22/12/43	05/05/45	0	17
U418	21/10/42	01/06/43	0	8	U484	19/01/44	09/09/44	0	8
U419	18/11/42	08/10/43	0	11	U485	23/02/44	05/05/45	0	15
U420	16/12/42	26/10/43	0	10	U486	22/03/44	12/04/45	2	13
U421	13/01/43	29/04/44	1	15	U487	21/12/42	13/07/43	SB	7
U422	10/02/43	04/10/43	0	8	U488	01/02/43	26/04/44	SB	14
U423	03/03/43	17/06/44	0	15	U489	08/03/43	04/08/43	SB	5
U424	07/04/43	11/02/44	0	10	U490	27/03/43	11/06/44	SB	15
U425	21/04/43	17/02/45	0	22	U501	30/04/41	10/09/41	1	5
U426	12/05/43	08/01/44	1	8	U502	31/05/41	05/07/42	16	14
U427	02/06/43	05/05/45	0	23	U503	10/07/41	15/03/42	0	8
U431	05/04/41	30/10/43	1M	30	U504	30/07/41	30/07/43	9	24
U432	26/04/41	11/03/43	22	23	U505	26/08/41	04/06/44	7	34
U433	24/05/41	16/11/41	1	6	U506	15/09/41	12/07/43	14	22
U434	21/06/41	18/12/41	0	6	U507	08/10/41	13/01/43	12	15
U435	30/08/41	09/07/43	6	23	U508	20/10/41	12/11/43	12	25
U436	27/09/41	26/05/43	7	20	U509	04/11/41	15/07/43	7	20
U437	25/10/41	04/10/44	1	36	U510	25/11/41	05/05/45	11	42
U438	22/11/41	06/05/43	0	18	U511	08/12/41	16/09/43	2	21
U439	20/12/41	03/05/43	0	17	U512	20/12/41	02/10/42	3	10
U440	24/01/42	31/05/43	2	16	U513	10/01/42	19/07/43	7	18
U441	21/02/42	18/06/44	3	28	U514	24/01/42	08/07/43	8	18
U442	21/03/42	12/02/43	7	11	U515	21/02/42	09/04/44	24	26
U443	18/04/42	23/02/43	2M	10	U516	10/03/42	05/05/45	12	38
U444	09/05/42	11/03/43	1	10	U517	21/03/42	21/11/42	7	8
U445	30/05/42	24/08/44	0	27	U518	25/04/42	22/04/45	11	36
U446	20/06/42	21/09/42	~	3	U519	07/05/42	10/02/43	0	9
U447	11/07/42	07/05/43	0	10	U520	19/05/42	30/10/42	0	5
U448	01/08/42	14/04/44	0	20	U521	03/06/42	02/06/43	8	12
U449	22/08/42	24/06/43	0	10	U522	11/06/42	23/02/43	12	8
U450	12/09/42	10/03/44	0	18	U523	25/06/42	25/08/43	1	14
U451	03/05/41	21/12/41	0	7	U524	08/07/42	22/03/43	4	8
U452	29/05/41	25/08/41	0	3	U525	30/07/42	11/08/43	1	13
U453	26/06/41	21/05/44	M	35	U526	12/08/42	14/04/43	0	8
U454	24/07/41	01/08/43	0	25	U527	02/09/42	23/07/43	2	10
U455	21/08/41	06/04/44	0	32	U528	16/09/42	11/05/43	0	8
U456	18/09/41	13/05/43	0	20	U529	30/09/42	15/02/43	0	5
U457	05/11/41	16/09/42	0	10	U530	14/10/42	05/05/45	3	31
U458	12/12/41	22/08/43	0	10	U531	28/10/42	06/05/43	0	7
U459	15/11/41	24/07/43	SB	20	U532	11/11/42	05/05/45	3	30
U460	24/12/41	04/10/43	SB	22	U533	25/11/42	16/10/43	0	11
U461	30/01/42	30/07/43	SB	18	U534	23/12/42	05/05/45	0	29
U462	05/03/42	30/07/43	SB	16	U535	23/12/42	05/07/43	0	7
U463	02/04/42	15/05/43	SB	13	U536	13/01/43	20/10/43	0	9
U464	30/04/42	20/08/42	SB	4	U537	27/01/43	09/11/44	0	22
U465	20/05/42	05/05/43	M	12	U538	10/02/43	21/11/43	0	9
U466	17/06/42	19/08/44	0	26	U539	24/02/43	05/05/45	2	27
U467	15/07/42	25/05/43	0	10	U540	10/03/43	17/10/43	0	7
U468	12/08/42	11/08/43	1	12	U541	24/03/43	05/05/45	3	26
U469	07/10/42	25/03/43	0	5	U542	07/04/43	28/11/43	0	7
U470	07/01/43	16/10/43	0	9	U543	21/04/43	02/07/44	1	15
U471	05/05/43	06/08/44	1	15	U544	05/05/43	17/01/44	0	8
U472	26/05/43	04/03/44	0	10	U545	19/05/43	11/02/44	1	9
U473	16/06/43	05/05/44	0	11	U546	02/06/43	24/05/45	0	22
U475	07/07/43	03/05/45	0	22	U547	16/06/43	31/12/44	1	18
U476	28/07/43	24/05/44	0	10	U548	30/06/43	30/04/45	2	22
U477	18/08/43	03/06/44	0	10	U549	14/07/43	29/05/44	0	10

Vessel	Com	De-com/sunk	Ships sunk	Months in active service	Vessel	Com	De-com/sunk	Ships sunk	Months in active service
U550	28/07/43	16/04/44	1	9	U612	05/03/42	24/08/42	0	5
U551	07/11/40	23/03/41	0	4	U613	12/03/42	23/07/43	2	16
U552	04/12/40	02/05/45	31	53	U614	19/03/42	29/07/43	1	16
U553	23/12/40	28/01/43	12	25	U615	26/03/42	06/08/43	3	17
U554	15/01/41	03/05/45	S	52	U616	02/04/42	14/05/44	1M	25
U555	30/01/41	—/05/45	S	52	U617	09/04/42	12/09/43	5M	17
U556	06/02/41	27/06/41	8	4	U618	16/04/42	14/08/44	3	28
U557	13/02/41	16/12/41	5M	10	U619	23/04/42	06/12/42	2	6
U558	20/02/41	20/07/43	20	29	U620	30/04/42	14/02/43	2	10
U559	27/02/41	30/10/42	2M	20	U621	07/05/42	18/08/44	12	27
U560	06/03/41	03/05/45	S	50	U622	14/05/42	24/07/43	0	14
U561	13/03/41	12/07/43	3M	28	U623	21/05/42	??/02/43	0	9
U562	20/03/41	19/02/43	2M	23	U624	28/05/42	07/02/43	6	9
U563	27/03/41	31/05/43	5	26	U625	04/06/42	10/03/44	0	21
U564	03/04/41	14/06/43	20	26	U626	11/06/42	15/12/42	0	6
U565	10/04/41	24/09/44	M	41	U627	18/06/42	27/10/42	0	4
U566	19/04/41	24/10/43	3	30	U628	25/06/42	03/07/43	8	13
U567	24/04/41	21/12/41	2	8	U629	02/07/42	08/06/44	1	23
U568	01/05/41	28/05/42	1M	12	U630	09/07/42	04/05/43	1	10
U569	08/05/41	22/05/43	3	24	U631	16/07/42	17/10/43	2	15
U570	15/05/41	27/08/41	0	3	U632	23/07/42	06/04/43	4	9
U571	22/05/41	28/01/44	8	32	U633	30/07/42	07/03/43	0	8
U572	29/05/41	03/08/43	5	27	U634	06/08/42	30/08/43	1	12
U573	05/06/41	02/05/42	M	11	U635	13/08/42	06/04/43	1	8
U574	12/06/41	19/12/41	0	6	U636	20/08/42	21/04/45	0	32
U575	19/06/41	13/03/43	11	21					
U576	26/06/41	15/07/42	7	13					
U577	03/07/41	09/01/42	0	6					
U578	10/07/41	10/08/42	7	13					
U579	17/07/41	05/05/45	0	46					
U580	24/07/41	11/11/41	0	4					
U581	31/07/41	02/02/42	0	7					
U582	07/08/41	05/10/42	6	14					
U583	14/08/41	15/11/41	0	3					
U584	21/08/41	31/10/43	3	26					
U585	28/08/41	29/03/42	0	7					
U586	04/09/41	05/07/44	1	34					
U587	11/09/41	27/03/42	2	6					
U588	18/09/41	31/07/42	8	10					
U589	25/09/41	14/09/42	0	12					
U590	02/10/41	09/07/43	2	21					
U591	09/10/41	30/07/43	6	21					
U592	16/10/41	31/01/44	0	27					
U593	23/10/41	13/12/43	2M	26					
U594	30/10/41	04/06/43	2	20					
U595	06/11/41	14/11/42	M	12					
U596	13/11/41	24/09/44	1M	34					
U597	20/11/41	12/10/42	1	11					
U598	27/11/41	23/07/43	0	20					
U599	04/12/41	24/10/42	0	10					
U600	11/12/41	25/11/43	6	23					
U601	18/12/41	25/02/44	0	26					
U602	29/12/41	??/04/43	M	16					
U603	02/01/42	01/03/44	4	26					
U604	08/01/42	11/08/43	7	19					
U605	15/01/42	13/11/42	1	10					
U606	22/01/42	22/02/43	5	13					
U607	29/01/42	13/07/43	5	18					
U608	05/02/42	10/08/44	4	30					
U609	12/02/42	07/02/43	1	12					
U610	19/02/42	08/10/43	6	20					
U611	26/02/42	10/12/42	0	10					

Below:
The promenade deck of *U405* (KK Rolf-Heinrich Hopman); in a quiet corner of the wartime sea the men took advantage of sunshine and fresh air. On the left some are lying on top of the saddle tanks.

Vessel	Com	De-com/ sunk	Ships sunk	Months in active service	Vessel	Com	De-com/ sunk	Ships sunk	Months in active service
U637	27/08/42	05/05/45	0	33	U716	15/04/43	05/05/45	0	25
U638	03/09/42	05/05/43	4	8	U717	19/05/43	05/05/45	SU	24
U639	10/09/42	28/08/43	0	11	U718	25/06/43	18/11/43	0	5
U640	17/09/42	17/05/43	1	8	U719	27/07/43	26/06/44	0	11
U641	24/09/42	19/01/44	1	16	U720	17/09/43	—/05/45	S	20
U642	01/10/42	05/07/44	1M	21	U721	22/07/43	05/05/45	S	22
U643	08/10/42	08/10/43	0	12	U722	15/12/43	27/03/45	1	15
U644	15/10/42	07/04/43	0	6	U731	03/10/42	15/05/44	0	19
U645	22/10/42	24/12/43	2	14	U732	24/10/42	31/10/43	1	12
U646	29/10/42	17/05/43	0	7	U734	05/12/42	09/02/44	0	14
U647	05/11/42	??/08/43	0	9	U735	28/12/42	28/12/44	1	24
U648	12/11/42	23/11/43	0	12	U736	16/01/43	06/08/44	0	19
U649	19/11/42	24/02/43	0	3	U737	30/01/43	19/12/44	0	23
U650	26/11/42	??/01/45	0	26	U738	20/02/43	14/02/44	0	12
U651	12/02/41	29/06/41	0	4	U739	06/03/43	05/05/45	0	26
U652	03/04/41	02/06/42	2M	14	U740	27/03/43	09/06/44	0	15
U653	25/03/41	15/03/44	1	36	U741	10/04/43	15/08/44	0	16
U654	05/07/41	22/08/42	3	13	U742	01/05/43	18/07/44	0	14
U655	11/08/41	24/03/42	0	7	U743	15/05/43	09/09/44	0	16
U656	17/09/41	01/03/42	0	6	U744	05/06/43	06/03/44	2	9
U657	08/10/41	14/05/43	1	19	U745	19/06/43	06/02/45	0	20
U658	05/11/41	30/10/42	0	11	U746	04/07/43	04/05/45	IS	22
U659	09/12/41	03/05/43	4	17	U747	17/07/43	01/04/45	IS	21
U660	08/01/42	12/11/42	4	10	U748	31/07/43	03/05/45	IS	22
U661	12/02/42	15/10/42	1	8	U749	14/08/43	04/04/45	IS	20
U662	09/04/42	21/07/43	5	15	U750	26/08/43	05/05/45	IS	21
U663	14/05/42	07/05/43	2	12	U751	31/01/41	17/07/42	5	18
U664	17/06/42	09/08/43	3	14	U752	24/05/41	23/05/43	9	24
U665	22/07/42	22/03/43	1	8	U753	18/06/41	15/05/43	6	23
U666	26/08/42	10/02/44	2	18	U754	28/08/41	31/07/42	9	11
U667	20/10/42	25/08/44	0	22	U755	03/11/41	28/05/43	1	18
U668	16/11/42	05/05/45	0	30	U756	30/12/41	03/09/42	1	9
U669	16/12/42	07/09/43	0	9	U757	28/02/42	08/01/44	3	23
U670	26/01/43	20/08/43	0	7	U758	05/05/42	11/03/45	6	34
U671	03/03/43	04/08/44	0	17	U759	15/08/42	26/07/43	1	11
U672	06/04/43	18/07/44	0	15	U760	15/10/42	08/09/43	0	11
U673	08/05/43	24/10/44	0	17	U761	03/12/42	24/02/44	0	14
U674	15/06/43	02/05/44	0	11	U762	30/01/43	08/02/44	0	13
U675	14/07/43	24/05/44	0	10	U763	13/03/43	24/01/45	1	22
U676	06/08/43	19/02/45	0	18	U764	06/05/43	05/05/45	1	24
U677	20/09/43	??/04/45	S	19	U765	19/06/43	06/05/44	0	11
U678	25/10/43	07/07/44	0	9	U766	30/07/43	21/08/44	0	13
U679	29/11/43	10/01/45	0	14	U767	11/09/43	18/06/44	0	9
U680	23/12/43	24/06/45	0	18	U768	14/10/43	20/11/43	0	1
U681	03/02/44	11/03/45	0	13	U771	18/11/43	11/11/44	0	12
U682	17/04/44	11/03/45	0	11	U772	23/12/43	30/12/44	5	12
U683	30/05/44	12/03/45	0	10	U773	20/01/44	06/05/45	0	16
U701	16/07/41	07/07/42	10	12	U774	17/02/44	18/04/45	0	14
U702	03/09/41	04/04/42	0	7	U775	23/03/44	06/05/45	1	14
U703	16/10/41	??/09/44	0	35	U776	13/04/44	05/05/45	0	13
U704	18/11/41	03/05/45	2	42	U777	09/05/44	15/10/44	0	5
U705	30/12/41	03/09/42	2	9	U778	07/07/44	05/05/45	0	10
U706	16/03/42	02/08/43	3	17	U779	24/08/44	05/05/45	0	9
U707	01/07/42	09/11/43	2	16	U801	24/03/43	17/03/44	0	12
U708	24/07/42	03/05/45	SU	34	U802	12/06/43	11/05/45	1	23
U709	12/08/42	01/03/44	0	19	U803	07/09/43	27/04/44	0	7
U710	02/09/42	24/04/43	0	7	U804	04/12/43	09/04/45	0	16
U711	26/09/42	04/05/45	0	32	U805	12/02/44	05/05/45	0	15
U712	05/11/42	05/05/45	0	30	U806	29/04/44	05/05/45	1	13
U713	29/12/42	24/02/44	0	14	U821	11/10/43	10/06/44	0	8
U714	10/02/43	14/03/45	2	25	U822	01/07/44	03/05/45	0	10
U715	17/03/43	13/06/44	0	15	U825	04/05/44	05/05/45	2	12

Vessel	Com	De-com/ sunk	Ships sunk	Months in active service	Vessel	Com	De-com/ sunk	Ships sunk	Months in active service
U826	11/05/44	11/05/45	0	12	U952	10/12/42	06/08/44	5M	20
U827	25/05/44	04/05/45	0	12	U953	17/12/42	05/05/45	1	29
U828	17/06/44	03/05/45	0	11	U954	23/12/42	19/05/43	1	5
U841	06/02/43	17/10/43	0	8	U955	31/12/42	07/06/44	0	18
U842	01/03/43	06/11/43	0	8	U956	06/01/43	05/05/45	0	28
U843	24/03/43	09/04/45	1	25	U957	07/01/43	21/10/44	0	21
U844	07/04/43	16/10/43	0	6	U958	14/01/43	??/08/44	0	19
U845	01/05/43	10/03/44	1	10	U959	21/01/43	02/05/44	0	16
U846	29/05/43	04/05/44	0	12	U960	28/01/43	19/05/44	1M	16
U847	23/01/43	27/08/43	LD	7	U961	04/02/43	29/03/44	0	13
U848	20/02/43	05/11/43	LD	9	U962	11/02/43	08/04/44	0	14
U849	11/03/43	25/11/43	LD	8	U963	17/02/43	20/05/45	0	27
U850	17/04/43	20/12/43	LD	8	U964	18/02/43	16/10/43	0	8
U851	21/05/43	03/04/44	LD	11	U965	25/02/43	27/03/45	0	25
U852	15/06/43	03/05/44	LD	11	U966	04/03/43	10/11/43	0	8
U853	25/06/43	06/05/45	1	23	U967	11/03/43	11/08/44	0M	17
U854	19/07/43	04/02/44	0	7	U968	18/03/43	05/05/45	0	26
U855	02/08/43	24/09/44	0	13	U969	24/03/43	06/08/44	0M	17
U856	19/08/43	07/04/44	0	8	U970	25/03/43	07/06/44	0	15
U857	16/09/43	07/04/45	1	19	U971	01/04/43	24/06/44	0	14
U858	30/09/43	05/05/45	0	20	U972	08/04/43	??/01/44	0	9
U859	08/07/43	23/09/44	LD	14	U973	15/04/43	06/03/44	0	11
U860	12/08/43	15/06/44	LD	10	U974	22/04/43	19/04/44	0	12
U861	02/09/43	06/05/45	LD	20	U975	29/04/43	05/05/45	0	25
U862	07/10/43	05/05/45	LD	19	U976	05/05/43	25/03/44	0	10
U863	03/11/43	29/09/44	LD	10	U977	06/05/43	—/05/45	S	24
U864	09/12/43	09/02/45	LD	14	U978	12/05/43	05/05/45	3	24
U865	25/10/43	19/09/44	0	11	U979	20/05/43	03/05/45	3	24
U866	17/11/43	18/03/45	0	16	U980	27/05/43	11/06/44	0	13
U867	11/02/43	19/09/44	0	19	U981	03/06/43	12/08/44	0	14
U868	23/12/43	05/05/45	0	17	U982	10/06/43	09/04/45	0	22
U869	26/01/44	28/02/45	0	13	U983	16/06/43	08/09/43	0	3
U870	03/02/44	30/03/45	0	13	U984	17/06/43	20/08/44	4	14
U871	15/01/44	26/09/44	LD	8	U985	24/06/43	15/11/44	1	17
U872	10/02/44	10/08/44	LD	6	U986	01/07/43	17/04/44	0	9
U873	01/03/44	05/05/45	LD	14	U987	08/07/43	15/06/44	0	11
U874	08/04/44	05/05/45	LD	13	U988	15/07/43	29/06/44	2	11
U875	21/04/44	30/05/45	LD	13	U989	22/07/43	14/02/45	2	19
U876	24/05/44	04/05/45	LD	12	U990	28/07/43	25/05/44	0	10
U877	24/03/44	27/12/44	0	9	U991	29/07/43	05/05/45	0	22
U878	14/04/44	10/04/45	0	12	U992	02/08/43	05/05/45	0	21
U879	19/04/44	19/04/45	0	12	U993	19/08/43	04/10/44	0	14
U880	11/05/44	16/04/45	0	11	U994	02/09/43	05/05/45	0	20
U881	27/05/44	06/05/45	0	12	U995	16/09/43	08/05/45	0	20
U883	27/03/45	05/05/45	LD	2	U997	23/09/43	05/05/45	0	20
U889	04/08/44	15/05/45	0	9	U998	07/10/43	27/06/44	0	8
U901	29/04/44	05/05/45	0	13	U999	21/10/43	05/05/45	0	19
U903	04/09/43	06/05/45	0	20	U1000	04/11/43	15/08/44	0	9
U904	25/09/43	05/05/45	0	20	U1001	18/11/43	08/04/45	0	17
U905	08/03/44	20/03/45	0	12	U1002	30/11/43	30/05/45	0	18
U906	15/07/44	31/12/44	0	5	U1003	09/12/43	23/03/45	0	15
U907	08/05/44	05/05/45	0	12	U1004	16/12/43	30/05/45	1	17
U921	30/05/43	30/09/44	0	16	U1005	30/12/43	30/05/45	0	17
U922	01/08/43	03/05/45	0	21	U1006	11/01/44	16/10/44	0	9
U923	04/10/43	09/02/45	0	16	U1007	18/01/44	02/05/45	0	16
U925	30/12/43	18/09/44	0	9	U1008	01/02/44	06/05/45	0	15
U926	29/02/44	05/05/45	0	15	U1009	10/02/44	10/05/45	0	15
U927	27/06/44	24/02/45	0	8	U1010	22/02/44	14/05/45	0	15
U928	11/07/44	05/05/45	0	10	U1013	02/03/44	17/04/44	0	1
U929	06/09/44	03/05/45	0	8	U1014	14/03/44	04/02/45	0	11
U930	06/12/44	05/05/45	0	5	U1015	23/03/44	19/05/44	0	2
U951	03/12/42	07/07/43	0	7	U1016	04/04/44	05/05/45	0	13

Vessel	Com	De-com/ sunk	Ships sunk	Months in active service	Vessel	Com	De-com/ sunk	Ships sunk	Months in active service
U1017	01/03/44	29/04/45	2	13	U1205	02/03/44	03/05/45	0	14
U1018	01/03/44	27/02/45	1	11	U1206	16/03/44	14/04/45	0	13
U1019	04/05/44	29/05/45	0	12	U1207	23/03/44	05/05/45	0	14
U1020	17/05/44	??/01/45	0	8	U1208	06/04/44	20/02/45	0	10
U1021	25/05/44	30/03/45	0	10	U1209	13/04/44	18/12/44	0	8
U1022	07/06/44	??/05/45	2	11	U1210	22/04/44	03/05/45	0	13
U1023	15/16/44	10/05/45	1	1	U1221	11/08/43	03/04/45	0	20
U1024	28/06/44	13/04/45	1	10	U1222	01/09/43	11/07/44	0	10
U1025	12/06/44	05/05/45	0	11	U1223	06/10/43	23/04/45	1	18
U1051	04/03/44	26/01/45	1	10	U1224	20/10/43	13/05/44	0	7
U1052	20/01/44	29/05/45	0	16	U1225	10/11/43	24/06/44	0	7
U1053	12/02/44	15/02/45	0	12	U1226	24/11/43	28/11/44	0	12
U1054	25/03/44	16/09/44	0	6	U1227	08/12/43	09/04/45	0	16
U1055	08/04/44	30/04/45	0	12	U1228	22/12/43	09/05/45	0	17
U1056	29/04/44	05/05/45	0	13	U1229	13/01/44	20/08/44	0	7
U1057	20/05/44	10/05/45	0	12	U1230	26/01/44	—/05/45	1	16
U1058	10/06/44	10/05/45	0	11	U1231	09/02/44	14/05/45	0	15
U1059	01/05/43	19/03/44	0	10	U1232	08/04/44	03/02/45	5	11
U1060	15/05/43	27/10/44	0	17	U1233	22/03/44	—/05/45	0	14
U1061	25/08/43	30/05/45	0	21	U1234	19/04/44	05/05/45	0	13
U1063	08/07/44	15/04/45	0	9	U1235	17/05/44	15/04/45	0	11
U1062	19/06/43	30/09/44	0	15	U1271	12/01/44	30/05/45	0	16
U1064	29/07/44	29/05/45	0	10	U1272	28/01/44	30/04/45	2	16
U1065	23/09/44	09/04/45	0	7	U1273	16/02/44	17/02/45	0	12
U1101	10/11/43	05/05/45	0	18	U1274	01/03/44	16/04/45	1	13
U1102	22/02/44	—/05/45	0	15	U1275	22/03/44	—/05/45	0	14
U1103	08/01/44	23/05/45	0	16	U1276	06/04/44	03/04/45	0	12
U1104	15/03/44	30/05/45	0	14	U1277	03/05/44	—/05/45	0	12
U1105	03/06/44	10/05/45	0	11	U1278	31/05/44	17/02/45	0	9
U1106	05/07/44	29/03/45	0	8	U1279	05/07/44	03/02/45	0	7
U1107	08/08/44	25/04/45	2	8	U1301	11/02/44	30/05/45	0	15
U1108	18/11/44	29/05/45	0	6	U1302	25/05/44	07/03/45	0	10
U1109	31/08/44	29/05/45	0	9	U1303	05/04/44	05/05/45	0	13
U1110	24/09/44	—/05/45	0	8	U1304	06/09/44	05/05/45	0	8
U1131	20/05/44	11/03/45	0	10	U1305	13/09/44	10/05/45	0	8
U1132	24/06/44	05/05/45	0	11	U1306	20/12/44	05/05/45	0	5
U1161	25/08/43	94/05/45	0	21	U1307	17/11/44	30/05/45	0	6
U1162	15/09/43	05/05/45	0	20	U1308	17/01/45	02/05/45	0	4
U1163	06/10/43	29/05/45	0	19					
U1164	27/10/43	26/04/44	0	8					
U1165	17/11/43	19/05/45	0	18					
U1166	08/12/43	28/07/44	0	7					
U1167	29/12/43	30/03/45	0	15					
U1168	19/01/44	05/05/45	0	16					
U1169	09/02/44	05/04/45	0	14					
U1170	01/03/44	03/05/45	0	14					
U1171	22/03/44	29/05/45	0	14					
U1172	20/04/44	27/01/45	2	9					
U1191	09/09/43	25/06/44	0	9					
U1192	23/09/43	09/04/45	0	19					
U1193	07/10/43	05/05/45	0	19					
U1194	21/10/43	24/05/45	0	19					
U1195	04/11/44	06/04/45	2	5					
U1196	18/11/43	??/08/44	0	9					
U1197	02/12/43	25/04/45	0	16					
U1198	09/12/43	??/05/45	0	17					
U1199	23/12/43	21/01/45	1	13					
U1200	05/01/44	11/11/44	0	10					
U1201	13/01/44	03/05/45	0	16					
U1202	27/01/44	10/05/45	1	16					
U1203	10/02/44	29/05/45	1	15					
U1204	17/02/44	05/05/45	0	15					

Ships sunk column:
Shows ships sunk in the *Atlantic*.

Abbreviations:
Ships sunk column

Some U-boats were not in positions to sink ships

S School boat
SU Used as school boat for part of the war. With operational flotilla for other part.
M Boat served in Mediterranean
E Experimental boat or a boat used for experiments
SB Supply U-boat
XB Minelayer
IS Served as school boat and also under Italian Command
LD Long distance boat — served as transporter
EU Used operationally and for experiments

Select Bibliography

Almann, Karl; *Ritter der sieben Meere*; Erich Papel Verlag, Rastadt, 1963

Beaver, Paul; *U-boats in the Atlantic*; Patrick Stephens Ltd, Cambridge, 1979

Beesly, Patrick; *Very Special Intelligence*; Hamish Hamilton, London, 1977 and Doubleday, New York, 1978

Bekker, Cajus; *The German Navy 1939-45*; Hamlyn, London, 1974

Bekker, Cajus; *Hitler's Naval War*; Macdonald and Jane's, London, 1974

Bödeker, Günter; *Die Boote im Netz*; Gustav Lübbe Verlag, Bergisch Gladbach, 1981

Bonatz, Heinz; *Seekrieg im Äther*; E. S. Mittler & Sohn, Herford, 1981
(The author was the commanding officer of the German Radio Monitoring Service)

Botting, Douglas; *The U-boats*; Time-Life Books, 1979

Bracke, Gerhard; *Die Einzelkämpfer der Kriegsmarine*; Motorbuch Verlag, Stuttgart, 1981

Brennecke, Jochen; *Jäger — Gejagte*; Koehlers Verlag, Jugendheim, 1956

Brickhill, Paul; *The Dam Busters*; Pan Books, London, 1967
(Includes information about the bombing of U-boat bunkers)

Brustat-Naval, Fritz; *Ali Cremer U333*; Ullstein, Frankfurt am Main, 1982

Brustat-Naval, Fritz and Suhren, Teddy; *Nasses Eichenlaub*; Koehlers, Herford, 1983

Buchheim, Lothar-Günther; *Ubootkrieg*; Piper, Munich, 1976

Busch, Harald; *So war der Ubootskrieg (U-boats at War)*; Deutsche Heimat Verlag, Bielefeld, 1954

Compton-Hall, Richard; *The Underwater War 1939-1945*; Blandford, Poole, 1982

Deutscher Marinebund; *Ubootmuseum U995*; Laboe

Dönitz, Karl; *Ten Years and Twenty Days*; Weidenfeld and Nicolson, London 1959

Dönitz, Karl; *Mein wechselvolles Leben*; Musterschmidt Verlag, Frankfurt, 1968

Dönitz, Karl; *Deutsche Strategie zur See im Zweiten Weltkrieg*; Bernard & Graefe, Frankfurt am Main, 1972

Frank, Dr Wolfgang; *Die Wölfe und der Admiral*; Gerhard Stalling Verlag, Oldenburg, 1953. Translated as *Sea Wolves — The Story of the German U-boat War*; Weidenfeld, London, 1955

Gabler, Ulrich; *Unterseebootsbau*; Wehr and Wissen Verlagsgesellschaft, Darmstadt, 1964
(Prof Gabler worked with Helmuth Walter on the development of new submarines towards the end of the war)

Gasaway, E. B.; *Grey Wolf, Grey Sea*; Arthur Barker, London, 1972
(About U124)

Giese, Fritz; *Die deutsche Marine 1920-45*; Bernard & Graefe, Frankfurt am Main, 1956

Giessler, Helmuth; *Der Marine-Nachrichten-und-Ortungsdienst*; J. F. Lehmanns Verlag, Munich, 1971

Görlitz, Walter; *Karl Dönitz*; Musterschmidt Verlag, Göttingen, 1972

Gretton, Sir Peter; *Convoy Escort Commander*; Cassell, London, 1964

Gretton, Sir Peter; *Crisis Convoy*; P. Davis, London, 1974
(The story of Convoy HX231, the first convoy to cross the Atlantic where the escorts managed to turn away every attacking U-boat. The author was the escort commander)

Gröner, Erich; Die deutschen Kriegsschiffe 1815-1945, Vol 3; *Uboote, Hilfskreuzer, Minenschiffe, Netzleger und Sperrbrecher*; Bernard & Graefe Verlag, Koblenz, 1985

Hadley, Michael; *U-boats against Canada*; McGill-Queen's University Press, Kingston and Montreal, 1985

Herzog, Bodo; *60 Jahre deutsche Uboote 1906-66*; J. F. Lehmanns Verlag, Munich, 1968

Herzog, Bodo; *U-boats in Action*; Ian Allan, Weybridge, 1971

Herzog, Bodo; *Die deutschen Uboote 1906-45*; J. F. Lehmanns Verlag, Munich 1959

Hirschfeld, Wolfgang; *Feindfahrten*; Neff Verlag, Vienna, 1982
(The author served as radio operator in U109, U234 and at the U-boat Command, and in this book he published his secret diary. This is probably the only wartime diary by a non-commissioned U-boat man and contains valuable material for anyone studying the war at sea)

Högel, Georg; *Embleme, Wappen, Malings deutscher Uboote 1939-45*; Hogel, Munich, 1984

Jones, Geoff; *The Month of the Lost U-boats*; William Kimber, London, 1977
(An account of May 1943)

Jones, Geoff; *Autumn of the U-boats*; William Kimber, London, 1984
(About the autumn of 1943)

Kludas, Arnold; *The U-boat Wilhelm Bauer Technology Museum*; Technikmuseum Uboot Wilhelm Bauer, Bremerhaven, 1985

Lenton, H. T.; Navies of the Second World War, Vols 1 and 2 *German Submarines*; Macdonald, London, 1965

Lohmann, W. and Hildebrand, H. H.; Kriegsmarine 1939-45; Podzun Verlag, Dorheim 1956-64
(These three volumes are the standard reference work on the administration and personnel of the German Navy)

Ludde-Neurath, Walter; *Regierung Dönitz*; Musterschmidt, Göttingen 1964

Macintyre, Capt Donald; *The Battle of the Atlantic*; Batsford, London, 1971

Macintyre, Capt Donald; *U-boat Killer*; Weidenfeld and Nicolson, London, 1956

Mordal, Jacques; *25 Centuries of Sea Warfare*; Abbey Press, London, 1959

Morison, Samuel Eliot; *History of United States Naval Operations in World War II*; Little, Brown and Co, Boston, 1970

National Archives and Records Administration; *Records Relating to U-boat Warfare 1939-45*; Washington DC, 1985

Peillard, Leonce; *Affäre Laconia*; Paul Neff, Vienna 1963. Translated as *U-boats to the Rescue*; Jonathan Cape Ltd, London, 1963

Pocock, Rowland F.; *German Guided*

Left:
Two men check the water distillation equipment. The photograph was taken on the port side of the central control room looking aft and the circular pressure door can be seen behind them.

Missiles; Ian Allan, Weybridge, 1967

Porten, Edward von der; *The German Navy in World War II*; Arthur Barker Ltd, London, 1969

Price, Alfred; *Aircraft versus Submarines*; William Kimber, London 1973

Prochnow, Günther; Deutsche Kriegsschiffe in zwei Jahrhunderten, Vol IV, *Unterseeboote*; Ernst Gades Verlag, Preezt, Holstein, 1969

Raeder, Dr Erich; *My Life*; US Naval Institute, 1960

Raeder, Dr Erich; *Struggle for the Sea*; William Kimber, London, 1959

Range, Clemens; *Ritterkreuzträger der Kriegsmarine*; Motorbuch Verlag, Stuttgart, 1974

Robertson, Terrence; *The Golden Horseshoe*; Pan Books, London, 1966

Rohwer, Dr Prof Jürgen; *Uboote: Eine Chronik in Bildern*; Gerhard Stalling Verlag, Oldenburg, 1962

Rohwer, Dr Prof Jürgen; *U107*; Profile Publications, Windsor, 1971

Rohwer, Dr Prof Jürgen; *Axis Submarine Successes 1939-45*; Patrick Stephens, Cambridge, 1983

Rowher, Dr Prof Jürgen; *The Critical Convoy Battles of March 1943*; Ian Allan, Weybridge 1977

Rohwer, Dr Prof Jürgen and Hümmelchen, Gerhard; *Chronology of the War at Sea* (Two volumes); Ian Allan, Weybridge, 1974

Rohwer, Dr Prof Jürgen and Jäckel, Eberhard; *Die Funkaufklärung und ihre Rolle im 2. Weltkrieg*; Motorbuch Verlag, Stuttgart, 1979

Roskill, Capt S. W.; *The War at Sea* (Four volumes); HMSO, London, 1954 and 1976

Roskill, Capt S. W.; *The Secret Capture*; Collins, London 1959
(About the capture of U110)

Rössler, Eberhard; *The U-boat*; Arms and Armour Press, London, 1981. Translated from *Geschichte des deutschen Ubootbaus*; J. F. Lehmanns Verlag, Munich, 1975

Rössler, Eberhard; *Die deutschen Uboote und ihre Werften*; Bernard & Graefe Verlag, Munich, 1979
(Two excellent volumes, both richly illustrated)

Rössler, Eberhard; *Die Torpedos der deutschen Uboote*; Koehler Verlag, Herford, 1984

Rössler, Eberhard; *Ubootstyp XXI*; Lehmanns Verlag, Munich 1967

Rössler, Eberhard; *Ubootstyp XXIII*; Lehmanns Verlag, Munich, 1967

Rössler, Eberhard; *Erprobungs-Unterseeboot Wilhelm Bauer*; Deutsches Schiffahrtsmuseum, Bremerhaven, 1984

Ruge, F.; *Sea Warfare 1939-45*; Cassel, London, 1957. Translated from *Der Seekrieg*; Koehlers Verlag, Stuttgart, 1954

Salewski, Michael; *Die deutsche Seekriegsleitung*; Bernard & Graefe Verlag, Frankfurt am Main, 1970 (Two volumes)

Schaeffer, Heinz; *U-boat 977*; William Kimber, London, 1952

Science and Industry Museum; *The Story of U505*; Chicago, 1969

Shelford, W. O.; *Subsunk*; George Harrap, London, 1960
(Has details of German submarine escape apparatus)

Showell, Jak P. Mallmann; *U-boats under the Swastika*; Ian Allan, Weybridge, 1973. Translated as *Uboote gegen England*; Motorbuch Verlag, 1974

Showell, Jak P. Mallmann; *The German Navy in World War Two*; Arms and Armour Press, London, 1979. Translated as *Das Buch der deutschen Kriegsmarine*; Motorbuch Verlag, 1980

Showell, Jak P. Mallmann; *Germania International*; German Navy Study Group, 78 Barnfield Crescent, Telford, Shropshire TF1 2EX, England
(Published at least quarterly)

Verband Deutscher Ubootfahrer; *Schaltung — Küste*; Hamburg

Waddington, C. H.; *OR in WW2*; Paul Elek, London, 1973

Wagner, G.; *Lagevorträge des Oberbefehlshaber der Kriegsmarine vor Hitler 1939-45*; J. F. Lehmanns Verlag, Munich, 1972

Waters, J. M.; *Bloody Winter*; Van Norstrand, New York, 1967

Watts, A. J.; *Axis Submarines*; Macdonald and Jane's, London, 1977; Arco, New York, 1977

Watts, A. J.; *The U-boat Hunters*; Macdonald and Jane's, London, 1976

Watson-Watt, Sir R.; *Three Steps to Victory*; Odhams, London, 1957

Werner, Herbert; *Iron Coffins*; Arthur Barker, London, 1970

Westwood, David; *Type VIIC*; Conway Marine Press, London, 1974

Witthöft, H. J.; *Lexikon zur deutschen Marinegeschichte*; Koehlers, Herford, 1977 (Two volumes)

Zienert, J.; *Unsere Marineuniform*; Helmuth Gerhard Schulz, Hamburg, 1970